COMMUNICATING
in **GEOGRAPHY**
and the
ENVIRONMENTAL
SCIENCES

Third Edition

IAIN HAY

OXFORD
UNIVERSITY PRESS
AUSTRALIA & NEW ZEALAND

OXFORD
UNIVERSITY PRESS
AUSTRALIA & NEW ZEALAND

253 Normanby Road, South Melbourne, Victoria 3205, Australia

Oxford University Press is a department of the University of Oxford.
It furthers the University's objective of excellence in research, scholarship,
and education by publishing worldwide in

Oxford New York

Auckland Cape Town Dar es Salaam Hong Kong Karachi
Kuala Lumpur Madrid Melbourne Mexico City Nairobi
New Delhi Shanghai Taipei Toronto

With offices in

Argentina Austria Brazil Chile Czech Republic France Greece
Guatemala Hungary Italy Japan Poland Portugal Singapore
South Korea Switzerland Thailand Turkey Ukraine Vietnam
OXFORD is a trade mark of Oxford University Press in the UK
and in certain other countries

National Library of Australia
Cataloguing-in-Publication data:

Hay, Iain, 1960– .
Communicating in geography and the environmental sciences.

3rd ed.
Bibliography.
Includes index.
ISBN 9 78019551 7613.
ISBN 0 19 551761 X.

1. Communication in geography. I. Title.

910.72

Typeset by Cannon Typesetting, Melbourne
Printed in Hong Kong by Sheck Wah Tong Printing Press Ltd

COMMUNICATING

in GEOGRAPHY
and the
ENVIRONMENTAL
SCIENCES

For Tania, Della & Roley

contents

list of figures

list of tables

list of boxes

acknowledgments

A large number of people have contributed to work that was eventually to become part of the pages which follow. I am very grateful to Cecile Cutler, Steve Fildes, Tom Jenkin, and Noel Richards for their patient, thoughtful, and constructive contributions to this edition and its predecessors. I would especially like to thank Tania for reminding me to look at the garden and Della and Roley for making sure I spend time in it! I am also grateful to Taylor and Francis for allowing sections of articles published in the *Journal of Geography in Higher Education* since 1994 to be presented in revised form here. Full acknowledgments of those earlier works are included in this book's 'References and further reading' sections. Readers are also advised that with the exception of the chapter 'Writing a media release', material published in this book is reproduced in Hay, Bochner, and Dungey's book *Making the Grade. A Guide to Successful Communication and Study* published by Oxford University Press. Finally, and again, to my parents—gifted teachers and learners—I owe special thanks.

introductory comments

Communicating in Geography and the Environmental Sciences, third edition, is about communicating effectively in academic settings. It discusses the character and practice of some of the most common forms of academic presentation skills used by students of geography and the environment. Chapters outline the 'whys' and 'hows' of essays, research and laboratory reports, reviews, media releases, summaries, annotated bibliographies, maps, figures, tables, posters, examinations, and talks. Information on the ways in which these forms of presentation are commonly assessed is another important part of the book.

Knowledge, information, and ideas remain the most highly valued currencies in universities. However, without the ability and means to communicate clearly and effectively, the value of one's thoughts and abstractions can be severely eroded. For that reason effective communication is a vital component of intellectual endeavour. One important ingredient of effective communication is an appreciation of the ways in which audiences make sense of the messages conveyed. Typically, audiences expect that certain conventions will be upheld or followed by people communicating to them through specific media. For instance, readers of an academic paper will usually expect some early introductory advice of the paper's purpose. People reviewing a scientific research report anticipate that information on supporting literature, research methods, and results will be set out in a customary order and will offer specific sorts of information. Unfortunately, however, many students do not know the accepted cues, clues, ceremonies, conventions, and characteristics associated with formal (academic) communication. In other words, some students do not know how to 'make the grade'. It is primarily because of that problem and because of the lack of specific, relevant advice to address it that this book was written.

In the pages which follow I have tried to demystify the conventions of communication associated with university exercises. By laying bare the criteria academic markers typically seek when evaluating specific forms of communication like essays, posters, and talks, this book lets everyone know how grades are made. Just as importantly, the following pages set out the means by which grade-making criteria may be fulfilled.

The book serves a number of other important purposes. It is intended to:

- *Help improve teaching, learning, and assessment within educational contexts of scarce resources.* Many academics now find themselves being asked to do more with less—to do more teaching, more research, more administration, and more community service with less money, less time, less public recognition, and less government support than ever before. One means of coping with this set of tensions is to teach more efficiently and effectively. This book is an attempt to contribute to those ends.
- *Help increasingly diverse student populations fulfil educational objectives.* Recent moves to mass tertiary education in many Western countries have brought to universities students with far more diverse educational and cultural backgrounds than ever before. By revealing the characteristics of academic communication and assessment this book represents one attempt to accommodate that shift. In serving this purpose the book may also be of value to those offering and undertaking distance education courses.
- *Provide students with useful vocational skills.* In the context of emerging patterns of work and work organisation, the ability of university graduates to communicate ideas and information is becoming increasingly important and surfaces repeatedly in the reports of government and business think-tanks and academic authors. In some recognition of vocational considerations, this book makes an effort to contribute to the development of communication skills. Although this third edition maintains its predecessors' focus on traditional academic communication skills and principles, it includes a chapter, co-written with Dr David Bass from the School of Geography, Population and Environmental Management at Flinders University, on preparing a media release. As argued in Hay & Israel (2001), it is important that geographers, environmental scientists, and managers make academic knowledge publicly accessible. One means of achieving this is through 'newsmaking'—engaging with the media to ensure that geographical and environmental issues are more effectively incorporated in public imagination and debate.
- *Codify and transfer teaching experience.* The book is one distillation of the experience and expertise possessed by those many people I have troubled over the years for comments on marking practice and communication conventions. With this book in hand, many new teachers and part-time teachers may find their teaching and assessment experiences simplified.

Most of the chapters have been written around a common framework comprising four parts. First, there is an explanation of the specific type of communication being discussed. This takes the form of an answer to a question such as 'Why prepare a poster?' This section is followed by a broad, conceptual statement of the key matters assessors seek when marking the particular type of communication under consideration. For instance, lecturers marking book reviews typically seek clearly expressed description, analysis, and evaluation of the text. An essay marker wishes to be told clearly what the author thinks and has learned about a specific topic. An outline of means of achieving effective contact with one's audience constitutes the third part of most chapters or sections. Where possible, this discussion is structured around an explicit statement of the sorts of criteria assessors have typically been found to use when marking student work. A statement of those assessment criteria forms the fourth part of most chapters. Lecturers may find these lists useful as marking guides (e.g. to ensure that a broad range of matters is considered during assessment; to offer consistency in marking practice) and they may be of considerable benefit to students seeking either a checklist which might be used in critical self-review or an indication of the sorts of things assessors are considering when marking work.

This edition reflects some of the technological shifts that have occurred since the first edition was published in 1996. Nowhere is this more evident than in the chapter on citing sources. This has been revised substantially to offer guidance on dealing with the wide array of new electronic-based resources now available. There is also material on passing online exams, using electronic aids to help communicate ideas and information, and making judicious use of electronic resources. While most chapters have been revised to update, clarify, and simplify their messages, the general structure and tone of the successful earlier editions have been maintained.

... FOR STUDENT READERS

If you are like many students in most universities, you have a mountain of textbooks to read, thousands of photocopied words to digest, and dog-eared collections of handwritten notes to absorb. On top of all that material directly related to your course, you now have a book on academic communication skills. Do not be discouraged. It is true that there is a lot to read and absorb in the pages that follow, but it is unlikely that you will have to use all of the material in this book in any single semester university course. Instead, this is a book written to be used throughout your entire degree (and for some post-degree experiences too). For example, in a first-year course, you might find the chapters on essay writing, graphics and exams most helpful. In third year, you might use the material on oral presentations for the first time while still using the material on essays and graphics. So, think of the book as comprising sections that will be important over three or four years, not just for one semester.

You might want to regard the book as something of a statement of achievement too. Let me explain that rather cryptic comment. If you use this text in the next few years at university, you should be able to complete a degree with a sound appreciation of almost all of the material in the book. Look at the book as an indicator of proficiency: 'this is what I will know', and not as something which says, 'this is what I have to know'.

The following pages discuss in detail the conventions of communicating effectively in an undergraduate academic setting. In part, the advice given is based on reviews of patterns of marking and comment by academic staff. The book was written to provide you with an insight into some of the expectations of people for whom you will be writing essays, giving talks, and drawing figures. Those expectations are reviewed fully in the chapters but they are also summarised in the assessment schedules. An understanding of your audience's expectation *before* you undertake an assignment ought to help you prepare better work than might otherwise have been possible.

You will find it helpful to review the assessment schedules (and the appropriate chapters) before you begin an assignment requiring some specific form of communication (e.g. writing an essay, giving a talk). You will then be able to undertake the assignment with an understanding of the appropriate conventions of communication. When you have finished a draft of your work, try marking it yourself using the checklist as a guide. If you have a patient and thoughtful friend, ask them if they will do this for you too. The checklist will help to ensure that you and your friend give consideration to the broad range of issues likely to be examined by any assessor, whether or not they actually use the schedules in their own marking practice. If something in the assessment schedule does not make sense to you, consult the material in the appropriate chapter for an explanation. In this way you may be able to illuminate and correct any shortcomings in your work before those problems are uncovered by your lecturer. The end results of this process ought to be better communication and better grades.

One thing needs to be stressed from the outset. The following pages are intended to offer advice only and not prescriptions for 'perfect' assignments. The guidelines are intended to assist you in preparing assignments, types of which you might be undertaking for the first time (e.g. an academic poster, a formal talk). As well as heeding the content of this book, you should read journal articles and other people's essays critically, pay attention to the ways in which effective and poor speakers present themselves and their material, and be critical of maps and graphs. See what works and what does not. Learn from your observations and attempt to forge your own distinctive approach to communicating. The style you develop may be very effective and yet transgress some of the guidelines set out in the following pages. This should not be a matter of concern: your individuality and imagination are to be celebrated and encouraged, not condemned and excised.

... FOR LECTURERS

Despite the revisions, this third edition is still not a book of magic. I do not wish to make wild claims about the benefits that might flow from student and teacher use of the pages that follow. However, on the basis of experiences with the earlier editions, I do have reason to believe that if material from this book is referred to and incorporated into teaching *and* assessment practice within a discipline or across a degree, there is likely to be an improvement in student communication skills. A number of simple and effective strategies for using this book have yielded positive results.

- Before the class undertakes an exercise, make available to students relevant copies of assessment schedules associated with most chapters. Alternatively, ask students as individuals or in groups to prepare their own criteria for establishing whether a specific piece of work is successful. Discuss these criteria within the class and compare them with the assessment schedules set out in this book. Perhaps produce a composite set of criteria that acknowledges the intentions and ambitions of both yourself and your students. In other words, use the assessment schedules provided here as a means of encouraging your students to think about their audience's expectations. This can also help you to simplify (where you consider it appropriate) the sometimes extended assessment schedules set out in this book.
- Encourage students, by whatever means you consider appropriate, to critically read assessment sheets and explanatory notes in the appropriate chapter of the book before they begin an assigned task.
- Apply strategies that encourage students to use marking schedules to assess their own work before submitting it for peer review or final assessment. Not only does this offer an opportunity for students to engage in critical self-reflection, but if submitted with work for instructor assessment, self-assessment sheets can be used as a 'diagnostic' tool, highlighting differences between students' perceptions of their own work and those of the assessor(s).
- Use peer review methods such as writing groups and student assessment of oral presentations as means of encouraging students to think critically about communication and the positions and expectations of author and audience. The assessment sheets associated with most of the chapters in this book are useful preliminary frameworks for peer review.
- Use the assessment sheets, and use them repeatedly, as the foundation for your own assessment practice.

These strategies, singly and in combination, while requiring little extra teaching effort, offer the potential for improvements in written, oral, and graphic communication skills. Why not give them a try?

FURTHER READING

Hay, I. & Israel, M. 2001, '"Newsmaking geography": Communicating geography through the media', *Applied Geography*, vol. 21, no. 2, pp. 107–25.

1

Writing an Essay

True ease in writing comes from art, not chance,
As those move easiest who have learned to dance.

Alexander Pope

KEY TOPICS

- Why write?
- How do I write a good essay?
- What are your essay markers looking for?

This chapter briefly **argues** the case for writing before going on to **discuss** how to write a good **essay**. Most of the material in the chapter is devoted to a **review** of those matters your essay markers might be looking for when they are **assessing** your work. Much of the information and advice in the following pages is structured around the essay assessment schedule included at the end of the chapter.

WHY WRITE?

You might think that essays and other forms of written work demanded by your lecturer are some sort of miserable torture inflicted on you as a part of an ancient academic initiation ritual. To tell the truth, however, there are some very good reasons to develop expertise in writing.

- It is an *academic and professional responsibility* to write. As an academic or practising geographer (perhaps labelled economist, planner, demographer) or environmental manager you should make the results of your work known to the public, to government, to sponsoring agencies, and the like. There is not only a moral obligation to make public the results of scientific inquiry, but you will probably be required to write—and to write well—as part of any occupation you take up.

- Writing is one of the most *powerful means we have of communicating*. It is also the most common means by which formal transmission of ideas and arguments is achieved.
- Among the most important reasons for writing is the fact that writing is a *generative, thought-provoking process*:

> I write because I don't know what I think until I read what I have to say.
>
> *Flannery O'Connor*

> You write—and find you have something to say.
>
> *Wright Morris*

> But I really write to find out about something and what is known about something … I write books to find out about things.
>
> *Dame Rebecca West*

As these quotes suggest, writing promotes original thought. It also reveals how much you have understood about a particular topic. (For a discussion of ideas on this point, see Game and Metcalfe's (2003) chapter on writing.)

- Writing is also a means by which you can *initiate feedback on your own ideas*. Through the circulation of your writing in forms such as professional reports, essays, letters to the editor, and **journal** or magazine articles you may spark replies that contribute to your own knowledge as well as to that of others. Writing (and other forms of communication) is critical to the development and re-shaping of knowledge.
- By forcing you to marshal your thoughts and present them coherently to other people, writing is also a *central part of the learning process*.
- Writing is a means of *conveying and creating the ideas of new worlds*. Writing is part of the process by which we give meaning to the world(s) in which we live. One of the ways in which we make sense of our world(s) is through the communications of others (e.g. journalists). In consequence, those who have power over communication have power over thought and, hence, power over reality.
- *Writing can be fun*. Think of writing as an art form or as story-telling. Use your imagination. Paint the world you want with words.

HOW DO I WRITE A GOOD ESSAY?

During your degree program, you might write twenty to fifty essays, totalling about 100,000 words—more words than there are in this book! You might as well spend a little time now ensuring that the 1000 to 2000 hours you spend writing those essays are as productive and rewarding as possible.

- *Read widely.* Reading the work of others, especially geographers and environmental managers, is essential. Not only will it increase your knowledge of your subject, it will also give you a feeling of how experts write about it.
- *Devote enough time to research and writing.* There is no formula for calculating the amount of time which you need to devote to writing essays of any particular length or 'mark value'. Some writers do their best work under great pressure of time; others work more slowly and may require several weeks to write a short essay. However, irrespective of your writing style, doing the research for a good essay does take time. So, do yourself a favour and devote plenty of time to finding and reading books and journal articles, and to consulting other sources germane to your essay.
- *Practise writing.* With most art forms, just as with sport, practice improves your ability to perform. Practice allows you to apply the 'conventions' of effective writing. It also provides you with the opportunity to seek feedback on the quality of your writing.
- *Plan.* Plan your work schedule to allow time for writing and, if you can, plan your essay.
- *Write freely at first,* suspending **editing** until you have a significant first draft of whatever part of your essay you are working on (Greetham 2001, pp. 176–7).
- *Seek and apply feedback.* Rewrite and rewrite again. Writing is an individual yet *social* process. Perhaps you have an image of a good writer sitting alone at a keyboard typing an error-free, comprehensible, and publishable first draft of a manuscript. Sadly, that image is unfounded. Almost every writer produces countless drafts, and seeks **comment** from peers and other reviewers. Listen to their comments carefully but remember that in the end, it is *your* essay.
- *Read your 'final' essay aloud.* No matter how many times you and your friends read over your work in silence, it will almost always be improved by correcting it after hearing it read aloud. You will hear repetitions you did not know were there. Unclear ideas and sentences will reveal themselves, and pompous, grandiloquent language will become evident.

When you write, remember that you are writing for an audience. It is vital that you understand the ways in which an audience might react to your work. A valuable means of gaining such

Write for your audience.

understanding is through allowing friends, tutors, and others to read and comment on draft copies of your work. You might even find it useful to form a group with some friends and agree to proofread one another's essays critically.

WHAT ARE YOUR ESSAY MARKERS LOOKING FOR?

Your lecturers are not looking for 'correct answers'. There is no 'line' for you to follow. They are concerned with how well you make your case. Whether they agree or disagree with your judgment is not essential to your mark. Disagreement does not lead to bad marks; bad essays do (Lovell & Moore 1992, p. 4).

The answer to the question 'what are your markers looking for?' is really quite simple.

> **BOX 1.1 ESSAY ASSESSORS WANT...**
>
> to be told clearly what you *think*
> and what you have *learned*
> about a *specific* topic.

The following guidelines and advice, which are written to match the criteria outlined in the assessment schedule at the end of this chapter, ought to help you satisfy the broad objective noted in the shaded box above. It is worth thinking seriously about these guidelines.

Quality of argument

Ensure that the essay fully addresses the question

If any one issue in particular can be identified as critical to a good essay, it is this one. Failure to address the question assigned or chosen is often a straightforward indicator of a lack of understanding of course material. It may also be seen as an indicator of carelessness in reading the question or of a lack of interest and diligence.

- Look closely at the wording of your essay topic: e.g. What does '**describe**' mean? How about '**analyse**' or '**compare** and **contrast**'? What do other key words in the assigned topic actually mean? (See the glossary for a discussion of terms used commonly in essay assignments.) The difference in meaning can be critical to the way you approach your essay. For example, an essay in which you are asked to 'critically discuss John Howard's role in post-2000

Australian race relations' requires more than a description of what he did. It asks you to **evaluate** the significance of his actions. Similarly, an essay which asks you to 'discuss the implications of tourism for Tongans' cultural integrity' requires that you give central attention to the issue of cultural integrity and not that you discuss the history of tourism in Tonga. You should be aware that most of your university essays will require you to think about material and weave it into an argument. Very few will ask you to simply recount all the facts you have discovered about some phenomenon or issue.

- Discuss the topic with other people in your class. See how your friends have **interpreted** it. Listen critically to the views of others but be prepared to stand up for your own and change them only if you are convinced you are wrong.
- Wherever necessary, clarify the meaning of an assigned topic with your lecturer. Do this *after* you have given the topic full thought, discussed it with friends, and established your own interpretation, but before you begin writing your paper.
- When you have finished writing, check that you have covered all the material required by the nature of the topic. The paragraph listing and rearranging technique outlined in the next section of this chapter may be helpful.

Ensure that your essay is logically developed

Nothing is more frustrating than to be lost in someone else's intellectual muddle. A paper that fails to define its purpose, that drifts from one topic to the next, that 'does not seem to go anywhere,' is certain to frustrate the reader. If that reader happens to be your lecturer, he or she is likely to strike back with notations scrawled in the margin criticising the paper as 'poorly organised,' 'incoherent,' 'lacking clear focus,' 'discursive,' 'muddled,' or the like. Most lecturers have developed a formidable arsenal of terms that express their frustration at having to wade through papers that … are poorly conceived or disorganised.

(Friedman & Steinberg 1989, p. 53)

In assessing an essay, markers will usually look for a coherent framework of thought underpinning your work. They are trying to uncover the conceptual skeleton upon which you have hung your ideas and see if it is orderly and logical. Throughout the essay readers need to be reminded of the connections between your discussion and the framework. Make clear the relationship between the point being made and any argument you are advancing.

For some topics—but not all—an essay framework can be formed before writing begins (see **Essay plan** and Sketch diagram discussions below). In other situations, the essay may take shape as it is being written (see **Freewriting** below).

Plan your essay.

BOX 1.2 WORKING OUT A STRUCTURE FOR YOUR ESSAY

Essay plan

If you can, try to set out an essay plan before you begin writing. That is, work out a series of broad headings that will form the framework upon which your essay will be constructed. Then, add increasingly detailed material under those headings until your essay is written: What will be the main ideas you might cover? What examples, data, quotes might be useful? What **conclusions** might you reach? As you proceed, you may find it necessary to make changes to the overall structure of the essay.

Sketch diagrams

A sketch diagram of the subject matter is also a good means of working out the structure of your essay. Write down key words associated with the material you will discuss, and draw out a sketch of the ways in which those points are connected to one another. Rearrange the diagram until you have formulated an outline. This can then be used in much the same way as an essay plan.

Freewriting

If you encounter 'writer's block', or are writing on a topic that does not lend itself to use of an essay plan, brainstorm and without hesitation write anything related to the topic until you have some paragraphs on the screen or page in front of you. Then remove the rubbish and organise the material into some coherent package. To be effective, this writing style requires good background knowledge of the material to be discussed. Freewriting can be a good way of making connections between elements of the material you have read about. It is not an easy option for people who have not got a clue about their essay topic.

When you have written the first draft of your essay, check the structure. You can do this quite easily:

- Go through the document giving each paragraph or section a heading which **summarises** that section's content.
- Write out the headings on a separate sheet of paper or on cards, or alternatively use the 'View Outline' option in your word processing software to list the headings used throughout the document. Read through the headings. Are they in a logical order? Do they address the assigned topic in a coherent fashion?
- If necessary, rearrange the headings until they do make sense and add new headings which might be necessary to fully cover the topic. If additional headings are required, you will also have to write some new sections of your paper. Of course, you may also find that you can remove some sections.

- Make your amendments and then go through this process of assigning and arranging headings again until you are satisfied that the essay follows a logical progression.
- Finally, rearrange the written material according to the new sequence of headings.

Make sure your essay structure is clear and coherent.

You might find that the summary of headings you have prepared supplies a framework upon which an informative **introduction** can be based. A reader provided with a sense of direction early in the paper should find your work easy to follow.

Ensure the writing is well structured through introduction, body, and conclusion

In almost all cases, good academic writing will have an introduction, a discussion, and a conclusion. You might combine this structure with the image of an essay taking the form of an hourglass. The introduction provides a broad outline, setting the topic in its context. The central discussion tapers in to cover the detail of the specific issue(s) you are exploring. The conclusion sets your findings back into the context from which the subject is derived and may point to directions for future inquiry.

Imagine your essay has an hourglass structure.

The following is not suggested as a recipe for essay writing, but these points of guidance should be of some assistance in constructing a good paper.

BOX 1.3 GUIDE TO THE CONTENTS OF AN ESSAY'S INTRODUCTION, BODY, AND CONCLUSION

In the *introduction:*

- **State** your aims or purpose clearly. What problem or issue are you discussing? Do not simply repeat or rephrase the question as this is one sure-fire way of putting any reader off your work.

Good essays get off to a good start.

- Make your **conceptual framework** clear. This gives the readers a basis for understanding the ideas which follow.
- Set your study in context. What is the significance of the topic?
- Outline the scope of your discussion (i.e. give the reader some idea of the spatial, temporal, and intellectual boundaries of your presentation). What case will you argue?
- Give readers some idea of the plan of your discussion—a sketch map of the intellectual journey they are about to undertake. Leave the reader in no doubt that your essay has a clear and logical structure (Burdess 1998).

- Be brief. In most essays an introduction that is about 10% of the total essay length is adequate.
- Capture the reader's attention from the outset. Is there some unexpected or surprising angle to the essay? Alternatively, attention might be caught with relevant and interesting quotes, amazing facts, and anecdotes. Make your introduction clear and lively, as first impressions are very important.

The best introductions are those which get to the point quickly and which capture the reader's attention (Bate & Sharpe 1990, p. 12). Like a good travel guide, an effective introduction allows readers to **distinguish** and understand the main points of your essay as they read past them (Greetham 2001, p. 184).

In the *discussion:*

> Convince your reader with logic, example, and careful structure.

- Make your case. 'Who dunnit?'
- Provide the reader with reasons and **evidence** to support your views. Imagine your lecturer is sitting on your shoulder (an unpleasant thought!) saying '**prove** that' or 'I don't believe you'. Disarm his/her scepticism.
- Present your material logically, precisely, and in an orderly fashion.
- Accompany your key points with carefully chosen, colourful, and correct examples and analogies.

In the *conclusion:*

- State your resolution of the problem or question set out in the introduction.

> Make sure the conclusion matches up with the introduction.

The conclusion ought to be the best possible answer to your essay question on the basis of the evidence that you have discussed in the main section of the paper (Friedman & Steinberg 1989, p. 57). It must match the strengths and balance of material you have presented throughout the essay (Greetham 2001, p. 197). Do not introduce new material.

- If appropriate, discuss the broad implication of the work (Moxley 1992, p. 68).
- Tie the conclusion neatly together with the introduction. When you have finished writing your essay, read just the introduction and the conclusion. Do they make sense together? Finally, ask yourself: have I answered the question? This may be evident only if you have the opportunity to review your essay some days after you have finished writing it. For this reason, if for no other, it is a good idea to plan to finish the penultimate draft of your essay some days or weeks before the due date. This will give you the opportunity to more dispassionately review your own work.
- Avoid clichéd, phoney, mawkish conclusions (Northey & Knight 1992, p. 73), e.g. 'The tremendous amount of soil erosion in the valley dramatically highlights the awful plight of the poor farmers who for generations to come will suffer dreadfully from the loss of the very basis for their livelihood'. Instead,

and if you can, leave your reader with something interesting to think about (Najar & Riley 2004, p. 56), such as wider implications or your informed perspective on future trends.

Some writers like to use *headings* throughout their essay. You are not compelled to use headings in essays—indeed, some lecturers actively discourage their use (check with your lecturer). However, for readers of an essay, headings may do several things (Snooks & Co. 2002, p. 44; Windschuttle & Elliott 1999). Headings help map the essay's structure; **show** readers where to find specific information within the essay; help group information into clearly defined sections; and they may also **indicate** to the reader what is to follow. These points provide a clue about the number and nature of headings that might be included in an essay. Provide sufficient headings to offer a person quickly scanning the essay a sense of the work's structure or intellectual 'trajectory'. To check this, write out the headings you propose to use. Is the list logical or confusing, sparse or detailed? Referring back to the essay itself, revise your list of headings until it provides a clear, succinct overview of your work.

> Headings show structure.

If you are writing a particularly long essay, you may need a hierarchy of headings. Three levels should be sufficient for most purposes, although up to five are **illustrated** in the examples below. Too many headings can add confusion rather than clarity.

BOX 1.4 HEADING STYLES

BOLD CAPITALS
MEDIUM CAPITALS
MEDIUM ITALIC CAPITALS
CAPITALS AND SMALL CAPITALS

or
BOLD CAPITALS
Bold lower case
Bold italic lower case
Italic lower case
Italic lower case. With text running on …

or
BOLD CAPITALS
Bold Upper and Lower Case
Bold italic lower case
Italic lower case

Take care to ensure that section headings are consistent throughout the essay.

Ensure the material is relevant to the topic

Don't waffle!

The material you present in your essay should be clearly and explicitly linked to the topic being discussed. To help clarify whether material is relevant or not, try the following exercise. When you have finished writing a draft of your essay, read each paragraph asking yourself two questions:

1   Does *all* of the information in this paragraph help answer the question?
2   *How* does this information help answer the question?

On the basis of your answers, edit. This should help you to eliminate the dross.

Ensure the topic is dealt with in depth

Have you simply slapped on a quick coat of paint or does your essay reflect preparation, undercoat, and good final coats?! Have you explored all of the issues emerging from the topic? This does not mean that you should employ the 'shot-gun' technique of essay writing. Such poor essay-writing style sees the author indiscriminately put as much information as they can collect on a subject onto the pages of their essay.

Instead, be diligent and thoughtful in going about your research, taking care to check your institution's library, CD-ROMs, statistical holdings, other libraries, and electronic information sources. Take notes/photocopies. Read. Read. Read. There is not really any simple way of working out whether you have dealt with a topic in sufficient depth. Perhaps all that can be said is that broad reading and discussions with your lecturer will provide some indications.

Quality of evidence

Ensure your essay is well supported by evidence and examples

You need relevant examples, statistics, and **quotations** from books, articles, and interviews, as well as other forms of evidence to support your case and substantiate claims. In addition, most readers seek examples which will bring to life or emphasise the importance of the points you are trying to make. You can draw information from good research (for example, by reading widely or by conducting interviews with appropriate people). Careful use of examples is also an effective indicator of diligence in research and of the ability to link **concepts** or theory with 'reality'.

Use sources other than the WWW.

When looking for evidence to include in your essay, do not confine your search to material available on the WWW. Your essay marker will most likely be very disapproving of this. Although the WWW is a remarkable and increasingly valuable source of information (see, for example, useful resources like Google Scholar and JSTOR which provide free access to scholarly works), using it solely and fundamentally indicates lazy scholarship and neglects vast amounts of high-quality material available from other sources—notably academic journals, reputable newspapers and magazines, and books.

Be critical of *all* your sources and particularly those on the WWW. Whose evidence and argument do you accept? Why? How do you know that your source is in any way credible or authoritative? Whose interests does it represent? By way of caution, **consider** anwr.org, a site promoting oil drilling in the Arctic National Wildlife Refuge. It takes some investigation to find that the site is supported by Arctic Power, a coalition of Alaskan industry groups pressing to open parts of the refuge to oil and gas development. Arctic Power is underwritten by the state of Alaska with funding from the oil industry.

> Make sure all of your sources are credible.

Table 1.1 provides some suggestions for scrutinising the credibility of **web pages**. Simply because something is published, or is on the Web, does not mean it is true. Indeed, as a 1993 Peter Steiner cartoon published in *The New Yorker* magazine observed, 'On the Internet, nobody knows you're a dog'.

Table 1.1   Evaluating web pages

Question	How do you answer it?	What does it imply?
Did you find the page or site through a sponsored link?	Some search engines will direct you to sponsored links first. These are usually identified as such.	Information distributed with commercial intent is not always 'balanced'.
From what domain does the page come?	Look at the **URL** (Uniform Resource Locator). Is the domain, for example: • commercial (.com) • educational (.edu) • government (.gov) • non-profit (.org), or • miscellaneous (.net)? What country is it from? (e.g., .au for Australia; .nz for New Zealand; .ca for Canada [note: USA-based sites typically have no country identifier]). A web search for country **domain names** will yield full lists. Consider whether the domain and country seem appropriate for the site.	Consider the appropriateness of the domain to the material. Is this kind of agency a fitting one for the material being presented? Is the material from the right place?

Table 1.1   *(cont.)*

Question	How do you answer it?	What does it imply?
Who or what agency wrote the page and why? Is the agency reputable?	Good places to start are the banner at the top of the page or any statement of copyright, which is typically located at the bottom of the page. Alternatively, look for information under links associated with the page and characteristically entitled 'About us', 'Who we are', or 'Background'. Authoring agency details are sometimes located in the URL between the http:// statement and the first / (forward slash), or immediately after a www statement (e.g. www.abs refers to the Australian Bureau of Statistics) and www.maf refers to the NZ Ministry of Agriculture and Fisheries). Try truncating back through the URL to find out about the authoring agency. That is, starting from the end of the URL, delete one by one each phrase ending with a / (forward slash), pressing enter after each deletion. This may generate new web pages that provide insights into the origins of the page you planned to use. It may also be useful to query the authoring institution's name through a search engine. This may reveal other information that points to funding sources and underlying agendas.	Web pages are written with intent or purpose—and it is not always the best of intent!
*Is this someone's personal web page or part of a **weblog** ('**blog**')?*	Look for a personal name in the URL. This is typically shown in the URL after a ~ (tilde), % (percentage), or /people/, /users/ statement (for example, /~jtrout/). Blogs are often identified as such through their title (e.g., Wired Campus Blog); their URL which may contain the word 'blog'; or in web page text introducing the blog.	The fact that information is presented on a personal page or 'blog' is not necessarily a bad thing. Indeed, some are of great value being written, for example, by people with media connections but without the oversight of an editor. However, you will need to find out whether the author is an expert, credible source. This information may be set out on the site you are looking through. If not, use a good search engine (e.g., Alexa, Google, Yahoo) to query the

		author's name. If you cannot get any insights to the author (e.g. their credentials, professional role), think seriously about whether you should use information from the page.
When was the page created or last updated?	Look at the bottom of the web page. This is usually where a 'created on' or 'last updated on' statement is located.	Old pages may contain outdated information. In almost every case, undated statistical or factual information should not be used.
Is the content and layout of high quality?	Check to see if the page looks well-produced and that the text is free of typographical errors and spelling mistakes (translated foreign sites may be an exception). Where possible, confirm the plausibility and accuracy of data or other information presented by comparing it with other good sources.	Scruffy, poorly set-out web pages do not necessarily contain inaccurate information but they should cause you to question the meticulousness of the author in their information gathering and presentation.

Adapted from: Barker (2005) and Beck (2005). Barker, in particular, offers very useful and detailed advice on assessing web pages.

Personal experience and observations may be incorporated as evidence in written work. For example, if you have spent several years as a police officer you may be able to offer penetrating insights in an assignment on the geographies of crime and justice. Women and men who have spent time caring for children in new suburban areas may have valuable comments to make on the issue of social service provision to such areas. It is certainly valid to refer to your own experiences, but be sure to indicate in the text that it is to those that you are referring, and provide the reader with some indication of the nature and extent of your experience: e.g. 'In my nineteen years as a police officer in central Melbourne … '. Where possible, support your personal observations with other sources which readers may be able to consult.

> Used judiciously, personal experience can be good evidence for an essay.

Avoid making unsupported **generalisations**: e.g. 'Crime is increasing daily' or 'Air pollution is the major cause of respiratory illness'. Unsupported generalisations are indicators of laziness or sloppy scholarship and will usually draw criticism from essay markers. Provide support for claims through use of empirical evidence or by citing recognised sources: e.g. 'The Australian Bureau of Statistics has recently released a report entitled *Crime in Australia* which **demonstrates** that crime rates in Australian urban areas have risen since comparable figures were last collected', or 'A new paper in the medical journal *Lancet* suggests that air pollution can be linked to 1054 deaths in Mexico City since 2002'.

Ensure accurate presentation of evidence and examples

When you use examples, take care to ensure that they:

- are relevant
- are as up-to-date as possible
- are drawn from reputable sources (fully identified in your text with an appropriate referencing system)
- include no errors of fact.

Keep a tight rein on your examples. Use only those details you need to make your case.

Use of supplementary material

Make effective use of figures and tables

You can use illustrations to make points more clearly, effectively, or succinctly than you can make them in words. People usually remember the information in illustrations more easily than in text. **Histograms**, **pie charts**, tables, schematic diagrams, and photos can supplement text but should not duplicate it (Mullins 1977, p. 40).

When evaluating your use of illustrative material, such as figures, tables, and maps, markers will check to see that you have made reference to the illustration in your discussion and that the illustration makes the point intended. Assessors also look to see whether you might have added additional illustrative material to support the points you are making or to organise better the information you have presented. Illustrations do not need to come from your reading. You can create your own illustrations where appropriate.

You should take care when incorporating tables and graphics into your essay. Make sure they are relevant and locate them as closely as possible to that part of the text in which they are discussed. Be sure to discuss each illustration some-where in your text. Unless you have a particularly good reason for doing so, do not put figures in an **appendix** at the end of the essay. Most readers find this very frustrating.

A picture is worth a thousand words.

Ensure the illustrations are presented correctly

Several types of illustrative material are commonly included in written work. These, and the accepted labels for each, are as follows:

Type of material	Label
Graphs, diagrams, and maps	Figure
Tables + word charts	Table
Photographs	Plate

Tables, figures, and plates can contribute substantially to the message being communicated in a piece of work. However, you must take care with their presentation.

BOX 1.5 USING ILLUSTRATIVE MATERIAL

Illustrative material should be:
- large (e.g. a figure can be expected to take up an entire page)
- comprehensible. Is the illustration easily understood and self-contained?
- legible
- customised to your work. Do *not* submit an essay laden with marginally relevant photocopied tables and figures lifted directly from texts and journals or pasted in from the WWW. Where appropriate, redraw, rewrite, or modify the material to suit your aims.
- correctly identified with sequential arabic numerals beginning with 1. For example, you should not photocopy Table 17.1 from a textbook and insert it in your essay as Table 17.1. Give it a number customised to your work (begin with Table 1 or Figure 1 etc.) and remove all trace of the photocopied numbering. When you place illustrative materials in your work, ensure that tables/figures etc. are put in correct numerical order. For example, Figure 3 should precede Figure 4.

Titles of illustrative material should be clear and comprehensive. The title must fully specify the *subject* of the illustration, its *location*, and the *time period* to which it refers. For example, 'Vietnamese Born Population as Percent of Total Population, Adelaide Statistical Division, 2006' is a good title, whereas 'Vietnamese Population' is not. The *source* from which you derived the illustration should be specified. Failing to correctly identify the source is one of the most common problems associated with student use of illustrations in written work. The source should be acknowledged with an appropriate reference.

Maps and other diagrams should have a complete and comprehensive *key* or *legend* which allows readers to comprehend/decode the material shown. *Labelling* should also be neat, legible, and relevant to the message being conveyed by the illustration.

Consult the other relevant chapters of this book for more information on the presentation of maps, figures, and tables.

Written expression and presentation

Your writing should be fluent and succinct

Write simply. Short words and sentences are best. Unless you deliberately wish to obfuscate, there is little room for grandiloquence in effective written communication. In your essay you should be conveying knowledge and information, not showing how many big words you know (Booth 1985, p. 13). One straightforward means of checking that communication is clear is to ask yourself whether your writing would be understood by someone whose first language is not English. If you know someone in that position who is willing to proofread your essay, give them a copy to look over.

Another, very effective, means of checking the fluency of your writing involves putting a draft of your work away for several days and then reading it afresh. Odd constructions and poor expression which were not evident before will leap out to greet you. This exercise is often even more revealing if you read the essay aloud. Yet another alternative is to make some mutual editing arrangements with friends. Make a deal. You will 'correct' their papers if they will 'correct' yours. Booth (1985, p. 6) notes that for over 2000 years it has been known that we see other people's mistakes more easily than we see our own.

> Reading your essay aloud can reveal clumsy expression, poor punctuation, and repetition.

Learning fluency in writing may seem impossible. There are, however, two fundamental secrets to success:

1 Take care to keep sentences short and as free of **jargon** as possible. Short sentences are easy to read. Short sentences convey ideas in a no-nonsense style.
2 Effective paragraphing is important. Although there are exceptions (see Clanchy & Ballard 1997 for a discussion) paragraphs typically comprise three parts (Barrett 1982, p. 118):

BOX 1.6 PARTS OF A PARAGRAPH

- *Topic sentence*—states the main idea (e.g. The depletion of Brazil's tropical rain forests is proceeding apace).
- *Supporting sentence(s)*—why, how, examples to support the topic or to prove the point (e.g. There is little government action to end land clearance in fragile environments and private incentives to clear the land remain attractive).
- *Clincher*—lets the reader know the paragraph is over. May summarise the paragraph, echo the topic sentence, or ask a question (e.g. There seems to be little hope for the forests of the Amazon region).

Most paragraphs are unified by a *single* purpose or a single theme (Moxley 1992, p. 74). That is, a paragraph is a cohesive, self-contained expression of one idea. If your paragraph conveys a number of separate ideas, rethink its construction.

Paragraphs should **relate** to one another as well as to the overall thrust of the text. Get into the habit of using transitional sentences at the end of paragraphs to carry the reader onto the next paragraph. For example, consider phrases such as:

Another problem associated with …	Elsewhere …
On the other hand …	Other common …
A similar explanation …	A significant consequence is …
From a different perspective …	A number of issues can be identified …

These are devices which allow you to lead your reader from one part of your essay to another.

Make every word count. Waffle is easily detected and it makes assessors suspect that you have little of substance to say. Prune unnecessary words and phrases from your work. Remember, the objective in an essay is to answer the question or to convey a body of information—not to write a specified number of words!

Use grammatical sentences

One simple way of detecting difficulties with grammar is to have that trusty friend read your essay out loud to you. If that person has difficulty and stumbles over sentence constructions, it is likely that the grammar is in need of repair. Another simple means of avoiding problems is to keep sentences short and simple. Not only are long, convoluted sentences often difficult to understand, they are also grammatical minefields.

Use correct punctuation

Check the material in chapter 10 for a review of common punctuation problems. Take particular care with the use of apostrophes! If there is anything you do not understand, ask your lecturer.

Use correct spelling throughout

Poor spelling brings even the best of work into question. Spelling errors emerge repeatedly as a problem in university-level essays. In these days when many papers are written with the help of a word-processing package, there is little excuse for incorrect spelling. If you write your essay on a computer with

> Spelling errors and sloppy presentation reflect poorly on your work.

a word-processing package be sure to use the spelling checker before you submit the essay for assessment but remember, distinctions between words such as there/their, too/two/to, and bough/bow will not show up. Check too that your spell-checker is using the appropriate form of English! (e.g. Australian English, rather than US English or Philippine English). If you write by hand or use a typewriter, go back to that friend you have been troubling for assistance. Have them look over your paper with an eye to the spelling and grammatical errors.

Make sure your work is legible and well set-out

> Poor presentation can prejudice your case by leading the reader to assume sloppiness of thought.
>
> (Bate & Sharpe 1990, p. 38)

Essays that are difficult to read because of poor handwriting can infuriate assessors. Frustrations emerge because it is very difficult to maintain a sense of your case, argument, or evidence if reading must be repeatedly interrupted to decipher individual words. Wherever possible use a typewriter or word-processor to produce the final copy of your paper.

To allow room for the assessor's comments, all work should be double-spaced and have a large left-hand margin (if in doubt, try 3.5–4 cm). Print your assignment on only one side of A4 pages.

Nicely presented work suggests pride of authorship. You are likely to find that presentation does make a difference—to your own view of your work as well as to the view of the assessor.

Your assignment should be a reasonable length

A key to good communication is being able to convey a message with economy (consider the communicative power of some short poems, such as *haiku*). Take care not to write more words than have been asked for. Most people marking essays do not want to read any more words than they have to. Avoid masking a scarcity of ideas with verbose expression. If you find you do not have enough to say in an essay, perhaps you need to do some more research—not writing.

Sources/referencing

An introductory word of advice on **references**: when writing an essay, be sure to insert **citations** as you go along. It is very difficult to come back to a paper and try to insert the correct references (Hodge 1994). Make sure too when you are collecting information for an essay that you record the bibliographic details of all your sources. This makes it easy to prepare the reference list.

Ensure you have an adequate number of sources

> Keep a full record of all your sources. It will save you a lot of time and work when you prepare your final reference list.

Markers will consider very carefully the quality of evidence you use in your work. You are expected to demonstrate that you have conducted extensive research appropriate to the topic and to the level of the course you are doing. For example, first-year essays might draw from secondary sources such as books, journals, and the Web, whereas third-year research essays might require library research, interviews, fieldwork, and information derived from other primary information sources.

You will be expected to draw your evidence from, and substantiate claims using, *up-to-date*, *relevant*, and *reputable* sources. Reputable sources might include scholarly journals, textbooks, high-quality web sites (see Table 1.1), major newspapers (e.g. the *Australian*, the *Age*, *Sydney Morning Herald*, *New Zealand Herald*, *Christchurch Press*, *Christian Science Monitor*, *New York Times*), and magazines (such as *Time*, *Far Eastern Economic Review*). Practise caution with all your sources, however. As noted earlier, simply because something is written in a journal, newspaper, or on the Web does not necessarily mean it is 'true'. Think critically about the trustworthiness of your sources—particularly if you are using material from the WWW. If you are in any doubt, ask your lecturer.

In much the same way as there is no answer to the question 'How long is a piece of string?', there is no specific number of sources you should consult for any particular kind or length of assignment. For instance, you cannot assume that twenty references is the right number for a first-year, 2000-word essay or that thirty is the correct number for a third-year, 4000-word research report. However, you should not rely on a small number of references or on references drawn too heavily from one source or type of information medium (e.g. WWW). Most assessors give some weight to the *number and range of references* you have used for your work. This is to ensure that you have established the soundness of your case by considering evidence from a broad range of possible sources. For example, the assessor might question the accuracy of an essay examining the consequences of hospital privatisation for Australian rural health care delivery if the essay were based largely on documents produced by the Liberal Party or by the Labor Party. Remember too: most markers will expect you to have consulted sources other than the WWW!

Make sure you adequately acknowledge your sources

Ideas, facts, and quotations *must* be attributed to the source from which they were derived. Failure to acknowledge sources remains a common and potentially dangerous error in student essays (see Burkill & Abbey 2004). Serious omissions may constitute **plagiarism** (see the notes on plagiarism in chapter 10). **Acknowledgment** should be made using an appropriate system of referencing.

Now, all of this business of acknowledging sources may seem to you to be a painful waste of time. But, like most things, there are reasons for it.

> Citing sources fully and correctly is an important academic skill. Take the time to learn how it is done.

BOX 1.7 REASONS FOR ACKNOWLEDGING SOURCES

People writing in an academic environment acknowledge the work of others for two main reasons:

- to attribute credit (and sometimes blame) for the acknowledged author's contribution to knowledge, and
- to allow interested readers the opportunity to pursue a line of inquiry should they be stimulated by something that has been cited. For example, in an essay on the economic geography of South Australian brewing, someone might write: 'Jones (2006, p. 16) observes that there is a great deal of money to be made by private investors by investing in the brewing business'. 'Aha' you think, 'I can make some quick dollars here. All I need to do is find Jones' book and read about how this might be done'. Thanks to the appropriate acknowledgment of Jones' idea in the essay you have read, you can rush to the nearest library and track down Jones' words of wisdom on money-making. Lo and behold, instant millionaire!

Quite often, people new to essay writing save all the acknowledgments of references contained in a paragraph until the end of that paragraph. There they place a string of names, dates, and page numbers. This is incorrect and annoying because the reader has no way of establishing which ideas/concepts/facts are being attributed to whom. References should be placed as close as possible to the ideas or illustrations to which they are connected.

If you are *quoting* someone *directly*, there are four golden rules to follow:

- *Reproduce the text exactly.* Spelling, capitalisation, and paragraphing must mirror that of the original source. If a word is misspelt or if there is an error of fact, put the word '**sic**' in square brackets immediately after the error. This lets your reader know that the mistake was in the original source and that you have not misquoted. Your main text and the quotation should be grammatically consistent. This sometimes requires that you add or remove words. If you find it necessary to omit unnecessary words, use three full stops (...), known as an ellipsis, to show that you have deleted words from the original text. If you need to add words, put those you have added within square brackets. Make sure you do not change the original meaning of the text through your omissions or additions.
- When making a direct quotation of less than about 30 words you should *incorporate the quote* into your own text, indicating the beginning and end of the quote with single quotation marks. The in-text reference or numerical

reference (see chapter 10) is usually placed after the closing quotation marks. For example:

> He described Hispaniola and Tortuga as densely populated and 'completely cultivated like the countryside around Cordoba' (Colon 2006, p. 165).

> He described Hispaniola and Tortuga as densely populated and 'completely cultivated like the countryside around Cordoba'.[5]

If you are making a direct quotation of more than 30 words, you should not use quotation marks, but rather *indent and use single-spacing* as shown in the example here:

One historian makes the point clear:

> Although it included a wide range of human existence, New York was best known in its extremes, as a city capable of shedding the most brilliant light and casting the deepest shadows. Perhaps no place in the world asked such extremes of love and hate, often in the same person. (Spann 2001, p. 426)

A blank line immediately precedes and follows the quote.

- *Use quotations sparingly.* Only use a quotation when it outlines an idea or example so well that you cannot improve on it, or when it contains a major statement you must document.
- *Integrate the quotation into your text.* **Justify** its inclusion. Let the reader know what it means for your work.

See chapter 10 for more details on acknowledging the works of others.

Make sure your in-text referencing style is correct and consistent

Full and correct acknowledgment of the sources from which you have derived quotations, ideas, and evidence is a fundamental part of the academic enterprise. Acknowledging the contribution of others to the essay you have written should not be difficult if you follow the instructions on referencing provided in chapter 10.

Make sure your reference list is correctly presented

The most common—and most easily rectified—problems in essay writing emerge from incorrect acknowledgment of sources. Repeatedly in students' essays, referencing is done improperly and reference lists are formatted incorrectly. Many of those people who mark essays consider that problems with the relatively simple matter of referencing reflect more serious shortcomings in the work they are reading. Consequently, it is advisable to follow carefully the instructions on referencing. If you do not understand how to refer to texts in an essay, see your lecturer.

Before you submit an essay for assessment, be sure that all in-text references have a corresponding entry in the list of *References Cited*. Further, in most cases, the list of *References Cited* should include *only* those references you have actually cited in the paper.

Demonstrated level of individual scholarship

'Scholarship' is one of the most important and perhaps the least tangible of the qualities that make a good essay. Above all, the essay should clearly be a product of *your* mind, of *your* logical thought. The marker will react less than favourably to an essay which is merely a compilation of the work of other writers. In considering matters of scholarship, then, essay markers are searching for judicious use of reference material combined with *your individual insights*.

While scholarship requires that you draw from the work of other writers, you must do so with discretion. Use direct quotations sparingly (if you do use quotations, be sure to integrate them with the rest of your text). Keep paraphrasing to a minimum.

> Essay markers want to know what you think and have learnt about a specific topic.

You might argue that novice status in the discipline means that you must rely heavily on other people's work. Obviously you might encounter problems when you are asked to write an essay on a subject that, until a few weeks ago, may have been quite foreign to you. But do not be misled into believing that in writing an essay you must produce some earth-shattering exposition on the topic you have been assigned. Instead, your assessor is looking for evidence that you have read on the subject, *interpreted* that reading, and set out appropriate evidence, based on that interpretation, which satisfactorily addresses the essay topic. Remember the advice from the beginning of the chapter. Your marker wants you to **explain** clearly what you think and what you have learnt about a specific topic.

Figure 1.1   Essay assessment schedule

Student Name: Grade: Assessed by:

The following is an itemised rating scale of various aspects of written assignment performance. Sections left blank are not relevant to the attached assignment. Some aspects are more important than others, so there is no formula connecting the scatter of ticks with the final grade for the assignment. Ticks in either of the two boxes left of centre mean that the statement is true to a greater (outer left) or lesser (inner left) extent. The same principle applies to the right-hand boxes. If you have any questions about the individual scales, comment, final grade, or other aspects of this assignment, please see the assessor indicated above.

Quality of argument

| The essay fully addresses the question | | | | | The essay fails to address the question |

Logically developed essay — Writing rambles and lacks logical continuity

Writing well structured through introduction, body and conclusion — Writing poorly structured, lacking introduction, cohesive paragraphing and/or conclusion

Material relevant to topic — Much material is not relevant

Topic dealt with in depth — Superficial treatment of topic

Quality of evidence

Essay well supported by evidence and examples — Inadequate supporting evidence or examples

Accurate presentation of evidence and examples — Much evidence incomplete or questionable

Effective use of figures and tables — Figures and tables rarely used or not used when needed

Figure 1.1 (*cont.*)

Illustrations effectively presented and correctly cited				Illustrations poorly presented or incorrectly cited

Written expression and presentation

Fluent and succinct piece of writing				Clumsily written, verbose, repetitive
Grammatical sentences				Many ungrammatical sentences
Correct punctuation				Poor punctuation
Correct spelling throughout				Poor spelling
Legible, well set out work				Untidy and difficult to read
Reasonable length				Too long/short

Sources/Referencing

Adequate number of references				Inadequate number of references
Adequate acknowledgment of sources				Inadequate acknowledgment of sources
Correct and consistent in-text referencing style				Incorrect and inconsistent in-text referencing style
Reference list correctly presented				Errors and inconsistencies in reference list

Demonstrated level of individual scholarship

High				Low

Assessor's comments

REFERENCES AND FURTHER READING

Allen, M. 1997, *Smart Thinking: Skills for Critical Understanding and Writing*, Oxford University Press, Melbourne.

Anderson, J. & Poole, M. 1994, *Thesis and Assignment Writing*, 2nd edn, Wiley, Brisbane.
A comprehensive review of essay writing mechanics.

Barker, J. 2005, *Evaluating Web Pages: Techniques to Apply & Questions to Ask* (online), Available: <http://www.lib.berkeley.edu/TeachingLib/Guides/Internet/Evaluate.html> (17 August 2005).
A very helpful practical resource for those seeking detailed guidance on assessing the quality of web pages.

Barrett, H.M. 1982, *One Way to Write Anything*, Barnes and Noble, New York.
Includes a detailed chapter on writing effective paragraphs.

Bate, D. & Sharpe, P. 1990, *Student Writer's Handbook*, Harcourt Brace Jovanovich, Marrickville, NSW.
This book provides a detailed review of the mechanics of essay writing e.g. essay outlines, paragraphs, English expression, and punctuation. (Perhaps a bit confused in its layout and not written in the correct language for its audience.)

Beck, S.E. 2005, *Evaluation Criteria* (online), Available: <http://lib.nmsu.edu/instruction/evalcrit.html> (17 August 2005).

Becker, H.S. & Richard, S.P. 1986, *Writing for Social Scientists: How to Start and Finish Your Thesis, Book or Article*, University of Chicago Press, Chicago.
Comprehensive and entertaining volume. Although written for graduate students and staff, this book contains useful advice for undergraduate students.

Bernstein, T.M. 1979, *The Careful Writer: A Modern Guide to English Usage*, Atheneum, New York.

Betts, K. & Seitz, A. 1994, *Writing Essays and Research Reports in the Social Sciences*, 2nd edn, Nelson, South Melbourne.
Chapter 3 is a helpful discussion on structuring an argument. It also includes sections on the nature of evidence in essays and ways of writing introductions and conclusions.

Booth, V. 1985, *Communicating in Science Writing and Speaking*, Cambridge University Press, Cambridge.
Includes a very helpful review of pre-writing and writing strategies. Enjoyable reading.

Burdess, N. 1998, *Handbook of Student Skills*, 2nd edn, Prentice Hall, Sydney.

Burkill, S. & Abbey, C. 2004, 'Avoiding plagiarism', *Journal of Geography in Higher Education*, vol. 28, no. 3, pp. 439–46.

Clanchy, J. 1985, 'Improving student writing', *HERDSA News*, vol. 7, no. 3, pp. 3–4, 24.
A short note arguing that literacy is discipline-specific and outlining five ways in which lecturers might improve the quality of student writing.

Clanchy, J. & Ballard, B. 1997, *Essay Writing for Students: A Practical Guide*, 3rd edn, Addison Wesley Longman, Melbourne.
A best-selling book that covers the entire essay writing process, including choosing a topic, taking notes, planning the answer, drafting and redrafting, assessment. Well worth reading.

Cottrell, S. 2003, *The Study Skills Handbook*, 2nd edn, Palgrave MacMillan, Hampshire.
Chapter 7 is a comprehensive, though sometimes confusing, discussion on university-level writing.

Dixon, T. 2004, *How to Get a First. The Essential Guide to Academic Success*, Routledge, London.
Includes a sometimes entertaining chapter on planning an essay that focuses on the importance of both thinking and planning before writing.

Fairbairn, G. & Winch, C. 1996, *Reading, Writing and Reasoning*, 2nd edn, Open University Press, Buckingham.

Fletcher, C. 1990, *Essay Clinic: A Structural Guide to Essay Writing*, Macmillan, South Melbourne.
This short book comprehensively outlines steps in the planning and construction of descriptive (word picture), narrative (story-telling), discursive (different viewpoints), expository (explanatory), analytical (dismantle and understand), and argumentative (persuasive) essays.

Friedman, S.F. & Steinberg, S. 1989, *Writing and Thinking in the Social Sciences*, Prentice-Hall, New York.
A valuable reference on all stages of the writing process.

Game, A. & Metcalfe, A. 2003, *The First Year Experience: Start, Stay and Succeed at Uni*, Federation Press, Leichhardt.
Includes a good chapter on writing that deals gently with the 'psychology' of writing as well as its mechanics.

Greetham, B. 2001, *How to Write Better Essays*, Palgrave Hampshire.
Includes useful material on writing effective paragraphs.

Hay, I. & Delaney, E. 1994, 'Who teaches, learns: Writing groups in geographical education', *Journal of Geography in Higher Education*, vol. 18, no. 3, pp. 317–34.

Hodge, D. 1994, Writing a good term paper, course handout, Department of Geography, University of Washington, Seattle.

Kay, S. 1989, *Writing Under Pressure: The Quick Writing Process*, Oxford University Press, New York.

Lester, J.D. 1998, *Writing Research Papers*, 9th edn, Longman, New York.
Extensive coverage of the essay writing process moving from finding a topic to writing a proposal, doing library research, writing note cards, and eventually, writing the paper.

Lovell, D.W & Moore, R.D. 1992, *Essay Writing and Style Guide for Politics and the Social Sciences*, Australasian Political Studies Association, Canberra.

Marshall, L. & Rowland, F. 1993, *A Guide to Learning Independently*, 2nd edn, Longman Cheshire, Melbourne.
Chapters 11 and 12 on essay writing are useful reading.

Miller, C. & Swift, K. 1981, *The Handbook of Non-sexist Writing for Writers, Editors and Speakers*, Women's Press, London.

Mohan, T., McGregor, H. & Strano, Z. 1992, *Communicating! Theory and Practice*, 3rd edn, Harcourt Brace, Sydney.
An overview of the communication process, with some detailed chapters on writing. Emphasis is given to the character of writing and audience responses, and the mechanics of writing particular styles of document (e.g. reports, essays, memos, faxes).

Moxley, J.M. 1992, *Publish Don't Perish: The Scholar's Guide to Academic Writing and Publishing*, Praeger, Westport, Connecticut.

Mullins, C. 1977, *A Guide to Writing and Publishing in the Social Behavioural Sciences*, Wiley, London.

Najar, R. & Riley, L. 2004, *Developing Academic Writing Skills*, MacMillan Languagehouse, Tokyo.

Northey, M. 1993, *Making Sense: A Student's Guide to Research, Writing, and Style*, 3rd edn, Oxford, Toronto.
Chapters 1, 2, 9, and 11 provide useful material on a variety of issues relating to essay writing.

Northey, M. & Knight, D.B. 1992, *Making Sense in Geography and Environmental Studies*, Oxford University Press, Toronto.
Chapters 2, 4, and 7 offer succinct advice on style in essay writing, editing, and the sensitive use of language.

Schwegeler, R.A. & Shamoon, L.K. 1982, 'The aims and process of the research paper', *College English*, vol. 44, no. 8, pp. 817–24.
The authors distinguish between, and discuss the implications of, the difference between students' views of essays (essays are an opportunity to show how much 'good' information you have collected and presented according to academic conventions) and academics' view of essays (an opportunity to analyse, interpret, and express an argument).

Snooks & Co. 2002, *Style Manual for Authors, Editors and Printers*, 6th edn, John Wiley & Sons Australia, Canberra.

Taylor, G. 1989, *The Student's Writing Guide for the Arts and Social Sciences*, Cambridge University Press, Cambridge.
A detailed and successful review of the essay writing process.

Windschuttle, K. & Elliott, E. 1999, *Writing, Researching, Communicating*, 3rd edn, McGraw-Hill, Sydney.

2

Writing a Report

Research is the process of going up alleys to see if they are blind.

Marston Bates

The great tragedy of science—the slaying of a beautiful hypothesis by an ugly fact.

T.H. Huxley

KEY TOPICS

- Why write a report?
- What are report readers looking for?
- What are the components of a good report? (including abstract and literature review)
- Writing a laboratory report

Your lecturer has assigned you a research project and, as if that was not difficult enough, you have been asked to report on your work—in writing. This chapter about writing research reports and laboratory reports is intended to help you complete that task. Indeed, by providing some guidance on how to write a particular kind of report, the following pages might also help you to undertake the research.

WHY WRITE A REPORT?

There are at least three good reasons for learning to write good research reports. These range from the practical to the principled.

First, there is a *vocational claim*. Academic and professional writing often involves the communication of research findings (Friedman & Steinberg 1989, p. 24). Indeed, as Montgomery (2003, pp. 138–9) notes, 'because of the tendency to outsource analysis and research these days, particularly in industry, the number and diversity of technical reports have gone through a burst of expansion'. Urban planners, market researchers, academics, environmental scientists, and intelligence analysts can all expect to undertake research and to write associated reports in the course of their employment. Indeed, getting and maintaining employment in areas related to geography and the environment often requires the effective conduct and communication of research. That communication is usually to an audience that anticipates answers to a certain set of questions that must nearly always be answered, irrespective of the character of the project. Consequently, it is important to be familiar with the ways in which research results are customarily conveyed from one person to another (i.e. the conventions of research communication).

Second, research reports and papers are a *fundamental and increasingly important building block of knowledge*. Each report is the final product of a process of inquiry. Through the communication of research findings we contribute to the development of practically adequate understandings of the ways in which the world works. 'Practically adequate' means those understandings will not necessarily be absolutely and forever right. Instead, they work and make sense here and now. Some event or discovery may see them change tomorrow.

Third, there is a *moral responsibility to present our research honestly and accurately*. Through our research writing we help to forge understandings about the ways in which the world works. Representing the world to other people in ways that we understand is to play an enormously powerful role. To a degree, people entrust us with the creation of knowledge. Given that trust, our actions must be beyond reproach. In part acknowledgment of that provision of trust we must provide peers, colleagues, and interested observers with accurate representations of our actions. Therein lies a critical role of research reports and a most important reason for writing them well.

WHAT ARE REPORT READERS LOOKING FOR?

Research and laboratory reports typically answer five classic investigative questions (Eisenberg 1992, p. 276).

BOX 2.1 FIVE INVESTIGATIVE QUESTIONS

- What did you do?
- Why did you do it?
- How did you do it?
- What did you find out?
- What do the findings mean?

The person reading or marking your report seeks clear and accurate answers to these questions. Because reports are sometimes long and complex, the reader will also appreciate some help in navigating their way through the document (Windschuttle & Elliott 1999). Make the report clear and easy to follow through easily understood language, a well-written introduction, suitable headings and subheadings, and, if appropriate, a comprehensive table of contents.

Some forms of report, especially lab reports, will answer the five investigative questions through a highly structured progression (e.g. introduction, methods, results, discussion) written in a way which would allow another researcher to repeat the work. For example, an environmental scientist reviewing present-day salinity levels in Australia's Murray River, or a demographer conducting a statistical study on the use of contraceptive measures in New Zealand, is likely to conduct the study as impartially as possible and to record their research procedures in sufficient detail to allow someone else to reproduce the study. For such forms of inquiry, repetition is an important means of verifying results. (This notion of reproducibility or **replication** is discussed fully in Sayer 1992.)

In other forms of research, such as those involving qualitative research methods (for example, interviews, participant observation, textual analysis), results are confirmed in different ways. As a consequence, the research report may be written differently. It will usually answer the five questions identified above, but less emphasis will be given to the business of ensuring replicability. It is more important that qualitative research reports be written in a way which allows other people to confirm the reliability of your sources and to check your work against other related sources about the same or similar topics. Consider, for example, the way a murder trial is conducted. The murder itself cannot be repeated to allow us to work out who the murderer was (replication). Instead, lawyers and police assemble evidence to reconstruct the crime as fairly and accurately as possible. This process is known as **corroboration**. Your report should be a fair and reasonable representation of events. (For fuller discussion of these and related matters, see Mansvelt & Berg 2005 and DeLyser & Pawson 2005.)

Now, geographers reporting on the social construction of an Australian city, or about gay men's perceptions of everyday places, will use different procedures and will write their research in different ways from coastal geomorphologists studying sand-grain size and longshore drift or economic geographers writing about the demographic characteristics of Australian country towns. Yet they will still usually answer the five basic investigative questions identified above, even though style and emphases may make the reports quite different in presentation.

The great diversity of research topics found within geography and environmental science means that you are likely to be asked to write research reports of different types throughout your degree. Reflecting that potential diversity, this chapter provides an introduction to report writing *in general*. Some specific references are made to laboratory writing. It is very helpful to have available an example of a high-quality report that satisfies the requirements of your lecturer or whoever else 'commissioned' the report (Montgomery 2003, p. 141). You can use this as a general model of the kind of style you should be adopting or as a precise blueprint, depending on the expectations of your audience. So, if you are preparing a report for your lecturer, ask if they have written reports you may consult as examples. Alternatively, try your library.

REPORT WRITING—GENERAL LAYOUT

It should be clear from the paragraphs above that although research and laboratory reports will usually answer Eisenberg's five investigative questions, there is no single correct research report style. The best way to organise a research report is determined by the type of research being carried out, the

> Find 'model' reports to help guide you through your first report-writing efforts.

character and aims of the author, and the audience for whom the report is written. Accordingly, the following guidelines for report writing cannot offer you a recipe for a 'perfect' research report. Keys to a good report include well-executed research and the will and skills to communicate the results of your work effectively.

Having acknowledged that there is no single 'correct' report writing style, it is fair to say that over time a common pattern of report presentation has emerged. That pattern reflects a strategy for answering the five investigative questions identified above. Through repeated use, it is also a structure of presentation many readers will expect to see. If you are new to report writing, and unless you have been advised otherwise, it may be useful to follow the general pattern outlined below. If you are more experienced and believe there is a more effective way of communicating the results of your work, try out your own strategy. Remember, however, that you are guiding the reader through the work: you will have to let your audience know if you are doing anything they might not expect.

Short research reports and laboratory reports generally comprise a minimum of seven sections which are outlined below. Long reports may add some or all of the extra materials listed. It is likely that most reports you are asked to write early in your university career will be short reports. By third or fourth year, longer reports might be expected.

Table 2.1   Contents of a report

Short report	Long report
• Title page	• Title page
	• Letter of transmittal
• Abstract/executive summary	• Abstract/executive summary
	• Acknowledgments (sometimes placed after Discussion or immediately before References)
	• Table of contents
• Introduction (what you did and why)	• Introduction
• Materials and methods (how you did it)	• Materials and methods
• Results (what you found out)	• Results
• Discussion (what the results mean)	• Discussion
	• Recommendations
	• Appendices
• References	• References

Although these headings point to an order of report presentation, there is no need to write the sections in any particular sequence. Indeed, you may find it useful to follow Woodford's (in Booth 1993, p. 2) advice to label several sheets of paper headed Title, Summary, Introduction, Methods, Results etc. and use these to jot down notes as you work through the project. Then begin your report by writing the easiest section (the methods section in many cases).

The following pages outline the form and function of the common components of research reports. Discussion also elaborates on some of the issues that contribute most significantly to effective research presentations in an academic setting. Those same issues form the basis of an assessment schedule for research reports and laboratory reports.

> There is no need to write your report in the same order it will be presented.

Preliminary material

Title page
The best titles are usually short, accurate, and attractive to potential readers. When you have finished writing your report, check that the title matches the results and discussion. An example of a functional and informative—though slightly bland—title is: 'Social consequences of homelessness for men in Adelaide, South Australia (1990–2006)'. This title lets the reader know the topic, place, and time period. An example of a poor title on the same subject matter is: 'Men and homelessness'.

The title page of a report should also include:

- your name, position, and organisational affiliation
- name of the person and/or organisation to whom the report is being submitted
- date the report was issued.

Modify these recommendations to suit the academic setting in which you find yourself. For example, date of issue might be the due date or the date you submit the assignment for assessment. The person to whom the report is submitted may be your lecturer.

Letter of transmittal

Reflecting the fact that reports are often commissioned, a letter of transmittal is sometimes included. This letter typically:

- explains the purpose of the letter (e.g. 'Enclosed is the final report on wetland management issues in the Lake Ngaroto region that was commissioned by your organisation.')
- sets out the main finding of the report and any other vital issues likely to be relevant
- acknowledges any significant assistance received (e.g. 'We are indebted to the Organisation of Lake Ngaroto Wetland Lovers for allowing us access to their extensive photographic records of post-1955 change in the lake.')
- offers thanks for the opportunity to conduct the research (e.g. 'We would like to thank the Department of Conservation for engaging us to conduct this research.')

(Mohan, McGregor & Strano 1992, p. 227; University of Canberra 2005)

Abstract/Executive summary

Of all sections of the report other than the title, this is the most likely to be read. It is important, therefore, to make it easy to understand. An **abstract** is a coherent and concise statement, intelligible on its own, which typically provides concise answers to each of the five investigative questions outlined at the beginning of this chapter: What did you do? Why did you do it? How did you do it? What did you find out? What do the findings mean?

Abstracts are limited in length (usually 100–250 words) and are designed to be read by people who may not have the time to read the whole report. They are *not* written in the form of notes. All information contained in the abstract must be discussed within the main report. Do not write an abstract as if it is the alluring back-cover blurb of a mystery novel. Let

> Many readers decide whether or not to read a report on the basis of its title and abstract; make sure they are clear and accurate.

your readers know what your research is about—do not leave them in suspense. Put the abstract at the beginning of your report, although it will usually be the last section you write.

Abstracts may be subdivided into two main types, *informative* and *indicative*, although they may be written in a style which combines features of each.

An *informative* abstract typically summarises primary research, and offers a concise statement of details of the paper's content, including aims, methods, results, and conclusions.

BOX 2.2 EXAMPLES OF INFORMATIVE ABSTRACTS

Example 1

Argent, N. & Rolley, F. 1999, 'Left Out on a Limb? Bank Branch Closures in Rural South Australia, 1981–1998', *South Australian Geographical Journal*, vol. 98, pp. 3–18.

Abstract

Amidst the growing recognition of the vital roles that local financial services play in the social and economic development of rural communities, the paper investigates the spatial and institutional pattern of bank branch closure since financial deregulation in rural South Australia. Using bank branch listings from 1981, 1986, 1991, 1996 and 1998 telephone directories, the paper finds that rural South Australia has lost one third of its 1981 branches, with 37 towns made branchless, over the study period. In assessing the options available to financially excluded communities the authors find that, in regional development terms, community banking offers one of the most appropriate responses to the banks' abandonment of face-to-face service delivery.

Example 2

Bren, L. & Sandell, P. 2004, 'Ecohydrology and Environmental Change to Lake Albacutya and Wyperfeld Park in North-Western Victoria, Australia', *Australian Geographical Studies*, vol. 42, no. 3, pp. 307-24.

Abstract

Lake Albacutya is a well-known intermittent lake in north-western Victoria. The lake is near the termination of the Wimmera River. From time-to-time the lake fills and flow passes down Outlet Creek into Wyperfeld National Park. The wetlands associated with the lake have a high biodiversity value and are named in international treaties. This paper examines the hydrologic factors associated with lake filling and flow into Wyperfeld. The lake has filled approximately six times since 1880 and has partially filled on other occasions. Examination of rainfall data from 1875 at Horsham gave no indication of long term rainfall decline, and showed that rainfall at Horsham can be viewed as representative of rainfall in the Wimmera River catchment. However a double-mass analysis showed that the relationship between the Wimmera River flow and rainfall has varied from 1890 to the present. Examination of data associated with six fillings of Lake Albacutya suggested that filling is a two-year event requiring at least 550 GL of flow passing Horsham over the two years immediately associated with the flood. A simple model based on rainfall and this threshold reproduced observed characteristics of the data reasonably well. This suggested that the flooding frequency of Lake Albacutya has dropped from about one in 25 years in the natural state to a substantially lower frequency under current river conditions. The results also suggested that because of changes in the Wimmera River the last filling and flood into Wyperfeld in 1976 was far smaller than it would otherwise have been. This is consistent with field mapping of the flood in relation to River Red Gum (*Eucalyptus camaldulensis Dehnh.*) stands. Analysis of the health of these stands showed major dieback with the severity of this being roughly proportional to the distance from the 1976 flood boundaries. An examination of values associated with the lake and adjoining Wyperfeld National Park suggested that biodiversity and economic values are and will be compromised by the reduction in flooding. In particular, an internationally-known provenance of Red Gum is at risk, and bird-breeding opportunities have diminished.

Example 3

Hill, R., Griggs, P. & Bamanga Bubu Ngadimunku Incorporated 2000, 'Rainforests, Agriculture and Aboriginal Fire Regimes in Wet Tropical Queensland', *Australian Geographical Studies*, vol. 38, no. 2, pp. 138–57.

Abstract
This paper challenges the hypothesis that Aboriginal fire-regimes in the coastal wet tropics of north Queensland have been responsible for significant rainforest decline in the past, and rejects the narrative that recent rainforest expansion is the result of the disappearance of Aboriginal people and their fire practices from the area. Mapping of vegetation in the Mossman district in c. 1890 from survey-ors' plans, and in 1945 and 1991 from aerial photography, demonstrates that the expansion of rainforest since 1945 represents a recovery following extensive rainforest destruction associated with sugar cane cultivation in the first 70 years of European occupation. Kuku-Yalanji Aboriginal people continued to occupy their traditional lands, and participated in the sugar industry, throughout this period. They adapted their fire management practices to the changed economic and social circumstances. Management of fire by the Kuku-Yalanji people prior to European occupation ensured the presence of extensive rainforest cover, while also providing access to fire-prone forests and their cultural resources.

An *indicative* abstract outlines the contents of a paper, report, or book, but does not recount specific details. It is commonly used to summarise particularly long reports and book chapters.

BOX 2.3 EXAMPLES OF INDICATIVE ABSTRACTS

Example 1

Macpherson, C. 1999, 'Will the "Real" Samoans Please Stand Up? Issues in Diasporic Samoan Identity', *New Zealand Geographer*, vol. 55, no. 2, pp. 50–9.

Abstract

This paper examines the circumstances in which ethnic labels and identities are constructed and the conditions that are producing socio-cultural convergence within them. Using Samoan identities as an example, it is argued firstly that categories based on descent will not necessarily reflect socio-cultural realities within them and, secondly, that Samoan identities constructed at various times for particular purposes may have given an impression of ethnic unity which masked considerable internal divergence. Finally, it is argued that it may be increasingly difficult for migrant Samoans to agree on symbols of Samoan identity, much less to agree whether or not these might be building blocks of a national identity. This fluid reality raises fundamental issues about the significance of the apparently fixed descent categories within which we routinely work.

Example 2

Moran, M.F. 2004, 'The Practice of Participatory Planning at Mapoon Aboriginal Settlement: Towards Community Control, Ownership and Autonomy', *Australian Geographical Studies*, vol. 42, no. 3, pp.339–55.

Abstract

The practice of participatory planning in discrete Indigenous settlements has been established since the early 1990s. In addition to technical and economic goals, participatory planning also seeks community development outcomes, including community control, ownership and autonomy. This paper presents an evaluation of one such planning project, conducted at Mapoon in 1995. The Plan successfully improved physical infrastructure and housing, but had mixed success in terms of community development. Despite various efforts to follow participatory processes, the Plan was essentially a passing event, community control progressively diminished after its completion, and outcomes fell short of notions of ownership and autonomy. This suggests some misunderstandings between the practice of participatory planning and the workings of governance.

Example 3
Thom, B.G. & Harvey, N. 2000, 'Triggers for Late Twentieth Century Reform of Australian Coastal Management', *Australian Geographical Studies*, vol. 38, no. 3, pp. 275–90.

Abstract
This paper identifies four triggers that underpinned the late 20th century reform of coastal management in Australia. These have operated across federal, state and local levels of government. The triggers are global environmental change, sustainable development, integrated resource management, and community awareness of management issues and participation in decision making. This reform has been driven by international and national forces. The number of inquiries into coastal management in Australia has culminated in the production of a national coastal policy in 1995. This has led to fundamental changes in coastal management and to the recognition of the inevitability of changes in coastal systems. Federal policies and programs are being translated into action at the state and local government levels through a variety of funding mechanisms and programs. These involve capacity building, a memorandum of understanding between all levels of government, an enhanced role for state advisory or co-ordinating bodies, and an increased role for public participation.

Abstracts usually comprise a single paragraph, although long abstracts may require paragraphing. They do not usually contain tables, figures, or formulae and they should not discuss anything not covered in the paper or report. All unfamiliar terms should be defined, as should **acronyms** (e.g. NATO, NAFTA) and non-standard abbreviations (e.g. dBA, pJ). Avoid referring to other works in an abstract. If you do refer to specific works or individuals they must, of course, be included in the list of references associated with the full paper.

It is a matter of common style that issues included or discussed in the main paper are presented in the present tense whereas what the author did and thought is written in the past tense, e.g. 'This report describes the nature of chemical weathering on … '; 'It was discovered that … '; 'Moreover, weathering had the effect of … '; 'The report concludes that … '.

Acknowledgments
If you have received valuable assistance and support from some people or organisations in the preparation of the report they should be acknowledged. As a general rule thank those people who genuinely helped with aspects of the work, such as proofreading, preparing figures and tables, solving statistical or computing problems, taking photos, or doing the typing.

Table of contents

This should accurately and fully list *all* headings and subheadings used in the report with their associated page numbers. The table of contents occupies its own page and must be organised carefully with appropriate spacing. Make sure that the numbering system used in the table of contents is the same as that used in the body of the report. Included after the table of contents, and on separate pages, are a list of figures and a list of tables. Each of these lists contains, for each figure or table, its number, title, and the page on which it is located. If your report uses many abbreviations and acronyms, provide a list of these too but make sure that you also define each one fully when it first appears in the text.

Introduction—why did you do this study?

> ### BOX 2.4 CONTENTS OF A REPORT'S INTRODUCTION
>
> The introduction of a report answers the following questions:
> - What question is being asked? (If appropriate, state your hypothesis.)
> - What do you hope to learn from this research?
> - Why is this research important? (What is the social, personal, and disciplinary significance of the work? This usually requires a literature review.)

When you write your introduction imagine that readers are unfamiliar with your work and that they really do not care about it. Let your audience know why this report is important and exactly what it is about, but do not include data or conclusions from your study. When readers know what you are going to discuss, they are better able to grasp the significance of the material you present in the remainder of your report.

Use the introduction to convince your audience to read the rest of your report.

When your readers have finished reading your introduction, they should know exactly what the study is about, what you hope to achieve from it, and why it is significant. If they have also been inspired to read the remainder of the report, so much the better!

Literature review

As part of, or soon after, your introduction you may need to write a literature review to provide the background to, and justification for, your research. The literature review is sometimes presented as a separate part of the report, after the introduction and before the discussion of materials and methods. A literature review is a comprehensive, but pithy and critical, summary of publications and reports related to your research. It should discuss significant other works written in the area and make clear your assessment of those works. Do you agree with them? What are their strengths and weaknesses? What questions have they left unanswered? How do they lead to the work your report discusses? (Cottrell 2003, p. 210)

As Macauley (2000) suggests, the literature review serves a number of functions. It may help:

- prevent you from 'reinventing the wheel' (i.e. replicating the earlier work of others)
- identify gaps in the literature and potential research areas
- increase your breadth of knowledge in the field and highlight information, ideas, and methods that might be relevant to your project
- identify other people working in the same area, and
- put your work into intellectual and practical perspective by identifying ways in which it may contribute to, fit in with, or differ from available work on the subject.

A good literature review makes clear the relationships between your work and that which has been done in the area before.

Starting a literature review can be difficult. It is probably useful to identify the parent discipline(s) with which your research is associated (e.g. geography, hydrology) and to then consult recent issues of the leading journals in the field to gather information on the topic area as broadly as it might be defined. Draw from the references in those articles to get some sense of the history of your research topic and to identify key authors, texts, and articles. Gather those texts and read them. You may also find it helpful to consult the Social Sciences Citation Index (SSCI) or the Sciences Citation Index (SCI) to **trace** the intellectual genealogy of key references through time (speak to your librarian about this helpful technique).

Once you have gathered and read relevant resources, you can begin writing the literature review. As a rule of thumb, a good literature review might normally discuss the truly significant books written in the field, notable books and articles produced on the broad subject in the past four or five years, and all available material on your specific research area. As noted above, the review should provide the reader with an understanding of the conceptual and disciplinary origins and significance of your study. It requires careful writing. As Reaburn (in Central Queensland University Library 2000) observes:

Students will get a pile of articles and will regurgitate what article one said, what article two said. I can't emphasise enough, a well written literature review must evaluate all the literature, must speak generally, with general concepts they have been able to lift from all the articles, and they must be able to evaluate and critically analyse each one, then link and make a flow of ideas. Rather than separate little boxes, each box representing an article, make a flow of ideas, generalise and use specifics from one or two articles to back up a statement.

Your literature review should not be a string of quotations or a review of findings of other authors' work. Do not make the mistake of trying to list and summarise all material published in your area of work. Rather, organise the review into sections that present themes and trends related to your research. Integrate all the little pieces of knowledge you have found in your reading into a coherent whole. Your completed literature review should be a critical analysis of earlier work set out in such a way that it becomes evident to the reader why your research work is being conducted (Behrendorff 1995, p. 4).

> Check to see that your literature review tells a coherent story about the development of research relevant to your topic.

You will probably find it helpful to look at examples of good literature reviews in your area of interest to gain a sense of how they are written. Short reviews are included as part of research papers in virtually every good academic journal. Have a look, for instance, at the articles by Lucas, Munroe, and Pigozzi in a single issue of *The Professional Geographer*.

Lucas, S. 2004, 'The images used to "sell" and represent retirement communities', *The Professional Geographer*, vol. 56, no. 4, pp. 449–59. Lucas confines her review to pages 450–3 in particular.

Munroe, D.K., Southworth, J. & Tucker, C.M. 2004, 'Modeling spatially and temporally complex land-cover change: the case of Western Honduras', *The Professional Geographer*, vol. 56, no. 4, pp. 544–59. The literature review in this paper is brief and confined largely to page 545.

Pigozzi, B.W. 2004, 'A hierarchy of spatial marginality through spatial filtering', *The Professional Geographer*, vol. 56, no. 4, pp. 460–70. Pigozzi's review is set out in the section entitled 'Introduction and context'.

Materials and methods—how did you do this study?

You should provide a precise and concise **account** of the materials and methods used to conduct the study, and why you chose them. Let your reader know exactly how you did the study and where you got your data. A good description of materials and methods should enable readers to duplicate the investigative procedure even if they have no source of information about your study other than your report. In qualitative studies, however, duplication of procedure is unlikely to lead to identical results. Instead, the outcome may be results which corroborate, substantiate, or, indeed, refute those achieved in the initial study.

> If your reader had no source of information other than your report, could they repeat your study?

Depending on the specific character of the research, the methods section of a report comprises up to three parts (Dane

1990, pp. 219–21), which may be written as a single section or presented under separate subheadings: sampling, apparatus, and procedure.

Sampling/subjects

An important part of the materials and methods section of a report is a statement of *how* and *why* you chose some particular place, group of people, or object to be the focus of your study. For example, if your research concerns people's fears and the implications those fears have for the use of urban space, why have you chosen to confine your study to some specific suburb of one Australian city? Having limited the study to that location, why and how did you choose a small group of people to speak to from the much larger total local population? Alternatively, in an examination of avalanche hazards in New Zealand's South Island high country, why and on what bases did you limit your study to those risks associated with one popular ski area?

> Explain and justify your sampling and case selection decisions.

In the sampling or subjects section of your report, your reader will appreciate answers to the following questions:

- *Who/what* specific group, place, or object have you chosen to study? You may have already stated in the introduction that you were exploring the attitudes of Papua New Guinean women to birth control, but you now need to identify the specific group and number of women you are going to interview or to whom you will administer questionnaires (e.g. 3000 urban-dwelling women of child-bearing age). Or, in your study about supernatural explanations of unusual landscape features, you might have determined that you will limit your study to Incan constructions in Peru within a 100-kilometre radius of the historically important town of Cuzco.
- *Why* did you make that choice? Why did you limit the study to 3000 Papua New Guinean women of child-bearing age and not to a smaller group of rural-dwelling women? Or in our other example, why Peru and not Easter Island? Why 100 kilometres? Why Cuzco and not Machu Picchu or Aguas Calientes?
- *How* did you select the unit(s) of study? That is to say, what specific sampling technique did you employ (e.g. snowball, simple random, typical case, cluster area, random traverse)? There is no need to go into great detail about the technique, such as describing any computer programs used in your sampling, unless the procedure was unusual.
- *What* are the limitations and shortcomings of the data or sources?

Of course, if you are reporting a field study, a general description of the study site is needed. Do not forget to include a map, for it may save you a great deal of writing and will almost

> Don't hesitate to illustrate.

certainly provide your reader with a clearer sense of the place you are describing than might the proverbial thousand words. Photographs may also be helpful.

Apparatus or materials

Provide a brief description of any special equipment or materials used in your study. For example, briefly describe any experimental equipment or questionnaires used in your work. In some more advanced studies you may also be expected to put the name and address of equipment manufacturers in **parentheses**. Do not hesitate to use figures and plates in your description of apparatus.

Procedure

This section contains specific *details* about how the data were collected, about response levels, and about the methods used to interpret the findings. For example, if your study was based on a questionnaire survey or experimental procedure, tell your readers about the process of questionnaire administration, or about the experiment, in enough detail to allow them to replicate your procedures. What statistical tests did you decide to use? It is important to *justify* your selection of data collection and statistical procedures in this section. Why did you choose one method over others? Give references to support your selection.

What are the advantages and disadvantages of the procedure you selected and how did you overcome any problems you encountered? You might consider it more appropriate to confine discussion of this last question to the discussion section of your report.

Where appropriate (e.g. in research involving human or animal subjects) your discussion of procedural issues should also indicate how the work satisfied relevant ethical guidelines.

Results—what did you find out?

The results section of a research report is typically a dispassionate, factual account of findings. It outlines what occurred or what you observed. State clearly whether any hypotheses you made can be accepted or rejected but, in general, you should not discuss the significance of those results here. That will be covered by the next section of the report. For example, you may have conducted a study which suggests that all koalas on a small offshore island will starve to death unless something is done to control their population. You would save your discussion of ways to resolve that problem for a later section of the report.

Although it is not customary to present conclusions and interpretations in the results section, in some qualitative and laboratory reports it is considered appropriate to combine the results with an interpretive discussion. If you have any doubt about what is appropriate, ask your lecturer.

A key to effective presentation of results is to make them as comprehensible to your readers as possible. To this end, it may be appropriate to begin your discussion of results with a brief overview of the material that is to follow before elaborating. You might also consider presenting your results in the chronological order in which you discovered them.

> Results are important, but save time, space, and energy to interpret them.

Use maps, tables, figures, and written statements creatively to summarise and convey key information emerging from the study. If you have provided results in figures and tables, do not repeat all the data in the text. Emphasise only the most important observations. You should place tables and figures close to the text in which they are mentioned without interrupting the flow of the text. However, if you have particularly detailed and lengthy data lists or figures which supplement the report's content, these may be better placed in an appendix.

The results section will often contain a series of subheadings. These usually reflect subdivisions within the material being discussed, but sometimes reflect matters of method. In general, however, try to avoid splitting up the results section on the basis of methods, since it may suggest that you are 'allowing the methods rather than the issues to shape the problem' (Hodge 1994, p. 2).

If you have not already done so in the report, the results section is an appropriate place in which to identify the limits of your data.

Discussion and conclusion—what do the findings mean?

> I am appalled by … papers that describe most minutely what experiments were done, and how, but with no hint of why, or what they mean. Cast thy data upon the waters, the authors seem to think, and they will come back interpreted.
>
> (Woodford 1967, p. 744)

The discussion is the heart of the report. Perhaps not surprisingly, it is also the part which is most difficult to write and, after the title, abstract, and introduction, is the section most likely to be read thoroughly by your audience. Readers and assessors will be looking to see if your work has achieved its stated objectives. So, take particular care when you are writing this part of your report.

The discussion has two fundamental aims:

- to explain the results of your study. Why do you think the patterns—or lack of patterns—emerged?
- to explore the significance of the study's findings. What do the findings mean? What new and important matters have been raised? Compare your results with trends described in

> Use the discussion to explain results and explore significance.

the literature and with theoretical behaviour. Embed your findings in their larger academic, social, and environmental contexts. Make explicit the ways in which your work fits in with studies conducted by other people and the degree to which it might have broader importance.

David Hodge makes the point:

> Remember that research should never stand alone. It has its foundations in the work of others and, similarly, it should be part of what others do in future. Help the reader make those connections.
>
> (Hodge 1994, p. 3)

The concluding sections of the report might also offer suggestions about improvements or variations to the investigative procedure which could be useful for further work in the field. Where do we go from here? Are there other methods or data sets which should be explored? Has the study raised new sets of questions? (Hodge 1994, p. 3) Any thoughts you have must be *justified*. Many students find it easy to offer suggestions for change, but few are able to support their views.

Recommendations

If your report has led you to a position where it is appropriate to suggest particular courses of action or solutions to problems, you may wish to add a recommendations section. This could be included within the conclusion or accorded a free-standing place. In some reports, recommendations are placed at the front, following the title page (Gray 1970, p. 6). Recommendations should be based on material covered in the report (Mohan, McGregor & Strano 1992, p. 228).

Appendices

Material which is not essential to the report's main argument and is too long or too detailed to be included in the main body of the report is placed in an appendix at the end of the report. For example, you might include a copy of the questionnaire you used or background information on your study area or pertinent data which is too detailed for inclusion in the main text. However, your appendix should *not* be a place to put *everything* you collected in relation to your research but for which there was no place in your report (Kane 1991, p. 187). Appendices are usually located after the conclusions but before the references. Each appendix contains different material and each should be numbered clearly.

Don't use appendices as a dumping ground for data.

References

For information on citing references in a research report, see chapter 10.

Written expression and presentation

Language of the report

Some audiences reading research and laboratory reports still expect the report to be written in 'objective', dispassionate, third-person language (e.g. 'it was considered' rather than 'I considered'). Consider that expectation when writing your report. If you choose to write in first-person style, which reflects the social creation of knowledge, some audiences may be distracted and unconvinced by your apparent 'personal bias'. Whatever choice you make, remember that simply writing a report in the superficially 'objective' third person does not render it any more accurate than a report written in the first person! (For a lengthy discussion of this, see Mansvelt & Berg 2005.) If you have any questions or concerns about the style of language you should use in your report, ask your lecturer.

Another matter of language which warrants attention is the use of **jargon**. The word 'jargon' has two popular applications. Most commonly, jargon refers to technical terms used inappropriately or when clearer terms would suffice. More accurately, it means words or a mode of language intelligible only to a group of experts in a particular field of study (Friedman & Steinberg 1989, p. 30). There will be occasions in report writing when you will find it necessary to use jargon in the second sense of the word. You should never be guilty of using jargon in the more common, first sense of the term. Remember, you are writing to communicate ideas to the intended audience as clearly as possible. Use the language which allows you to do that. KISS (that is, Keep It Simple, Stupid) your audience. For a more detailed discussion of jargon, see chapter 10.

Two final points include checking that your report's text and figures 'move from the general to the specific ... for individual sections and for the report as a whole' (Montgomery 2003, pp. 143-4) and ensuring that your report—despite its many sections—reads as a single, integrated document. This

> Make sure your report is coherent and formatted consistently.

is an especially important issue if your report is the output of a group project and sections have been written by different people or teams. It may involve the sometimes lengthy tasks of rewriting some sections, reordering elements of the report, ensuring all references, figures, and tables are formatted uniformly.

Presentation

Be sure that your report is set out in an attractive and easily understood style. Care in presentation suggests care in preparation. *Care* in presentation is to be emphasised here, not gaudiness and decoration. People tend to be suspicious of overly 'decorated' reports, and in a professional environment, such as consulting, they may also question the costs of production. Get the fundamental matters straight. For instance:

• Use the same-sized paper throughout. There may be some occasions, however, when the use of same-sized sheets is impractical (for example, when you are using maps).
• Number all pages.
• Be sure the different parts of your report stand out clearly.
• Use lots of white space—but do be judicious about your use of paper.
• Use SI (*Système International*) units (that is, metric) in describing measures.
• Use a clear and consistent hierarchy of headings. An example is set out below.

BOX 2.5 EXAMPLE OF HEADING HIERARCHIES IN A REPORT

1. **Introduction**
   1.1 Background
   1.2 Aims
   1.3 Objectives
2. **Methods**
   2.1 The questionnaire
   2.2 Sample group
3. **Results**
   3.1 Response rate
   3.2 Findings
       3.2.1 Who is fearful in urban space?
       3.2.2 Precautionary strategies taken to avoid perceived threats
       3.2.3 Residents' views on means to reduce levels of fear
4. **Conclusions**
5. **Recommendations**
   5.1 Public solutions to fear of violence in urban space
   5.2 Individuals' solutions
6. **Appendices**
   (i)   The questionnaire
   (ii) Tabulated responses
7. **References**

WRITING A LABORATORY REPORT

A laboratory report is a particular form of research report. Hence, the preceding advice is applicable. Typically, a lab report dispassionately and accurately recounts experimental research procedures and results. A good report is written so that another student-researcher could repeat the experiment in exactly the same way as you did (assuming, of course, that you employed correct procedures) and could compare their results with yours. You must be both meticulous in outlining methods and accurate in your presentation of results. Meticulous does not mean tedious. Try not to overdo the detail. In the context of the specific experiment that you are doing, record those things which are important. What did you need to know to do the experiment? Let your reader know that. One could almost argue that the best 'Materials and methods' sections in laboratory reports ought to be written by novices who are less likely to make assumptions about readers' understanding of experimental methods than are more experienced researchers.

By convention, laboratory reports follow the order of research report presentation outlined earlier in this chapter, that is:

- Title page
- Abstract
- Introduction
- Materials and methods
- Results
- Discussion
- Appendices
- References.

Depending on the specific nature of your experiment, your lab supervisor may not require all these sections. For example, if your report is simply an account of work you undertook during a single laboratory class it is possible that there will be no need for you to include an abstract, references, and appendices. However, your lecturer may be impressed if you take the care and attention to relate your day's laboratory work to appropriate reference or lecture material. Clearly, though, if your lab work is conducted over a longer period than a single class, you will have the opportunity to consult relevant reference materials.

Figure 2.1 Research report assessment schedule

Student Name: Grade: Assessed by:

The following is an itemised rating scale of various aspects of research report performance. Sections left blank are not relevant to the attached assignment. Some aspects are more important than others, so there is no formula connecting the scatter of ticks with the final grade for the assignment. Ticks in either of the two boxes left of centre mean that the statement is true to a greater (outer left) or lesser (inner left) extent. The same principle is applied to the right-hand boxes. If you have any questions about the individual scales, comment, final grade, or other aspects of this assignment, please see the assessor indicated above.

Purpose and significance

Statement of problem or purpose is clear and unambiguous					Statement of problem or purpose is unclear or ambiguous

Research objectives outlined precisely					Research objectives unclear

Disciplinary, social and personal significance of the research problem made clear					Problem not set in context

Documentation fully outlines the evolution of the research problem from previous findings					No reference to earlier works or incorrect references

Description of method

Most appropriate research method selected					Research method selected is inappropriate

'Sample', cases or study area appropriate to purpose of inquiry					'Sample', cases or site unsuitable

Complete description of study method					Inadequate description of study method

Quality of results

Evidence of extensive primary research					Little or no evidence of primary research
Limitations of sources made clear					Inappropriate sources accepted without question
Relevant results presented in appropriate level of detail					Relevant results omitted or suppressed

Discussion & interpretation

No errors of interpretation (e.g. logic, calculation) detected					Many errors of interpretation
Limitations of findings made clear					Limitations of findings not identified
Discussion connects findings with relevant literature					No connection between findings and other works

Conclusions

Significance of findings made clear					Little or no significance identified
Conclusions based on evidence presented					Little or no connection between evidence and conclusions
Stated purpose of research achieved					Little or no contribution to solution of problem or achievement of purpose

Use of supplementary material

Effective use of figures and tables					Illustrative material not used when needed or not discussed in text
Illustrations presented correctly					Illustrations poorly presented

Figure 2.1 (*cont.*)

Detailed statistical analyses and tables placed in appendices				Excessively detailed findings in text

Written expression and presentation

Document follows assigned report format conventions				Little or no adherence to report presentation
Clearly and correctly written				Poor written expression
Report carefully produced				Sloppy presentation

Sources/referencing

Adequate number of sources				Inadequate number of sources
Adequate acknowledgment of sources				Inadequate acknowledgment of sources
Correct and consistent in-text referencing style				Incorrect or inconsistent referencing style
Reference list correctly presented				Errors and inconsistencies in reference list

Assessor's general comments

REFERENCES AND FURTHER READING

Baylis, P. 1993, 'Writing skills and the scientific world I: Reports', in *Communication for Scientific, Technical and Medical Professionals*, eds V. Hoogstad & J. Hughes, Macmillan, South Melbourne.

Beer, D.F. (ed.) 1992, *Writing and Speaking in the Technology Professions: A Practical Guide*, IEEE Press, New York.
This valuable edited collection comprises over 60 short papers on a wide variety of communication skills, including technical report writing. Other topics include oral presentations, running meetings, writing resumes, preparing illustrations, and writing proposals.

Behrendorff, M. 1995, Practical aspects of producing a level three report for the Department of Mechanical Engineering, Department of Mechanical Engineering, University of Adelaide.

Betts, K. & Seitz, A. 1994, *Writing Essays and Research Reports in the Social Sciences*, 2nd edn, Nelson, Melbourne.

Blicq, R.S. 1987, *Writing Reports to Get Results: Guidelines for the Computer Age*, IEEE Press, New York.

This book, of more than 200 pages, offers a serious, no-nonsense review of different report types and how to go about compiling them. Numerous examples are provided. Do not be misled by the volume's publishers, the Institute of Electrical and Electronics Engineers. This book is useful to students and practitioners in other fields.

Booth, V. 1993, *Communicating in Science. Writing a Scientific Paper and Speaking at Scientific Meetings*, 2nd edn, Cambridge University Press, Cambridge.

Chapter 1 of Booth's readable and brief book offers helpful advice on writing a scientific paper. Particular attention is devoted to the mechanics and detail of scientific presentation.

Brower, J.E., Zar, J.H. & von Ende, C.N. 1990, *Field and Laboratory Methods for General Ecology*, 3rd edn, W.C. Brown, New York.

Central Queensland University Library 2000, *Why do a Literature Review?* (online), Available: <http//www.library.cqu.edu.au/litreviewpages/why.htm> (27 March 2001).

Cooper, B.M. 1964, *Writing Technical Reports*, Penguin, Harmondsworth, Middlesex.

Cottrell, S. 2003, *The study skills handbook*, 2nd edn, Palgrave Macmillan, Hampshire.

Chapter 9 provides some helpful, though slightly chaotic, material on report writing.

(CUTL) Centre for University Teaching and Learning and Faculty of Engineering, 1995, *Report Writing Style Guide for Engineering Students*, Faculty of Engineering, University of South Australia, Adelaide.

Dane, F.C. 1990, *Research Methods*, Brooks/Cole, Pacific Grove, California.

Day, R.A. 1994, *How to Write and Publish a Scientific Paper*, 4th edn, Cambridge University Press, Cambridge.

Several chapters of this book are devoted to writing the various sections of a research report.

DeLyser, D. & Pawson, E. 2005, 'From personal to public: communicating qualitative research for public consumption', in *Qualitative Research Methods in Human Geography*, 2nd edn, ed. I. Hay, Oxford University Press, Melbourne, pp. 266–74.

Eisenberg, A. 1992, *Effective Technical Communication*, 2nd edn, McGraw-Hill, New York.

Freeman, T.W. 1971, *The Writing of Geography*, Manchester University Press, Manchester.

Now somewhat dated, this book provides a broad overview of fieldwork and writing in geography. Chapter 3 is more narrowly focused on the written presentation of research results and, although emphasis is given to thesis writing, much of the advice is applicable to report writing.

Friedman, S.F. & Steinberg, S. 1989, *Writing and Thinking in the Social Sciences*, Prentice-Hall, New York.
Chapter 3 includes useful discussions of the role of writing in the research process and the three components of the rhetorical stance: subject, audience, and voice. Take care, however, for in their consideration of voice, the authors imply that sufficient evidence and emotive language are mutually exclusive. Clearly this is incorrect. There is also a helpful review of the appropriate and inappropriate uses of jargon in technical writing.

Gray, D.E. 1970, *So You Have to Write a Technical Report. Elements of Technical Report Writing*, Information Resources Press, Washington, D.C.
A very helpful book providing basic guidance on report writing. Set out in the order in which reports are typically written rather than the order in which they are read, chapters provide straightforward advice on how to write specific sections of a report.

Hodge, D. 1994, Guidelines for Professional Reports. Course handout for GEOG 426, Department of Geography, University of Washington, Seattle.

Holloway, S.L. & Valentine, G. 2001, 'Making an argument: writing up human geography projects', *Journal of Geography in Higher Education*, vol. 25, no. 1, pp. 127–32.

Kanare, H.M. 1985, *Writing the Laboratory Notebook*, American Chemical Society, Washington, DC.
Chapter 3, 'Organizing and writing the notebook', offers detailed advice on keeping a comprehensive laboratory notebook. Other parts of the text discuss matters such as the legal and ethical aspects of note-taking, patents, and invention protection.

Kane, E. 1991, *Doing Your Own Research*, Marion Boyars, London.

Lindsay, D. 1984, *A Guide to Scientific Writing*, Longman Cheshire, Melbourne.

Lucas, S. 2004, 'The images used to "sell" and represent retirement communities', *The Professional Geographer*, vol. 56, no. 4, pp. 449–59.

Macauley, P. 2000, *The Literature Review* (online), Available: <http//www.deakin.edu.au/library/litrev.html> (27 March 2001).

Mansvelt, J. & Berg, L. 2005, 'Writing qualitative geographies, constructing geographical knowledges', in *Qualitative Research Methods in Human Geography*, 2nd edn, ed. I. Hay, Oxford University Press, Melbourne, pp. 248–65.

Marshall, L. & Rowland, F. 1993, *A Guide to Learning Independently*, 2nd edn, Longman Cheshire, Melbourne.
Chapter 13 is a useful introductory overview of report writing.

Mohan, T., McGregor, H. & Strano, Z. 1992, *Communicating! Theory and Practice*, 3rd edn, Harcourt Brace, Sydney.
Chapter 9 offers an overview of report types, functions, format, and style.

Montgomery, S. L. 2003, *The Chicago Guide to Communicating Science*, The University of Chicago Press, Chicago.
Chapter 10, on 'Technical Reports', is a very helpful discussion on the context within which reports are written and the form they should take.

Moxley, J.M. 1992, *Publish, Don't Perish. The Scholar's Guide to Academic Writing and Publishing*, Praeger, Westport, Connecticut.
Contains two chapters that outline different ways of writing reports based on qualitative and quantitative research.

Munroe, D.K., Southworth, J. & Tucker, C.M. 2004, 'Modeling spatially and temporally complex land-cover change: the case of Western Honduras', *The Professional Geographer*, vol. 56, no. 4, pp. 544–59.

Northey, M. & Knight, D.B. 1992, *Making Sense in Geography and Environmental Studies*, Oxford, Toronto.
This book has a short chapter on writing lab reports.

Pigozzi, B.W. 2004, 'A hierarchy of spatial marginality through spatial filtering', *The Professional Geographer*, vol. 56, no. 4, pp. 460–70.

Procter, M. 2000, *The Literature Review: A Few Tips on Conducting It* (online), Available: <http//www.utoronto.ca/writing/litrev.html> (6 April 2001).

Sayer, A. 1992, *Method in Social Science. A Realist Approach*, 2nd edn, Routledge, London.
Sayer's very influential book includes a useful chapter entitled 'Problems of explanation and the aims of social science' which introduces differences between 'intensive' (essentially qualitative) and 'extensive' (essentially quantitative) research and their implications for the process of research and the communication of results. However, this chapter is challenging reading.

Sides, C.H. 1992, *How to Write and Present Technical Information*, 2nd edn, Cambridge University Press, Oakleigh, Victoria.

University of California – Santa Cruz University Library 2005, *How to ... Write a Literature Review* (online), Available: <http://library.ucsc.edu/ref/howto/literaturereview.html> (17 July 2005).
A very helpful practical resource for those seeking additional guidance on writing a literature review.

University of Wisconsin – Madison Writing Centre 2004, *Review of Literature* (online), Available: <http://www.wisc.edu/writing/Handbook/ReviewofLiterature.html> (17 July 2005).
Another very helpful practical resource for those seeking additional guidance on writing a literature review.

Walker, J.R.L. 1991, 'A student's guide to practical write-ups', *Biochemical Education*, vol. 19, no. 1, pp. 31–2.

Windschuttle, K. & Elliott, E. 1999, *Writing, Researching, Communicating. Communication Skills for the Information Age*, 3rd edn, McGraw-Hill, Sydney.
This long, comprehensive book has a number of useful, short chapters on writing administrative, management, and annual reports.

Woodford, F.P. 1967, 'Sounder thinking through clearer writing', *Science*, vol. 156, no. 3776, p. 744.

3

Writing an Annotated Bibliography, Summary, or Review

I was so long writing my review that I never got around to reading the book.

Groucho Marx

Some books are to be tasted, others to be swallowed and some few to be chewed and digested.

Francis Bacon, 1625

KEY TOPICS

- Preparing an annotated bibliography
- Writing a summary or précis
- How to write a good review

Your academic endeavours will often require you to summarise and make sense of the works of other people. This chapter provides some advice on writing annotated bibliographies, summaries or précis, and book, article and WWW-site reviews—exercises which specifically require you to interpret and abridge longer pieces of work comprehensibly. Where appropriate, the discussion sets out the criteria which readers and assessors usually consider in evaluating this kind of work. You will find assessment criteria for different types of summary assignments in Figures 3.1 and 3.2.

PREPARING AN ANNOTATED BIBLIOGRAPHY

An **annotated bibliography** is a list of reference materials, such as books, articles, and WWW sites in which you provide author, title, and publication details for each item (as in a **bibliography**) and a short review of that item. The review might typically be up to 150 words long. Annotated bibliographies are customarily set out with the items in alphabetical order (by authors' surnames). Some annotated bibliographies are, however, written in the form of a short essay which quickly and concisely offers the same bibliographic material and **critique**, but in a more literary style than an annotated list.

Following are examples of items from annotated bibliographies.

BOX 3.1 EXAMPLES OF ANNOTATED BIBLIOGRAPHIES

Example 1—from Weintraub (1994)

Bullard, R.D. 1990, *Dumping in Dixie: Race, Class, and Environmental Equity*, Westview Press, Boulder, CO.

Dumping in Dixie is an in-depth study of environmental racism in black communities in the South. Bullard explores the barriers to environmental and social justice experienced by blacks and the factors that contribute to the conflicts, disparities, and the resultant growing militancy. He provides case studies of strategies used by grassroots groups who wanted to take back their neighborhoods in Houston's Northwood Manor neighborhood; West Dallas, Texas; Institute, West Virginia; Alsen, Louisiana; and Emelle-Sumter County, Alabama.

In these predominantly Black communities, grass roots organizing was carried out to protest against landfills, incinerators, toxic waste, chemical industries, salvage yards, and garbage dumps. Strategies included demonstrations, public hearings, lawsuits, the election of supporters to state and local offices, meetings with company representatives, and other approaches designed to bring public awareness and accountability. Bullard offers action strategies and recommendations for greater mobilization and consensus building for the ensuing environmental equity struggles of the 1990s.

Example 2—from Cottingham, Healey & Gravestock (2002)

Haigh, M.J. 1996, 'Empowerment, ethics, environmental action: a practical exercise', *Journal of Geography in Higher Education*, vol. 20, no. 3, pp. 399–411.

Just as active learning creates a deeper understanding than passive learning, so active geography grants a deeper understanding of geographical processes than passive geography. Geography students may be empowered to use their knowledge to improve the world they inhabit. However, to be effective they also need a holistic appreciation of both the ecological and ethical implications of their actions. They must become attuned both to their own internal preconceptions and to those which direct and constrain others. They must become capable of seeing their actions through the eyes of others. The exercise reported here tries to highlight these issues through the systematic critical analysis of a technical land reclamation project. Simulation is employed to encourage students to match practical solutions in landscape reclamation to wider issues in environmental ethics. In particular, students are encouraged to examine their own motivation for advocating particular technical solutions, to consider the value systems implicit in technical solutions proposed by others, and to examine environmental actions in context.

Example 3—from Gould (1993, p. 215)
(This is an example of an annotated bibliography written in essay form.)
I know of no geographical research on the condom, and virtually nothing on the geography of sexual relations, although the fine and pioneering work by a geographer: Symanski, R. 1981, *The Immoral Landscape: Female Prostitution in Western Societies*, Butterworths, Toronto; is increasingly referenced by other human scientists. Numerous short reports on condom use and propagation are given in almost all issues of *World–AIDS*, while many articles and reports in the 'AIDS Monitor' of *New Scientist* deal with condom use.

A good place to see examples of annotated bibliographies is the WWW. Some of these include, for example, Cottingham, Healey and Gravestock's (2002) collection on fieldwork in geography and environmental sciences, and the US Federal Railroad Administration's Office of Policy (1992) work on transport and the environment.

What is the purpose of an annotated bibliography?

Annotated bibliographies provide people in a particular field of inquiry with some commentary on books, articles, WWW sites, and other resources available in that field. They discuss the content, relevance, and quality of the material reviewed (Engle, Blumenthal & Cosgrave 2004). Annotated bibliographies may also provide a newcomer to a body of work with an insightful review of material available. Your instructor might ask you to write an annotated bibliography to make you familiar with some of the literature in your discipline area.

What is the reader of an annotated bibliography looking for?

Although the content may vary depending on the purpose of the list, readers of annotated bibliographies typically expect to see the following three sets of information, although many annotated bibliographies exclude the element of critique.

> ### BOX 3.2 KEY INFORMATION IN AN ANNOTATED BIBLIOGRAPHY
>
> **Details:** full bibliographic details (see chapter 10 for details)
>
> **Summary:** a clear indication of the content (and argument) of the piece. Consider including, for example: material on the author's aim in writing the piece; their intended audience; their claim to authority; and key arguments they use to support points.
>
> **Critique:** critical comment on the merits and weaknesses of the publication or on its contribution to the field of study. Some of the things you might also consider evaluating are: appropriateness of the article to its intended audience; whether it is up-to-date; and importantly, its engagement with other important literature in the field.

WRITING A SUMMARY OR PRÉCIS

Summaries (sometimes called **précis**) restate the essential contents of a piece of writing in a much more limited number (usually specified) of words than the original text. Abbreviation of the text is accomplished by presenting the main ideas in alternative wording, leaving out most examples and minor points.

Your précis must accurately *re-present* the text in condensed form. It should be a scaled-down version of the original text. Unlike a review, a précis does *not* contain interpretation of the issues raised. It is *not* evaluative. There is no need for you to provide your reaction to the ideas of the author.

Brevity and clarity are critical ingredients of a summary or précis. Let your reader or assessor know, in as few words as possible, what the summarised text is about. Do not prepare a précis which is as long as the article itself. Imagine your audience sitting opposite you with a bored glaze about to appear across their eyes. Spare them the details. Give them enough information to understand what the text is about but not so much that they might just as well have read the original.

> A good précis spares the details and focuses on key matters.

This leads us to one of the most common shortcomings of a summary or a précis: the failure to say what the original author's *main argument* is. Imagine someone has asked you to tell them about a movie you have recently seen. One of the most important things they will want to know, and in relatively few words, will be *essential details of the plot*. For example, readers probably do not want to know the names of Cinderella's evil sisters, the colour of her ballgown, or the temperament of the horses. Instead, they want to know the essence of the story which brought Cinderella together with her Prince Charming.

Once you have written your summary, reread it with the following question in mind: 'Could I read this précis aloud to the author in the honest belief that it accurately summarises his or her work?' If the answer is 'no', modify your work. You might also ask yourself: 'Would someone who has not read the original text have a good sense of what it is about after reading this précis?' Again, if the answer is 'no', you have some repairs to make.

What is the reader of a summary or précis looking for?

The criteria in the précis assessment schedule in Figure 3.1 can be used as guidelines for successfully completing your précis.

Figure 3.1 Précis assessment schedule

Student Name: Grade: Assessed by:

The following is an itemised rating scale of various aspects of a précis. Sections left blank are not relevant to the attached assignment. Some aspects are more important than others, so there is no formula connecting the scatter of ticks with the final grade for the assignment. Ticks in either of the two boxes left of centre mean that the statement is true to a greater (outer left) or lesser (inner left) extent. The same principle is applied to the right-hand boxes. If you have any questions about the individual scales, comment, final grade, or other aspects of this assignment, please see the assessor indicated above.

Description

Full bibliographic details of the text provided					Insufficient bibliographic details
Text's subject matter identified clearly					Text's subject matter poorly or inadequately defined
Purpose of the text identified clearly					Text's purpose not stated or unclear
Emphases in the précis match emphases in original text					Little or no correspondence with text's emphases
Order of presentation in précis matches that of original text					Little or no correspondence with text's order of presentation

Key evidence supporting the original author's claims outlined fully				Little or no reference to original text's evidence
Précis written in own words				Précis constructed largely from quotes

Written expression and presentation

Fluent piece of writing				Clumsily written, verbose, repetitive
Grammatical sentences				Many ungrammatical sentences
Correct punctuation				Poor punctuation
Correct spelling throughout				Poor spelling
Legible, well set out work				Untidy and difficult to read
Reasonable length				Too short/long
Correct and consistent in-text referencing style				Incorrect and/or inconsistent in-text referencing style
Reference list correctly presented				Errors and inconsistencies in reference list

Assessor's comments

Provide full bibliographic details of the text

At the start of your précis, you should provide the reader with a full reference to the work you are summarising. This includes details of:

- authors' names
- date of publication

- title
- edition
- publisher
- place of publication.

For example:

Aplin, G. 2002, *Australians and their Environment: An Introduction to Environmental Studies*, 2nd edn, Oxford University Press, Melbourne.

Clearly, if you are writing a précis of a WWW site or page, you would need to provide the equivalent electronic details. You will probably find it helpful to see chapter 10 for detailed information on correct referencing techniques.

Clearly identify the text's subject matter

After you have written the reference, you should provide a short statement informing your readers what the reviewed text is about. Make it clear, for instance, that you are reviewing a book on 'advances in water quality testing for environmental management' or another on 'recent developments in political geography'.

Clearly identify the purpose of the text

Having stated what the text is about, you need to let the reader of your summary know precisely what the *aim* of the text is. The distinction between a text's subject matter and its purpose is illustrated by the following introductory passage from Ley and Bourne's edited collection on the social geography of Canadian cities:

> This is a book *about* the places, the people and the practices that together comprise the social geography of Canadian cities. Its *purpose* is both to describe and to interpret something of the increasingly complex social characteristics of these cities and the diversity of living environments and lived experiences that they provide.
>
> (Ley & Bourne 1993, p. 3, emphasis added)

In his **preface** to *Recent America*, Dewey Grantham also distinguishes between the aim and the purpose of the text:

> *Recent America* seeks to provide a relatively brief but comprehensive survey of the American experience since 1945. The emphasis is on national politics and national affairs, including international issues and diplomacy, but some attention is given to economic, social, and cultural trends. I hope that this volume will serve as a useful introduction to a fascinating historical epoch ...
>
> (Grantham 1987, p. x)

You must think carefully about the distinction between a text's subject matter and its purpose. Usually a book or article will discuss some topic or example in order to make or illustrate a particular point or to investigate a specific theme. For example, a volume exploring the transmission of inherited housing wealth to women in Hobart may actually be attempting to contribute to broader discussions of Australia's political economy. You need to be sure you have not confused the subject matter and the purpose.

> Be sure to distinguish between the subject matter and purpose of the text you are summarising.

Ensure emphases in the précis match emphases in the original text

In the summary you should give the same relative emphasis to each area as do the authors of the original text (Northey & Knight 1992, p. 59). If, for example, two-thirds of a paper on monitoring water pollution from New South Wales' ski fields is devoted to a discussion of the legalities of obtaining the water samples, your précis should devote two-thirds of its attention to that issue. This helps to provide your reader with an accurate view of the original text.

Ensure that the order of presentation in the précis matches that of the original text

Just as you should give the same emphasis to each section as did the author of the original text, you should also follow the article/book's order of presentation and its chain of argument (Northey & Knight 1992, p. 59; South Australian College of Advanced Education 1989). Make sure you have presented enough material for a reader to be able to follow the logic of each important argument. You will not be able to provide every detail. Present only the critical connections.

If you are reviewing a web site, this advice on following the order of presentation may be redundant given the non-linear structure of some Web resources. Consider instead trying to follow the order of the site indicated by the layout of hotlinks on the site's homepage.

> Summarising a web site presents unique challenges.

Outline fully the key evidence supporting the original author's claims

You should briefly mention the critical evidence provided by the author to support his/her arguments (Northey & Knight 1992, p. 59). There is no need to recount all the data or evidence offered by the author. Instead, refer to the material which was the most compelling and convincing.

Ensure that the précis is written in your own words

Write the précis in your own words although you may, of course, elucidate some points with quotations from the original source. Do not construct a précis from a collection of direct quotations from the text you are summarising.

WRITING A REVIEW

A review is an honest, concise and thoughtful description, analysis, and evaluation of some text, such as a book, journal article, research report, or WWW site. Reviews serve an important role in the professional and academic world and for that reason you will see book review sections in almost every major journal of environmental studies or geography (e.g. *Geographical Research, New Zealand Geographer*). Reviews let people know of the existence of a particular text as well as pointing out its significance. They also warn prospective users about errors and deficiencies (Calef 1964). So many new publications and WWW resources are appearing that we need to be selective about what we read.

Lecturers usually ask you to write reviews for one or several of the following reasons:

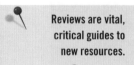

Reviews are vital, critical guides to new resources.

- to familiarise you with a significant piece of work in the field
- to allow you to evaluate the importance of a text to the discipline you are studying
- to allow you to practise your capacity for critical thought.

What are your review markers looking for?

People who read reviews, including those marking your review, typically want *honest* and *fair* comments on:

- what the reviewed item is about (*description*)
- details of its strengths and weaknesses (*analysis*)
- its contribution to the discipline (*evaluation*).

Figure 3.2 shows the criteria for assessment of a book/article/web site review. The next few pages of guidelines and advice will help you to deal with these issues.

A review should be interesting as well as informative. So, while your assessor will probably expect you to deal with the following issues in the course of your review, there are no rules concerning the order in which you should present them. Instead, you should set out the material in a manner which is both comprehensive and interesting. You should read a few reviews in professional journals in your discipline area to see how they have been laid out and ordered before you write your own.

Figure 3.2   Book/article/web site review assessment schedule

Student Name: Grade: Assessed by:

The following is an itemised rating scale of various aspects of a review. Sections left blank are not relevant to the attached assignment. Some aspects are more important than others, so there is no formula connecting the scatter of ticks with the final grade for the assignment. Ticks in either of the two boxes left of centre mean that the statement is true to a greater (outer left) or lesser (inner left) extent. The same principle is applied to the right-hand boxes. If you have any questions about the individual scales, comment, final grade, or other aspects of this assignment, please see the assessor indicated above.

Description

Left				Right
Full bibliographic details of the text provided				Insufficient bibliographic details
Sufficient details of author's background				No details of author's background
Text's subject matter identified clearly				Text's subject matter poorly or inadequately identified
Purpose of the text identified clearly				Text's purpose not stated or unclear
Author's conceptual framework identified correctly				Little or no attempt to identify conceptual framework
Succinct summary of the text's content				Excessive/inadequate summary of content provided
Intended readers identified accurately				Readership not identified

Analysis

Left				Right
Text's contribution to understanding of the world/discipline identified clearly				Little or no reference to text's contribution
Clear statement on achievement of text's aims				Text's aims not identified or identified incorrectly

Figure 3.2   (*cont.*)

Text's academic/ professional functions identified clearly	☐☐☐☐	Text's functions not identified or identified incorrectly
Text's organisation commented on fairly	☐☐☐☐	Little or no comment on organisation
Text's evidence evaluated critically	☐☐☐☐	Little or no comment on evidence
Text's references evaluated critically	☐☐☐☐	Little or no comment on references
Style and tone of presentation evaluated critically	☐☐☐☐	Little or no comment on style and tone
Quality of supplementary material (e.g. tables, maps, plates) reviewed competently	☐☐☐☐	Little or no comment on supplementary material
Other deficiencies/strengths in the text identified correctly and fairly	☐☐☐☐	Other evident weaknesses/strengths not identified

Evaluation

Text compared usefully with others in the field	☐☐☐☐	Little or no effort to compare text with other texts in the field
Valid recommendation on the value of reading the text provided	☐☐☐☐	No recommendation provided or recommendation inconsistent with earlier comments

Written expression, references, and presentation of the review

Various sections of the review of appropriate length	☐☐☐☐	Major imbalances evident
Fluent piece of writing	☐☐☐☐	Clumsily written, verbose, repetitive
Grammatical sentences	☐☐☐☐	Many ungrammatical sentences

Correct punctuation				Poor punctuation
Correct spelling throughout				Poor spelling
Legible, well set-out work				Untidy and difficult to read
Reasonable length				Too short/long
Correct and consistent in-text referencing style				Incorrect and/or inconsistent referencing style
Reference list correctly presented				Errors and inconsistencies in reference list

Assessor's comments

Description: what is the reviewed item about?

Description or summary is an important part of a review. You should imagine that your audience has not read the text you are discussing and that their only knowledge of it will come from your review. Give them a comprehensive but concise outline of the text's content and character. However, do not make the mistake of devoting almost all of the review to description—if you do that, your reader might as well go to the original text! As a rule of thumb, try to keep the summary to less than half the total length of your review.

Provide full bibliographic details of the text

You should provide a full and correctly set out reference to the work under review so that others may consult or purchase it (and so that your marker knows that you have reviewed the correct text). Readers of your review will be interested to know:

- who the work's authors/editors are
- the name of the book's publisher (if it is a book you are reviewing)
- where and when the volume was published.

It is sometimes helpful to state how many pages are in the text. (If you are reviewing a book, it is also useful to state its purchase cost, its International

Standard Book Number (ISBN), and whether the volume includes figures and other useful material, although these are rarely required for classroom reviews.) An example of a complete book review reference is provided below:

Moulaert, F., Rodriguez, A. & Swyngedouw, E. (eds) 2002, *The Globalized City: Economic Restructuring and Social Polarization in European Cities*, Oxford University Press, New York, pp. xxii and 279pp., plates, tables, figs, and index. US$85.00 cloth (ISBN 0-19-926040-0).

The text referred to in this example has 279 pages plus an additional 22 pages of introductory material (e.g. acknowledgments, title page, contents pages, notes on contributors). The hardback edition costs US$85.00. If a paperback existed its price would also be recorded here. This book also includes photos, tables, diagrams, and an **index**. It does not appear to have a bibliography, maps, or a glossary. These might have been listed if present.

If you are reviewing a WWW site, you should follow the same bibliographic principles but, of course, the detail will be a little different. An example of a WWW-site reference for a review[1] is set out below:

ABC-CLIO 2000, *World Geography* (online), Available: <www.abc-clio.com>, Date reviewed: 15 November 2000. Market@abc-clio.com, US$499 per year.

Both the author and publisher of this site are ABC-CLIO. Among the details included are the site's URL (Universal Resource Locator or, more simply, its 'address') and the date of the review. The date is useful given the ease and frequency with which WWW sites can be revised. Subscriptions to the site can be ordered through the **email** address provided. This one costs US$499 each year.

Bibliographic details are normally placed at the top of the review. The book review section of almost any geography or environmental management journal will provide an example for you to follow.

Give sufficient details of the authors' background

If you consider it appropriate, and know of the authors' expertise in the area they are writing about, provide a brief overview of their backgrounds and reputations (Marius & Page 2002, p. 213; Northey & Knight 1992, p. 60). It may also be helpful to consult the WWW or a *Who's Who* publication to find out a little more about any specific author's affiliation and credentials. You might consider whether the authors have written many other books and articles in this

---

1. Note that more information is provided in a review reference than is required in the list of references at the end of a document (see chapter 10). In this example, the price and selling agent's/publisher's email addresses are included. They would not normally be part of a list of references.

area and whether they have any practical experience. Readers unfamiliar with the subject area will often appreciate some information on the authors' apparent credibility or areas of expertise.

Clearly identify the text's subject matter
See the previous section, 'Writing a Summary or Précis', for details.

Clearly identify the purpose of the text
This was also discussed in the section above. See the notes for 'Writing a Summary or Précis' for details.

Correctly identify the author's conceptual framework
Texts are written from a particular perspective. Authors have a way of viewing the world and of arranging their observations into some specific and supposedly comprehensible whole. That way of thinking about the world is known as a *conceptual framework*. You might imagine a conceptual framework to be rather like the text's skeleton upon which the flesh of words and evidence is supported. As a reviewer, one of your tasks is to expose that skeleton, letting your reader know how the authors have interpreted the issues they discuss. How have the authors made sense of that part of the world they are discussing?

> Try to uncover the intellectual scaffolding that gives the book you are reviewing coherence.

In your review, you might combine identification of the conceptual framework with a critique of it. Does the author make inappropriate assumptions, and are there inconsistencies, flaws, or weaknesses in the intellectual skeleton? For example, an author might argue that massive job losses, associated with the adoption of new labour-saving technologies in industry, have been a particular feature of capitalism in Australia. A reviewer might suggest that this reflects a simplistic view of human–technology relations under capitalism and go on to argue that service-sector employment has risen at the same time as industrial job losses have occurred. Moreover, the reviewer might suggest that while some industries have atrophied, others have emerged and grown.

Provide a succinct summary of the text's content
Readers want some idea of what is in the book, article, or web site. Describe the content in sufficient detail for them to understand what the text is about. This might require stating what is in the various parts of the text and how much space is devoted to each section. You might want to integrate the summary of content with your evaluation of the text or you might prefer to keep it separate (Northey & Knight 1992, p. 61). If you are new to review writing, it is usually safer to keep the two separate. Write the summary first, then the analysis.

Accurately identify the intended readers of the text under review

The reader of a review is usually interested to know what sort of audience the author of the original text was addressing. In many cases the author will include a statement on the intended readership early in the volume—often in the preface. For example, in the preface to *The Slow Plague*, Peter Gould says that his book is:

> … one of a series labelled [sic] *liber geographicus pro bono publico*—a geographical book for the public good, which sounds just a bit pretentious until we translate it more loosely as 'a book for the busy but still curious public.'

> (Gould 1993, pp. xiii–xiv)

Howitt, Connell and Hirsch (1996, p. v) suggest that readers of their edited collection, *Resources, Nations and Indigenous People*, are likely to include students, Aboriginal organisations, and mining company staff. In the preface to their book, *Introducing Human Geography*, Gordon Waitt et al. (2000, p. vii) explicitly recognise their readers: 'This textbook introduces first-year university students to contemporary themes and practices in human geography'.

> **Be sure to identify a text's intended audience and that you review it with that audience in mind.**

Identifying the intended audience of the reviewed text serves at least two important purposes. First, you will be helping your readers decide whether the original text is likely to be of any relevance to them. Second, you will be providing yourself with an important foundation for writing your critique of the text. For example, from Gould's statement above, it is reasonable to conclude that his book ought to be easy to read, stimulating, and written for a lay audience. If it is not, there is an important flaw in the book. A book or article intended for experts in the field may legitimately use technical terms and express complex ideas. A version of the same information for children, on the other hand, may be simplified with a completely different vocabulary. You should write your review with the relationship between content/style and intended audience in mind.

Analysis: details of strengths and weaknesses

So far you have let your reader–assessor know a few basic descriptive details about the text you are reviewing. Now you need to let everyone know what you consider to be the weaknesses *and* strengths of the text. Being negative about a volume under review does not necessarily suggest that you are smarter than the author. Indeed, it can be more difficult and challenging to demonstrate how good a text is. If you believe that the material you are reviewing has no significant weaknesses, you should say so. However, you should also point out its specific strengths.

As Calef observes, analysis is usually the weakest feature of book reviews:

> All authors deserve sympathetic, appreciative analyses of their books; too few authors get them. Many reviewers concentrate on the authors' mistakes and discuss the books as they should have been written.
>
> (Calef 1964, p. 1)

It is essential that when you write your review you consider the aims of the authors. *Analyse the text on the authors' terms.* Have the authors achieved their aims?

In your analysis you should above all '*be fair, be explicit, be honest*' (Calef 1964, emphasis added). To these ends you should explain why you agree or disagree with the authors' methods, analysis, or conclusions.

> Be fair, be explicit, and be honest when you write a review.

In organising their analysis of a text, many reviewers point out the utility and successes of the book, article, or WWW site first and then move on to point out its deficiencies. You may find that pattern a useful one to follow.

Clearly identify the text's contribution to your understanding of the world/discipline

In evaluating the text's contribution to the discipline you should begin with the assumption that the author has something useful to say, rather than trying to explain whether you agree or disagree with that contribution. What is that contribution? Has the author helped *you* to make sense of things? What has been illuminated?

State clearly whether or not the text achieved its aims

Think carefully about the authors' objectives and compare those with the content of the text. Do they match one another? You would be derelict in your duty as a reviewer if you had stated what the reviewed text's aims were, but failed to say whether or not they had been met. (Imagine how frustrated you would feel if someone told you there was an article in a magazine about how to make a lifetime fortune in twenty-one days and when you read those pages you found that the article failed to deliver what it promised.)

Clearly identify the text's academic/professional functions

Ask what educational, research, or professional functions the text might fulfil. For example, is the book, article, or web site likely to be a useful resource for people in the same class as you, for other undergraduate students, or for leaders in the field?

Accentuate the positive. For example, an author may think that the book's audience ought to be final-year undergraduate students, but you—as an undergraduate student reviewer—believe the book would better serve a first-year audience. Rather than simply stating that the text is inappropriate for its intended audience, let your reader know which audience the text might best serve.

> Try to be helpful in your analysis, not negative.

Comment fairly on the text's organisation

Say whether you believe the reviewed text is well organised or not. In this context, think about the ways in which the book/paper is subdivided into chapters/sections or how easy it is to navigate around the web site. Do the subdivisions, chapters, or hotlinks advance the text's purpose or are they obstructive? Do they break up or upset an intellectual trajectory? Support your standpoint with examples.

Critically evaluate the text's evidence

An author's evidence should be reliable, up to date, drawn from reputable sources (such as official statistics, Hansard, international journals, experts in the field, or links to credible and relevant web sites), and should support claims made in the text. Would the results of the original text stand up to replication (i.e. if the study were done again, is it likely that the results would be the same?) or corroboration (are the results of the study substantiated by other related evidence?)?

Give a clear assessment of the evidence used in the text. Is the evidence compelling, or not? If, for example, you are sceptical about the repeated use of quotations drawn from *National Enquirer* to support a discussion of gerrymandering and electoral bribery in Queensland, you should let the reader know. Back up your assessment of the evidence with reasons for your conclusion. If you are able, and if it is necessary, suggest alternative and better sources of evidence.

Critically evaluate the text's references

Readers and assessors of your review will wish to know if the reviewed work has covered the available and relevant literature to a satisfactory degree. If you are reviewing a web site, you might expand your notion of references cited to include hotlinks from the reviewed site to other relevant web sites and pages. If there are major shortcomings in the references acknowledged, it is possible that the text's authors may not be fully aware of material which might have illuminated their work. If you are new to your discipline you might protest, sometimes quite justifiably, that you cannot offer a meaningful judgment about the strength of the reference material. Nevertheless, you ought to be thinking about this question and answering it where possible.

Critically evaluate the style and tone of presentation

Among other things, readers of a review may be trying to work out whether to buy, read, or consult the reviewed text. Therefore, questions foremost in the mind of some will be whether the text is written clearly and if it is interesting to read. Is the writing repetitious? Detailed? Not detailed enough? Boring? Is the style clear? Is it tedious, full of jargon, offhand? Particularly if you think there are problems with the style of writing, it is appropriate to support your criticisms with a few examples.

If you are reviewing a WWW site, you might also consider commenting on the visual character and quality of the site. Is judicious use made of electronic wizardry or has technology stolen the show?

You should also comment on the tone of the text. Let your reader or assessor know if the text is only accessible to experts in the field or if it is a 'coffee-table' publication. Of course, criticisms about the tone of the text should be written with reference to the intended audience. It would probably be unfair, for instance, to condemn a text on the grounds that it used technical language if it was written for an audience of experts.

Ensure that the quality of supplementary material is reviewed competently

Many books, articles and WWW sites make extensive use of supplementary material such as tables, plates, maps, and figures. In reviewing the text, you should comment on the quality of these materials and their contribution to the text's message. Graphic and tabular material in the text under review should be relevant, concise, large enough to read, comprehensible, and should provide the details of sources.

Correctly and fairly identify any other deficiencies/strengths in the text

After a close reading of the text, you should be able to identify any weaknesses and strengths you have not already discussed. Remember: you do not *have* to find things wrong with the text you are reviewing. Being critical does not require you to be negative. Similarly, you should not pick out minor problems within the text and suggest that they destroy the entire book. However, if there are genuine problems, be explicit about what they are, providing examples where possible.

> Support criticisms in your review with evidence.

Evaluation: contribution to the discipline

In the first section of the review you described the text being reviewed. You then went on to outline the text's strengths and flaws. Now you have to make a judgment. Is the text any good? You may find it useful to be guided by the central question: *'Would you advise people to read (or buy) the text you have reviewed?'*

Compare the text's usefulness with that of others in the field

If you have sufficient expertise in the field, **appraise** the text being reviewed in terms of its use as an alternative to work already available. It may be helpful to consult library reference material to see, for example, how many other volumes on the same or a similar topic have been produced recently. If you are reviewing a web site, search for competitors and compare them.

> Think about how the text you are reviewing stacks up against its competition.

Compare the text you are reviewing factually with its predecessors. What subjects does it treat that earlier volumes did not? What does it leave out? (Northey & Knight 1992, p. 60) Remember to cite correctly any additional sources you use.

Make a valid recommendation on the value of reading the text

A fundamental reason for writing reviews is to let readers know whether a particular book, article, or web site is worth consulting. Your recommendation should be consistent with the preceding analysis of its strengths and weaknesses. For example, it would be inappropriate to **criticise** a text mercilessly and then conclude by saying that it is an important contribution to the discipline and should be consulted by everyone interested in the area. It is worth restating a point made earlier: in your review *be fair, be explicit, be honest.*

Written expression, references, and presentation of the review

Make sure the various sections of the review are of appropriate length

Assessors will consider the balance between description, analysis, and evaluation when marking a review. A description of the text is important, but it should not dominate your review. As noted earlier, unless there are special reasons, the description should usually be less than half of the total length of the review.

Your own writing should be clear, concise, and appropriate for your audience. Detailed advice on the assessment criteria used for written expression (which is shown in the assessment schedule for reviews in Figure 3.2) can be found in chapter 1.

Some examples of reviews

Before you start writing a review, you will find it helpful to look to high-quality academic journals (e.g. *Area, Geographical Research, Professional Geographer*) for good examples. Below, and as a preliminary guide, are some slightly revised versions of reviews published in the *Library Journal*. You will see that, despite their brevity, the reviews address many of the issues discussed in this chapter. The last review is of a WWW site.

BOX 3.3 EXAMPLES OF REVIEWS

Example 1

Mommsen, H. 1996, *The Rise and Fall of Weimar Democracy*, trans. E. Forster & L. E. Jones, University of North Carolina, Chapel Hill, pp. 608.

This translation makes available to the English-speaking world an important historical work published in 1989 by a prominent German historian. The period from 1919 to 1933 was a time of great political, social, economic, and artistic upheaval in Germany. In this magisterial work, the author looks at the Weimar period from the viewpoint of social and economic history, providing a lucid yet detailed account of the complexities of this era without attempting to pull the strands out of their context in order to find the 'roots' of the Nazi period that followed. By doing so, he both sheds light on this interesting period and provides a convincing overall picture of Germany's road from parliamentary democracy to dictatorship during the interwar years. Because of its depth and detail, this book is not for casual readers, but it covers a complex subject with admirable clarity and is certain to become a classic. Everyone interested in European history should read this book.

Adapted from: *Library Journal* 1996, vol. 121, no. 12.

Example 2

Meredith, M. 2005, *The Fate of Africa: A History of Fifty Years of Independence*, PublicAffairs Perseus Publishing, New York, pp. 800.

A scholar of Africa necessarily becomes an expert on death. In Meredith's tome, death comes in huge numbers and in many ways: through famine, ethnic strife, and racial injustice and at the hands of ruthless dictators. It came in the days of European colonialism, but in postcolonial Africa, death pervades the continent. Meredith (*Our Votes, Our Guns: Robert Mugabe and the Tragedy of Zimbabwe*) writes with sobriety, intelligence, and a deep knowledge of Africa as he describes individuals responsible for deaths unimaginable to much of the rest of the world. A well-known example is the carnage among Hutus and Tutsis in Rwanda, claiming 800,000 lives in 100 days in 1994—more people were killed more quickly than in any other mass killing in recorded history. Much of this tragic history has been told in part elsewhere, but Meredith has compiled the text covering the entire continent. Only in the last few pages does Meredith answer the question of Africa's fate—and he thinks it's bleak. This is a valuable work for those who wish to understand Africa and its besieged peoples.

Adapted from: *Library Journal* 2005, vol. 130, no. 12.

Example 3

Rossi, J. 2000, *The Wild Shores of Patagonia: The Valdes Peninsula and Punta Tombo*, Abrams, New York, pp. 224.

Neither an experienced author nor a photographer, Rossi discovered Patagonia while on short leave from her job with the European Parliament and promptly turned her fascination into a two-year encampment to prepare this book. About half the book is devoted to a detailed discussion of southern right whales, southern elephant seals, and killer whales (including their unique beach hunting methods). Less detail is given to South American sea lions, and dusky and bottlenose dolphins. The author describes Magellanic penguins but provides limited information on 12 other kinds of birds, sometimes furnishing just one picture and caption per species. Rossi also discusses eight land animals in about 25 pages, giving short shrift to some unique creatures. Reader interest in this area may grow, since the United Nations has recently declared the Valdes Peninsula a World Heritage Site, and ecotourist visits are increasing. Although the photographs are merely average, this readable volume is recommended for members of the general public and for academic audiences interested in environmental and life sciences.

Adapted from: *Library Journal* 2001, vol. 126, no. 1.

Example 4

ABC-CLIO 2000, *World Geography*, ABC-CLIO, Available: <www.abc-clio.com>, Date reviewed: 15 November 2000. Market@abc-clio.com, US$499 per year.

World Geography aims to be the place students go to research a number of themes and look up facts (many nongeographical) on all countries. There are three major sections providing access to the data: Home, Student, and Reference. The site includes more than 10,000 entries, including biographies, histories, maps, documents, statistics, video clips, and photographs. At Home students can select a country to study; search the text by keyword or choose to catch up on world events; read a Feature Article (Why Is the Price of Gas Rising?); or answer three questions to a Where in the World? quiz. The Feature Article portion is well researched; one hopes ABC-CLIO plans to archive these essays.

In the Reference section, country selection is via a world map or drop-down menu. Text can be searched by keyword or in advanced search, where searches can be limited by type. A noteworthy inclusion here is Ask the Cybrarian, in which students can ask reference questions of ABC-CLIO.

The Student section can be used in the classroom. Students can read the syllabus, class announcements, the word of the day, and take review tests. A nice feature here is regional overviews that cover Landforms, Climate, Vegetation and Animal Life, People, and Natural Resources and Agriculture. Other overviews cover people, news events, and organizations for the selected country.

There are also a few problems. Though country maps are clear, city maps are unfortunately excluded. Data presented are only for one year, although often more historical data are needed. News events in the Home section are listed incompletely, e.g., 'Experts Investigate Possible ...' Possible what? Forcing users to click to see if a story is worth reading is inefficient. The icon used to designate a link to a map is a small map of the United States—for all countries. Sources for news articles are not always provided, nor are clear directions on how to cite information found here. Information included is sometimes mystifying; for example, under Organizations in the United States section, corporations such as Apple, Walt Disney, AT&T, and Exxon are included. Pierre Trudeau's death is noted, but no biography is available. The Tools section offers two excellent features: the Merriam-Webster's Collegiate Dictionary and the Merriam-Webster's Collegiate Thesaurus, and ClioView allows students to select, sort, and view a country and topic (18 from which to choose, including Literacy, Population Density, and Active Armed Forces).

The bottom line: World Geography is not exactly what its name implies. It is ABC-CLIO's successor to Exegy and is better described as a good source for beginning country studies. In that context, it is a useful resource. This site is recommended for members of the general public and for children entering secondary school.

Adapted from: *Library Journal* 2001, vol. 126, no. 1.

REFERENCES AND FURTHER READING

Association of College and Research Libraries. 1994, Guidelines for reviewing electronic media, *Choice Current Review for Academic Libraries*, American Library Association, Middletown, Connecticut.

Bergman, B.A. 1978, 'Do's and don'ts of book reviewing', in *Book Reviewing*, ed. S.E. Kamerman, Writer, Boston.

Berry, B.J.L. 1993, 'Canons of reviewing revisited', *Urban Geography*, vol. 15, no. 1, pp. 1–3.

Burdess, N. 1998, *The Handbook of Student Skills for the Social Sciences and Humanities*, 2nd edn, Prentice Hall, New York.
Chapter 3 includes short sections on writing abstracts and book reviews.

Calef, W.C. 1964, *Canons of Reviewing*, Illinois State University.

Clanchy, J. & Ballard, B. 1991, *Essay Writing for Students: A Practical Guide*, Longman Cheshire, Melbourne.
Chapter 9 includes a succinct description of how to write a review. Appendix 10 also outlines some of the criteria used by staff in the disciplines of political economy and women's studies when assessing book reviews.

Cottingham, C., Healey, M. & Gravestock, P. 2002, *Fieldwork in the geography, earth and environmental sciences higher education curriculum* (online), Available: <http://www2.glos.ac.uk/gdn/disabil/fieldwk.htm> (15 July 2005).

Day, R.A. 1989, *How to Write and Publish a Scientific Paper*, Cambridge University Press, Cambridge.

Engle, M., Blumenthal, A. & Cosgrave, T. 2004, *How to prepare an annotated bibliography*, Cornell University (online), Available: <http://www.library.cornell.edu/olinuris/ref/research/skill28.htm> (13 July 2005).

Federal Railroad Administration, Office of Policy 1992, *Transportation and the Environment: An Annotated Bibliography* (online), Available: <http://ntl.bts.gov/DOCS/tea.html> (15 July 2005).

Friedman, S. & Steinberg, S. 1989, *Writing and Thinking in the Social Sciences*, Prentice-Hall, Englewood Cliffs, New Jersey.

Gould, P. 1993, *The Slow Plague: A Geography of the AIDS Pandemic*, Blackwell, Cambridge, Massachusetts.

Grantham, D.W. 1987, *Recent America*, Harlan Davidson, Arlington Heights.

Howitt, R., Connell, J. & Hirsch, P. (eds) 1996, *Resources, Nations and Indigenous Peoples: Case Studies from Australasia, Melanesia and Southeast Asia*, Oxford University Press, Melbourne.

Kamerman, S.E. (ed.) 1978, *Book Reviewing*, Writer, Boston.

Kenny, H.A. 1978, 'The basics of book reviewing', in *Book Reviewing*, ed. S.E. Kamerman, Writer, Boston.

Kirsch, R. 1978, 'The importance of book reviewing', in *Book Reviewing*, ed. S.E. Kamerman, Writer, Boston.

Ley, D.F. & Bourne, L.S. 1993, 'Introduction: The Social Context and Diversity of Urban Canada', in *The Changing Social Geography of Canadian Cities*, eds L.S. Bourne & D.F. Ley, McGill-Queen's University Press, Montreal & Kingston.

Marius, R., & Page, M.E. 2002, *A Short Guide to Writing About History*, Longman, New York.

McEvedy, M.R. & Wyatt, P. 1990, *Presenting an Assignment*, Nelson, Melbourne.

Northey, M. & Knight, D.B. 1992, *Making Sense in Geography and Environmental Studies*, Oxford University Press, Toronto.
See chapter 6, especially, which provides advice on writing summaries/précis, analytic book reports, and literary reviews (i.e. focusing on a theme and requiring coverage of several books).

Ormondroyd, J., Engle, M. & Cosgrave, T. 2001, *How to Critically Analyze Information Sources* (online), Available: <http//www.library.cornell.edu/okuref/research/skill26.htm> (27 March 2001).

Smith, J. 1995, Review of 'A Continent Transformed: Human Impact on the Natural Vegetation of Australia', *Australian Geographical Studies*, vol. 33, no. 1, pp. 133–4.

South Australian College of Advanced Education 1989, Article reviews and annotated bibliographies, Adelaide.

Waitt, G., McGuirk, P., Dunn, K., Hartig, K. & Burnley, I. 2000, *Introducing Human Geography*, Longman, French's Forest.

Weintraub, I. 1994, 'Fighting environmental racism: a selected annotated bibliography', *Electronic Green Journal*, vol. 1, no. 1, unpaged.

4

Writing a Media Release

How is the world ruled and how do wars start? Diplomats tell lies to journalists and then believe what they read.

Karl Kraus

KEY TOPICS

- What is a media release and what are users of media releases looking for?
- How to make a media release effective
- Following up on your media release and being interviewed

Geographers and environmental managers are often interested in ensuring that the media and thereby the general public know of their work and their views on important issues. This chapter provides some guidance on how to prepare material for the print media, and offers some short comments on conducting a successful radio interview. If you find yourself in a position where you are asked to give a radio or television interview, Mathews (1981) provides some very helpful advice. There are also a growing number of WWW sites that offer guidance. See, for example, Berger (1992) and Telg (2000).

> The mass media provide access to vast, valuable, and powerful audiences.

BOX 4.1 WHY WRITE FOR THE MEDIA?

There is a wide variety of reasons for writing for the media. A written piece may:
- inform and raise awareness among the general public about geographical and environmental management issues

- communicate the results of your scholarly activities to broad and interested audiences
- offer your selection of facts and views on a particular situation or issue (agenda setting)
- help establish a favourable public profile for your work, your discipline, and the organisation for which you work. This may help find sponsors and other forms of support.
- promote and secure support for activities (e.g. presentations, public meetings, research in progress, funding)
- help develop your local profile as someone with something useful to say about some specific topic (become an 'authorised knower' (Hay & Israel 2001)), and
- help reporters get their facts right.

WHAT IS A MEDIA RELEASE AND WHAT ARE USERS OF MEDIA RELEASES LOOKING FOR?

The most commonly employed means of communicating with the media is through a media release (also known as a press release). Media releases are a major source of information used by journalists. They generally set out the core information about something you hope will get favourable editorial coverage.

A media release is often your first contact with the media about any story. It may be your only contact. You should try to ensure that the release is well-written, comprehensive, and captivating. Try to provoke interest and set the tone for the ways in which the story might subsequently be covered.

A media release is a vital bridge between your academic and professional work and the mass media.

BOX 4.2 WHAT ARE USERS OF MEDIA RELEASES LOOKING FOR?

Remember, mass media is essentially a profit-driven business. Staff at newspapers, radio and television stations aim to sell as much of their news product (and associated advertising) to as many readers, listeners, or viewers as possible. For this reason, they are most likely to be interested in stories that are:

- new or up to date (e.g. an economic geographer's explanation for a recent rise/fall in national currency)
- unusual or unexpected (e.g. discovery of a new species of tuatara on an offshore island of New Zealand; heterosexual couple thrown out of gay bar for kissing publicly)

- captivating (e.g. an oceanographer's professional views on how to make America's Cup yachts sail faster by taking advantage of local knowledge)
- relevant to a large part of the medium's audience (e.g. a forecast by an urban geographer of plummeting real estate values in Sydney is likely to be of deep interest to readers of the *Sydney Morning Herald*—and perhaps the Melbourne *Age* but for quite different reasons!). It is useful to recall that most media outlets have specific markets to which they aim to make their stories interesting and relevant. Thus, a small country town's newspaper may carry stories on environmental issues relating to the surrounding region which a larger metropolitan paper will not be interested in covering.
- local and or regional relevance, and
- accurate.

TARGETING YOUR RELEASE

Despite all of the above, the success of a news release also depends on it being directed at the correct outlet. You are unlikely to get much coverage if you direct your great story about revolutionary applications of Global Positioning Systems (GPS) for sheep tracking in the New Zealand high country to the Brisbane *Courier Mail*! Accordingly, you should consider familiarising yourself with media outlets you think might be relevant to your work and interests. Assess the market.

Selecting the right media outlet is vital to the success of your story.

BOX 4.3 TARGETING A MEDIA RELEASE

Direct your attention to matters such as:
- What relevant papers and magazines exist?
- How often do these publications appear (daily, weekly, monthly ...)?
- To what audiences is the content relevant (e.g. local, state, national, international; conservative, wealthy, left-wing)?
- How much space/time is devoted to specific issues?
- Do the stories that are run challenge or uphold the status quo?
- What are the characteristic styles of writing used by the paper?

Check the regular features pages or sections within the publications you are targeting. Many metropolitan newspapers have special sections on specific days of the week (e.g. Monday sport; Tuesday environment; Wednesday real estate; Thursday higher education and so on). Not only might this be of significance in terms of the timing of your press release, but it will also point out the sorts of issues the publication considers most important.

WRITING A MEDIA RELEASE

Layout and presentation

- Type the media release on one side of a sheet of paper, double-spaced, justified left and right with wide margins. This allows it to be subedited and passed on immediately to a printer or announcer.
- Use letterhead paper if possible. If this is not available to you, be sure to type your name, that of the organisation with which you are associated, and full address and contact details at the top. If your letterhead is 'over-the-top' it may pay to tone it down. In the main, editors are not impressed by glossy, embossed, or colour logos with exotic fonts. All they want is clear, concise, clean, crisp news. Glamour is no substitute for substance.
- Date the media release.
- Mark the document 'media release' and add a short, attractive title that explains what the release is about.
- Number the pages of the release and associated information.

Structure

In many respects, a media release does not follow the principles of good writing. It is certainly different from other forms of written communication with which you might become familiar at university. It does, however, require attention to structure. The media release must catch the reader's attention (hook the reader), provide a context, and deliver easily digested quotes. In writing a media release it is all too tempting to write too much. You do not just want to target potential news readers, you also have to get the message past the journalist and the editor's desk. This is not an easy task as even small circulation papers may receive forty to fifty releases per day (Minnis & Pratt 1995).

> A media release follows an inverted pyramid structure so that whole paragraphs near the end can be deleted without losing the story's central message.

- Use a catchy headline and set it out in large, bold capital letters (e.g. **CAT LOVERS SPITTING MAD**).
- Make your most important points first; and then provide others in declining order of importance. News stories are written according to a fairly rigid top–down formula, known as the 'inverted pyramid'. They commence with the most important, central information first and then go on to provide explanatory paragraphs with other details in declining order of importance.

There are several reasons for this. First, the reader's attention is captured immediately. Second, because most people do not have time to read the entire newspaper, it is helpful to them if they can gain a broad overview of the news of the day by reading headlines and introductory paragraphs. Third, stories often have to be edited down to fit available space. With the inverted pyramid structure, subeditors can be fairly confident that by removing material from the end of the story, they are not removing any vital information. For this reason, check any release you write to ensure that it will still make sense if paragraphs are removed from the end.

- Keep the opening paragraph ('intro') brief. Aim for fewer than 40 words. Williams (1994) suggests the ideal length is 17–25 words. Be sure the intro makes an impact and highlights the newsworthy angle of the story. This forces the writer to focus on the main story hook.

- The opening paragraph provides the 'story hook' (Williams 1994) and should include the *who, what, when, where,* and *why* of a story. For example, 'Angered by recent proposals to end domestic cat ownership by 2030 [WHY], the Cat Appreciation and Taming Society (CATS) [WHO] has convened a public meeting [WHAT] to discuss new pet ownership regulations. The meeting will be held at the Onsley Town Hall [WHERE] on 12 December [WHEN].' If you deal with the 'so what' issue, so much the better.

- The second paragraph can provide a 'secondary hook' (Williams 1994) and should explain in more detail the information from the first paragraph. For example, 'CATS has convened the meeting in response to radical proposals by the Member for Onsley, Mr Jim Nopsis, to make it illegal to own cats in the state.'

- Keep paragraphs short. Try limiting them to a single sentence.

- The release should conclude with END to let the journalist know what is media release and what is subsidiary information, like contact details and photographs.

- End the release with the names and full contact details of a minimum of two reliable people who can be contacted for more details. It is helpful to include daytime and evening phone numbers. If the journalist finds no one to talk to about the release, the story may be abandoned. After-hours contact details, including weekends, are essential.

> Make yourself available to journalists following up on your release.

Evidence and credibility

> Quotes from key figures lend authority to a media release.

- Near the top of your story, provide a few details about yourself or your organisation, such as the function it serves and its number of members.

- Do not assume reporters are familiar with you or the organisation with which you are associated. Mention its full name early in the release with the initials in parentheses.
- Use quotes wherever possible. These give the story vitality and credibility. Be aware that many quotes in media releases are in fact entirely manufactured. No one actually said them! If this is the case with your release at least run the quote past the person to whom the quote is attributed to see if they are happy with its style and content.
- Attribute statements to a particular person and not to some anonymous spokesperson. Give the spokesperson's full title, name, and position (e.g. Dr Felicity Sealpoint, President of the Cat Appreciation and Taming Society). It is often helpful if the people quoted are prominent within the community in some way or are leaders in their field.
- Provide each person's full name and be sure to include some phrase that makes it clear to readers what that person's claim to authority in this story is (e.g. 'Local breeder of Singapura cats, Mrs Mee Yeo, said ...').
- Support statements and claims with 'hard' evidence such as statistics, quotes, and references to government documents and other reports.
- Be accurate.

Language

- Be sure the release is clear, concise, and arresting. Try to keep it to a page or less (i.e. about 300–400 words). Keep the sentences short. Leave out unnecessary words. Readership can fall off by as much as 80% after the third or fourth paragraph of a news story (Williams 1994, p. 6). With this in mind, short and to-the-point releases should be the goal.
- Keep language simple and concise (e.g. 'now', not 'at this point in time'; 'here' not 'hereabouts').
- Avoid jargon and clichés 'like the plague'.
- Use colourful quotes. Statements like 'The Honourable member for Onsley is a despicable cat-killer' is likely to get good coverage! Do let people know that you plan to quote them!
- Use the word 'said' when attributing quotes to people. Although there is a wide variety of options such as 'exclaimed', 'declared', 'stated', 'expressed', and so on, try to avoid them. Although they may not be aware of it, most newspaper readers expect to see 'said'. Anything else may prove disruptive.
- Be sure all spelling is correct and that all names and titles are accurate.
- Unless the story is about something that is yet to happen, use the past tense.

- Use the active rather than the passive voice. In the passive voice, the subject receives the action expressed by the verb (e.g. the tree was hit by the moving car), whereas in the active voice the subject performs the action of the verb (e.g. the moving car hit the tree). In general, the active voice is more lively and succinct.
- Use positive rather than negative statements.

Engaging with the media can be tiresome and disheartening. A media release that may have taken many hours for you to construct may not even make it beyond the waste bin of a newspaper office. If the story does make it into the public arena it may look nothing like your original. Walters et al. (1994) reported that, on average, press releases were halved in size by journalists and editors from a mean of 434.8 words to 209.8; 13.5 paragraphs to 6.3; and 18.4 sentences to 9.3. The reading level of releases was lowered ('dumbed-down'), with the Flesch-Kincaid-Grade level reduced from 14.98 to 13.60 and the average length of words reduced from 5.28 to 5.05 letters. In these cases the journalist and editor are making your story more palatable and hence more digestible for the audience. Do not regard the changes as a slight against your professionalism and integrity. It is simply a case of 'horses for courses'.

Photographs and supplementary information

- It can be very helpful to submit a good quality, relevant photograph (or other illustrative material such as a map) with your story, particularly if you are submitting it to a small paper or newsletter with limited resources. Photographs should be black and white where possible, of very high standard, and about 150 × 100 mm in dimension. While larger newspapers may not use your photo, it might give their staff some ideas for pictures of their own. Include a typed **caption** for the photograph (be sure the caption answers what, where, when, and who questions). Attach the caption to the back of the picture.

Consider including a high-quality, relevant photo with your media release.

- In some cases a picture can make a story. For instance, a recent close-up photograph of a Tasmanian tiger (*Thylacinus cynocephalus*), regarded as extinct since 1936, is likely to make the front page of most Australian national newspapers, whereas an unillustrated report of its sighting is unlikely to figure prominently in any newspaper.
- Try to avoid large group photos. When reduced in size for publication these tend to lose relevant details.
- If you find that the complexity of the story warrants it, consider including with your release a separate 'fact sheet' that explains complicated matters clearly. If your release describes a paper or research report you have written,

it may be helpful to send in a copy of the report with your press release. Do not expect to receive the report back, though!

Timing matters

- If you have any concerns about when the release should be published, state at the top either 'For immediate release' or if you prefer later public disclosure, say 'Embargoed until [time], [date]'.

> Timing your media release can be critical to its success so learn about your local media schedules.

- Consider sending your news release to newsrooms on Saturday or Sunday as these are usually the quietest days of the week. This may require that you provide after hours (AH) contact details on your release. Mobile telephones can be a real bonus here but make sure your batteries are charged and you have good coverage!
- Give the journalists plenty of time to react to your media release (days rather than hours if possible).
- Daily papers are typically busiest in the morning and early afternoon. For morning papers, the deadline for most stories is late afternoon (only major stories are likely to be published after that). Unless you have a story of tremendous significance and urgency, do not call a journalist after about 4 p.m. You are unlikely to get a warm reception. The best time is likely to be between noon and 2.30 p.m. Contact staff on evening papers between 7.00 and 8.30 a.m.
- Weekly papers, such as those published on Sundays, typically face a Wednesday or Thursday deadline—unless the story is of major note.
- On public holidays and in major holiday seasons such as Christmas and early January (in the southern hemisphere), newsrooms are often desperate for new stories.
- Where possible, try 'piggybacking' your story onto some significant local or international event. If, for instance, you have been conducting research work on strategies to curb the impact of feral cat populations on native fauna, and you see the 'Cat Lovers Spitting Mad' article in your local paper, it might be timely to send in a news release about your work. Keep a close eye on those current events that might make your release topical.
- While piggybacking may be helpful, try to avoid clashing with a foreseeable event of such magnitude that it will dominate the news.

MEDIA RELEASE FORMAT

Although not all media releases will follow it exactly, the basic outline for a media release is as follows:

BOX 4.4 SUGGESTED LAYOUT OF A MEDIA RELEASE

Letterhead
FOR IMMEDIATE RELEASE [or Embargoed until time, date]
Date
Headline
Introductory paragraph that answers *Who, When, Where, What*, and *Why?*
A second paragraph explaining in more detail the information from the first paragraph.
Third paragraph that includes a quote attributed to some prominent person.
Fourth paragraph that includes some more information, perhaps another quote.
Subsequent paragraphs add supplementary information that can be removed by a subeditor without making the earlier parts of the release incomprehensible.
-END-
For Further Information Contact:

Full Title and Name of Contact	Full Title and Name of Contact
Direct Phone Number (BH)	Direct Phone Number (BH)
Direct Phone Number (AH)	Direct Phone Number (AH)
Email Address	Email Address
URL [if appropriate]	URL [if appropriate]

Following are examples of (a) a fictitious media release written according to this format and (b) a verbatim copy of a release prepared in an Australian university to bring public attention to work carried out there on the geographical dimensions of racism.

BOX 4.5 EXAMPLE OF A FICTITIOUS MEDIA RELEASE

The Cat Appreciation and Taming Society
27 March 2006
MEDIA RELEASE for immediate release
CAT LOVERS SPITTING MAD

Adelaide, Australia. Angered by recent proposals to end domestic cat ownership by 2030, the Cat Appreciation and Taming Society (CATS) has convened a public meeting in Onsley to discuss new pet ownership regulations.

CATS has convened the meeting in response to radical proposals by the Member for Onsley, Mr Jim Nopsis, to make it illegal to own a cat after 2030.

According to CATS, Mr Nopsis's proposals arise from misguided concerns about the effect of cats on native wildlife.

Commenting on the proposed regulations, CATS president Dr Felicity Sealpoint described Mr Nopsis as 'an ill-informed and despicable cat killer'.

'Not only are these proposals frighteningly cruel, they are also a flagrant infringement on our civil rights,' Dr Sealpoint said.

The CATS meeting will be held in the Onsley Town Hall at 7 pm on 1 April.

-END-

For further media enquiries please contact:

Dr Felicity Sealpoint

President, Cat Appreciation and Taming Society

Tel: 8123-9876 (BH), 8765-1234 (AH)

Email: sealpoint@tinroof.com

Or

Mr Rex Cornish

Secretary, Cat Appreciation and Taming Society

Tel: 8381-3456 (BH), 8123-4567 (AH)

BOX 4.6 EXAMPLE OF A MEDIA RELEASE ABOUT GEOGRAPHICAL RESEARCH

THE GEOGRAPHY OF RACISM

The occurrence of racism in NSW is regionally specific, according to new research from UNSW. The regional variations are associated with average educational attainment, the distribution of cultural groups, and the distinct histories of inter-communal relations in each region.

'Areas of relative affluence in NSW appear to be places where there is less racism. We believe it is education levels which are the most substantial contributor to this class-based geography of racism,' say Drs Kevin Dunn and Amy McDonald from the UNSW School of Geography.

'Contrary to popular belief, there are regions in Sydney where people harbour more racist sentiment than rural areas of NSW. The areas where the respondents were the most 'racist' were outer western Sydney, the mid north coast and the major industrial cities of the Illawarra and the Hunter.'

'Intolerance of people with an Asian background is very high among both urban and rural Australians. Anti-Asian sentiment was not only widespread, but there appears to be little urban and rural variation,' says Dr Dunn. 'Anti-Indigenous feeling was higher among respondents from rural Australia. The anti-Indigenous sentiment that was found to exist in areas such as Richmond-Tweed and the north-western part of the state are likely to be due to the history of community relations in those areas.'

The study found that although a region demonstrated intolerance of a specific group this did not necessarily translate to high levels of opposition to multiculturalism. Also, the geographies of anti-Asian and anti-Indigenous sentiment do not match. In contrast to their anti-Indigenous sentiment, residents of the Richmond-Tweed and the Murrumbidgee areas were not overly concerned about multiculturalism.

'An urban-rural divide is only confirmed in so far as affluent Sydney, and to a lesser extent inner-western Sydney, are concerned,' says Dr Dunn. 'The survey generally shows that people in outer western Sydney, the Hunter and Illawarra are more intolerant of cultural difference than those in rural areas. Inner, eastern and lower northern Sydney were areas in which respondents exhibited lower levels of racism.'

Dr Dunn ascribes the variations on the different cultural make-up of each region of NSW, the different needs and resources of the cultural groups in each place and the different problems and tensions in each locality. 'This variation must be taken in to account when formulating anti-racism initiatives,' says Dr Dunn.

This pilot study feeds into a three-year project (2000–2003), funded by the Australian Research Council, which involves a survey of 10,000 Australians. CONTACT DETAILS: Dr Kevin Dunn, School of Geography, tel. (02) 9385 5737

or

Victoria Collins, Public Affairs and Development, tel. (02) 9385 3644.
Date: 16 October 2000

SENDING THE MEDIA RELEASE

Find out who you should send your media release to.

Once the release is written, what then? For large newspapers, send the release to the Chief of Staff as well as to the relevant 'environment', 'economy', 'education', 'police', or 'local government' rounds writer—unless you already have a working relationship with a specific journalist. If you do direct your release to a media friend, take care to ensure that he or she is not unwell or on holiday as your story may otherwise go unattended. For small newspapers, send the release to the Editor. And for television and radio, send the release to the News Director or Chief of Staff. Do not make the mistake of sending your media release to the Chief Executive Officer, Managing Editor, Managing Director, or someone else at 'the top', unless you know them personally. All this is likely to achieve is a delay, as the release filters its way down to the Chief of Staff.

In general, it is probably best to fax a news release (although you can also hand-deliver, email, or post them), particularly if there is some urgency associated with the story. If you are sending photographs or discussing an event/issue that is not urgent, it may be more appropriate to mail the materials. If you do this, consider printing the release on coloured paper. That may make it less likely to get lost on a copy-room floor! If you live in a town with a small local newspaper, or a radio or television station, there may be some advantage in delivering the story yourself. You may then get the opportunity to make your case personally and begin to develop a working relationship with a local journalist.

It is important to note that staff change, offices relocate, and newspaper enterprises are bought and sold. As a result your contacts at various outlets may change. No one is going to return your release with a 'return to sender' on it. It will go into the bin. Keep your media contacts file up to date.

BEING INTERVIEWED

After you have sent out a media release, you may be contacted by a reporter seeking follow-up information. This is likely to be by phone. Although you might be a bit nervous about this, you should agree to speak—especially if you wish to develop an ongoing professional relationship with the journalist. However, do not allow the interview to proceed at a faster pace than you feel comfortable with. If you have been caught at a bad time (e.g. dinner is burning) or you need a few moments to gather your thoughts and notes, tell the reporter that you will call them back in a few minutes. Use that short time to get clear in your head what you want to say and then be sure to call the reporter back *when you said you would*. During the interview take time to explain your points but try not to 'waffle on' or dwell on marginal issues. If you have discussed an issue that is critical to the story, ask the reporter to read back their notes to ensure that 'we've got it right'. You are unlikely to encounter an objection as it will help the journalist avoid disputes about material after the paper has been published.

While it might be considered unethical in some academic work to quote material from interviews without the speaker having the opportunity to preview the ways in which their words will be used, reporters will not normally let you see a copy of the story they plan to publish before it goes to subeditors or to print. Asking to scrutinise the story before publication is unlikely to achieve much other than upsetting the reporter.

Sometimes your release will find its way to a radio station. Usually a radio program producer has a very tight timing schedule and will arrange for an on-air interview to be held with you later that same day or on the following day. This kind of interview can be fairly unnerving and a few precautions are always worthwhile.

> Before you do a media interview, get clear in your mind the key messages you want to convey.

- If the interview is to be conducted over the phone, make sure that you are available to receive the call. You will have been scheduled in and other interviews cannot be rescheduled.
- Try to ensure that there are no barking dogs, rustling paper, unexpected visitors, or mischievous friends to interrupt you (a DO NOT DISTURB sign can be very useful). On no account should you have a radio on in the room. In the same vein do not move your chair, tap your pen, or tap your fingers on the desk during the interview.
- Have your press release and a note pad in front of you. Jot down the most important parts of your story so you can get straight to the point and not be drawn into a discussion of insignificant details. The prompts you include on your note pad might also include reminders to greet the interviewer and to refer to him/her by name. Radio interviewers will appreciate the recognition as it confirms their importance to their audience. Remember to say thank you. These simple prompts can put you at ease. Many people unused to being interviewed in such an immediate atmosphere become nervous and can forget key issues and day-to-day courtesies. Those omissions can make you seem ill-versed in your subject matter, and cold and distant to a listening audience. You might also find your note pad useful for writing brief notes on questions that are asked.
- During the interview, when the interviewer repeats some facts (usually directly from your release), make a point of saying 'that's absolutely correct' or 'you've got straight to the main cause of the problem'. This again makes the interviewer feel comfortable and welcoming towards you.

If the radio interviewer and producer both like you then you may become a regular guest on their show. You are now well on your way to fame and perhaps even fortune!

FOLLOWING UP

If you do not hear back from the media outlet to which you sent your release, consider contacting them to see if the story is of any interest to them and to see if they need more information. This is also a good opportunity to convince the reporter that your story is worth covering. Try not to badger the poor journalist, though!

It is often difficult to anticipate whether any particular story will get coverage. Some stories will be reported. Others will not. If your story did not make it, share your disappointment with the reporter, but do not get angry about it. That is unlikely to do your case any good—in either the short term or the long term.

Developing a rapport with journalists can be a mutually beneficial exercise. For the author of a release it can help improve writing style. For the journalist it can be a regular and productive source of interesting news stories.

If you are favoured by good media coverage, phone or write to the reporter and express your appreciation to them. Like anyone else, they will welcome positive feedback. If, on the other hand, there are errors or problems with your story, be courteous in any complaints you make. Remember, journalists are ordinary people whose mistakes are more public than most people's!

> Try developing a good long-term relationship with journalists. They may eventually see you as an expert and seek you out for stories and comment.

CONCLUDING COMMENTS

The end results of writing and sending media releases can be enlightening, both to you and to the general public. At worst you will have explored an alternative genre of writing. At best you will have achieved your bit of fame and sparked interest in, and knowledge about, your activities as a geographer or environmental manager within the wider community. The various media are vital vehicles by which we can endeavour to communicate the results of our labours to audiences larger than the common group of markers, colleagues, families, and friends. If we want larger audiences within the general public to value our work and other contributions to the community, it is essential that we develop and refine our skills in presenting information to and through the media.

REFERENCES AND FURTHER READING

Berger, J. 1992, 'Teaching media interview skills', in *Teaching Public Relations*, ed. T. Hunt, Public Relations Division of the Association for Education in Journalism and Mass Communication, Available: <http://lamar.colostate.edu/~aejmcpr/27berger.htm> (15 April 2005).

Hay, I. & Israel, M. 2001, '"Newsmaking geography": Communicating geography through the media', *Applied Geography*, vol. 21, no. 2, pp. 107–25.

Lee, R.C. 1985, *A Geographer's Map of the Media*, Joint Committee for Geography in Higher Education, Geographical Association/Institute of British Geographers/Royal Geographical Society, Scottish Association of Geography Teachers, London.

Marken, G.A. 1994, 'Press releases: when nothing else will do, do it right', *Public Relations Quarterly*, Fall, pp. 9–11.

Mathews, I. 1981, *How to Use the Media in Australia*, Fontana, Melbourne.

Minnis, J.H. and Pratt, C.B. 1995, 'Let's revisit the newsroom: What does a weekly newspaper print?', *Public Relations Quarterly*, Fall, pp. 13–18.

Mondo Code LLC 2006, *Mondo Times*, Available: <http://www.modotimes.com/index. html> (1 February 2006).
A worldwide, searchable guide to print, audio and visual media.

Pesman, S. 1983, *Writing for the Media: Public Relations and the Press*, Crain, Chicago.

Telg, R. 2000, *Media Interview Skills for Environmental Education Programs*, Available: <http://edis.ifas.ufl.edu/WC036> (15 July 2005).

Walters, T.N., Walters, L.M. and Starr, D.P. 1994, 'After the highwayman: Syntax and successful placement of press releases in newspapers', *Public Relations Review*, vol. 20, no 4, pp. 345–56.

Williams, D. 1994, 'In defense of the (properly executed) press release', *Public Relations Quarterly*, Fall, pp. 5–7.

5

Preparing a Poster

One picture is worth ten thousand words.

Frederick R. Barnard, 1927

KEY TOPICS

- Why prepare a poster?
- What are poster markers looking for?
- Guidelines for preparing a good poster

Posters are a useful way of presenting the results of research and other scholarly enterprise. They are an effective and swift means of presenting an idea or set of ideas, finding increasing use at professional conferences and other gatherings (Pechenik 2004, p. 237). Producing a good poster can be challenging, as you need to provide an effective combination of graphic and written communication. This chapter outlines some of the keys to poster production. Discussion covers layout, visibility, and the use of colour and type style. While there is also a brief reference to the use of figures, extended discussions on the production of maps and graphical devices can be found in chapters 6 and 7.

WHY PREPARE A POSTER?

Physically, a poster is a piece of stiff card about 90–100 × 60–75 cm in size (some may be much larger) to which graphic materials, such as maps, graphs, and photos, are affixed and linked together by a small amount of text. Figures 5.1 and 5.2 show examples of posters completed by two first-year university students.

Figure 5.1   Example of a poster completed by a first-year university student

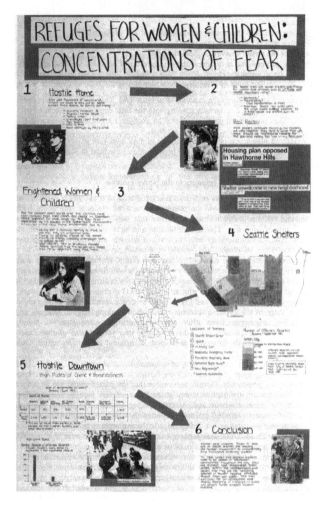

A poster presents an argument or explanation, summarises an issue, or outlines the results of some piece of research in succinct visual form. Posters are especially good for promoting informal discussion and showing results which require more time for interpretation than is possible in, say, an oral presentation. However, they are not useful for reviewing past research or presenting the results of 'textual' research (Lethbridge 1991, p. 14).

Assessors may ask you to prepare a poster for a variety of reasons. Posters:

- add variety and new challenges to the course
- encourage the expression of complex information and ideas through careful combinations of text and graphics

Figure 5.2   Example of a poster completed by a first-year university student

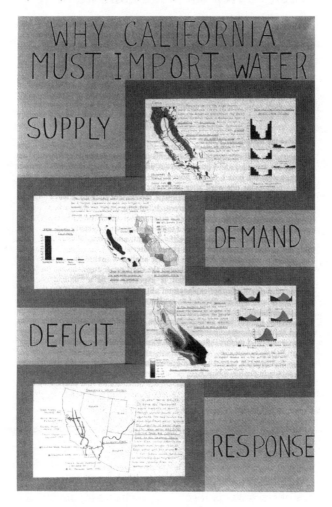

- develop and test skills in graphic communication
- stimulate critical thought
- offer the prospect of encouraging student–staff interaction (see Hay & Thomas 1999, Howenstine et al. 1988, Knight & Parsons 2003, and Vujakovic 1995 for a discussion).

If you are assigned a poster exercise, do not make the mistake of thinking that it involves little more than crayons, colouring-in, and collage! Posters are a challenging means of communicating information. They require you to express complex ideas with brevity and grace, and to balance text with graphics of high quality.

WHAT ARE YOUR POSTER MARKERS LOOKING FOR?

Poster production is not an explicit test of your artistic abilities, but if you have such aptitudes you should take advantage of them. A few central principles are critical to creating a successful poster.

BOX 5.1 PRINCIPLES OF POSTER PRODUCTION

Your markers are looking for performance with respect to principles which could be called the ABC of poster production:

- **Attention-getting:** the poster should make a good first impression. It should grab the viewer's attention. Achieve this through layout, colour, title, and other devices.
- **Brevity:** the poster should make its point(s) quickly.
- **Coherence:** an effective poster makes a logical, unified statement requiring no further explanation. It should be intellectually accessible to the intended audience and must be capable of 'standing alone'.
- **Direction:** does the poster have a clear trajectory through the subject matter? Keep the poster simple. Keep it focused. Overcomplicated posters discourage and confuse readers.
- **Evidence:** the poster should present an argument which is supported by accurate, referenced evidence.

Not surprisingly, these principles are very similar to the keys which unlock successful written and oral communication.

Whereas many of the essays you may be required to produce as part of your university degree will be read by an audience of one—your lecturer—posters are sometimes produced with other (hypothetical) audiences in mind. For example, you might be asked to produce a public information poster on strategies for making best use of green waste. If you have such an assignment, always consider your target audience and ensure that your language, ideas, and choice of graphics suit that audience. Perhaps more commonly though you will be working on 'academic' posters. In addition to the ABC of poster production as set out above, these may require that you:

> Academic posters are quite different from promotional posters.

- express a problem and resolve it
- argue or explain an issue, and/or
- evaluate evidence concerning a chosen topic (Howenstine et al. 1988, p. 144).

Your poster should reflect critical thinking rather than simply your capacity to describe some phenomenon. If you are given free choice of poster topic by your lecturer, you would be wise to check that the approach to the topic you have selected is appropriate before you proceed too far. Make sure that you are satisfying the intellectual demands of the exercise as well as the graphic requirements. The poster assessment schedule in Figure 5.3 indicates the general criteria for assessing posters. You will probably find it productive to continually assess your poster against these criteria as you work on it. This should help you produce a high-quality piece of work.

Figure 5.3   Poster assessment schedule

Student Name: Grade: Assessed by:

The following is an itemised rating scale of various aspects of written assignment performance. Sections left blank are not relevant to the attached assignment. Some aspects are more important than others, so there is no formula connecting the scatter of ticks with the final grade for the assignment. Ticks in either of the two boxes left of centre mean that the statement is true to a greater (outer left) or lesser (inner left) extent. The same principle applies to the right-hand boxes. If you have any questions about the individual scales, comment, final grade, or other aspects of this assignment, please see the assessor indicated above.

Quality of argument

Clear statement of question of relationship being investigated					Ambiguous or unclear statement of purpose
Poster fully addresses the question					Poster fails to address the question or issue posed/issue raised
Poster 'stands alone' requiring no additional explanation					Poster is difficult or impossible to comprehend without additional information
Logical/orderly explanation of the issue under investigation					Illogical/inadequate explanation
All components in presentation given appropriate level of attention					insufficient/ unbalanced treatment of components

Figure 5.3   (*cont.*)

Quality of evidence

Argument well supported by evidence and examples				Inadequate supporting evidence or examples
Accurate presentation of evidence and examples				Incomplete or questionable evidence

Use of supplementary material

Effective use of figures, tables, and other illustrative material				Illustrative material not used when needed or not discussed in text
Illustrations presented correctly				Illustrations presented incorrectly

Poster appearance

Poster carefully produced				Sloppy presentation
All text legible from 1.5 m				Text illegible from 1.5 m

Sources/Referencing

Adequate number of sources				Inadequate number of sources
Adequate acknowledgment of sources				Inadequate acknowledgment of sources
Correct and consistent referencing style				Incorrect or inconsistent referencing style
Reference list correctly presented				Errors or inconsistencies in reference list

Assessor's comments

While a completed poster should require no additional information for the viewer to be able to understand the content, there may be some occasions when your lecturer will ask you to stand by your poster and answer questions about it—as is the practice at an increasing number of academic and professional conferences.

> A good poster should stand alone comprehensibly, requiring no further explanation.

DESIGNING YOUR POSTER

Layout and research

Because thoughtful composition and layout are such important parts of effective communication (Vujakovic 1995, p. 254), it is worth reserving a big chunk of time for setting out your poster. Work that may have taken many hours to prepare can be ruined by an ill-conceived layout. It is also a good idea, therefore, to design your poster at the same time as you are conducting the research associated with the exercise. Produce sketches or mock-ups of poster layouts before deciding on the final set-up. Discuss these sketches with friends and your lecturer, who will all bring their fresh, critical eyes to your work. You will probably find that this will save you time and that it will help you to make sense of the issue under discussion in your poster. For example, in designing the poster you will probably find weaknesses and gaps in any argument you are developing or in any relationships you are exploring. These discoveries should prompt you to undertake additional enquiry which will contribute to the production of a better project. Of course, this means that you cannot leave poster production to the night before the assignment is due, no matter how straightforward the project may initially appear!

Guiding the reader through poster components

Careful composition is critical to good poster communication. Your poster should have a logical and clearly apparent structure (see Figure 5.4 (a)). To this end, it is useful to note that, besides graphics, posters usually comprise five (occasionally six) important components:

1 *title and subheadings*, which should be meaningful, visible, brief, and memorable. The title should normally also include the names of the poster's authors.
2 *abstract*, summarising the poster's key content. Some posters neither have nor need an abstract. Detailed information about writing abstracts is provided in chapter 2.

3 an *introduction*, in which you provide a short statement of the problem investigated and the approach used.

4 the *body* of the presentation. If your poster is presenting the results of some research, this section might be split into a number of parts. The first might commonly be *materials and methods*, where you explain any research techniques used in sufficient detail for readers to work out the scope of your study, the precision with which it has been done, and the validity of the data obtained. The second is likely to be a statement of *results*. This is a vital part of the poster. It enables readers to examine the data on which your conclusions are based and to critically evaluate their validity. Most readers need to see the information on which conclusions are based before they are able to accept them.

5 a *statement of conclusions* and/or *directions for future research*. The conclusions let readers know what interpretations you have made of the information presented in the poster, drawing together information from the introduction on its significance. You might also explain how future work could follow up on some particular aspect of your findings.

6 *references*, placed on the front of the poster or, in some cases, attached to the reverse side.

Evidently, then, posters are little different structurally from essays and other forms of expression. However, unlike written forms of communication, posters do not have to be set up in a linear form, with readers moving from top left to bottom right. 'Spider' diagrams (see Figure 5.4 (b)), showing factors contributing to social power in a community, and cyclical diagrams, showing the hydrological cycle or the cycle of poverty, are just two alternatives to the linear structure. However, while posters do offer this flexibility of presentation, it is important that you provide your readers with a clear sense of direction. To this end, readers must usually be guided through the poster with informative subheadings, numbers, or arrows. Readers do not know their way around your poster as you do. Lead them along. Be aware, however, that after reading the title and scanning the poster many people move straight to the conclusions (Simmonds & Reynolds 1989, p. 95). If the conclusions seem important, the viewer may then decide to read the rest of the poster. In view of this, give some hard thought to your title and to the way you present your conclusion(s).

> Make sure your poster's structure is clear to readers.

Posters may also be set up to be interactive (Vujakovic 1995, p. 254). Readers might be asked questions to which the answers are revealed by lifting flaps or overlays, or by turning circles of cardboard. Devices such as these will almost certainly encourage your audience to interact with the poster. They should be kept uncomplicated and robust.

Figure 5.4   Examples of different poster formats

(a)

Title and Author		
Introduction	Results—Year A	Conclusions
Project's Significance		Further Research
Materials and Methods	Results—Year B	References

(b)

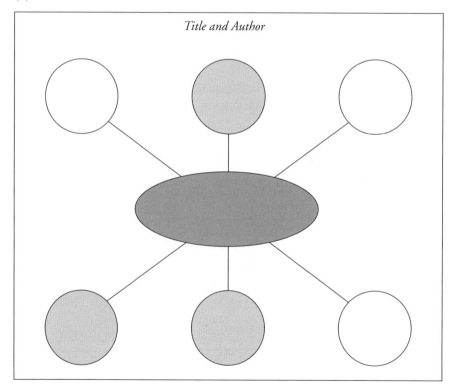

Source Hay & Thomas (1999, p. 211)

Text

Number of words and level of detail

Unlike posters advertising airlines or alcohol, academic posters almost always contain some amount of text. Together with the graphics, text contributes to the introduction, explanation, and discussion of your work. It is important, however, to keep text to a minimum. Lethbridge (1991, p. 18) suggests a maximum word count of 500, but makes the point that a poster will be much more effective if it uses only 250–400 words. Confine the text you do use to short sections which complement the poster's graphic components. Make sure no single block of text takes longer than 30 seconds to read (Knight & Parsons 2003, p. 155). Poster viewers do not enjoy reading long texts. Bad posters are often bad because they contain too much text or because all the text is presented in a small number of blocks.

> Use small amounts of text on your poster and be sure it is visible from at least 1.5 metres.

You do not need to provide all the intricate details of a project discussed in a poster. In much the same way as a talk highlights points which can later be explored by interested members of the audience, so a poster can be used to present the most important elements of your work. Onlookers, whose interest has been aroused, might then speak to you about details (Day 1989, p. 145). Having said this, an earlier point bears repetition: the poster must still be comprehensible without further elaboration.

Visibility of text

Given the amount of work you will have to do to get the number of words you use in your poster down to an acceptable level, you will, no doubt, want your audience to be able to read each carefully selected letter! To this end, ensure that:

- all materials on your poster are clearly legible from a distance of about 1.5 metres
- titles and headings are discernible to viewers several metres away
- upper and lower case letters are used throughout headings and poster text. Do not just use capitals. THEY ARE A LOT MORE DIFFICULT TO READ QUICKLY
- textual material is confined to a number of brief statements. Do not write an essay and paste it to the board! Few people, if any, will read it.

Use larger fonts and/or display faces for short headings, and smaller and/or less decorative type for longer titles. Twelve point—a common size for typed essays and reports—is much too small a point size for the body of the text.

If you need to use 12 point type to fit all your text on the poster, the poster probably contains too much text. The solution to this problem is to abbreviate and rewrite the text.

BOX 5.2 SUGGESTED POSTER TYPE SIZES

For posters, suggested type sizes are:

• main headings	96–180 point	(27–48.5 mm)
• secondary headings	48–84 point	(12.9–25.4 mm)
• section headings	24–36 point	(5.9–8.7 mm)
• text and captions	14–18 point	(3.2–4.6 mm)

Type is one of the most important aspects of visual design, especially for headings, and you should use a typeface that relates to the subject material. While the body of the text needs to be clear and simple, you may be able to add extra graphic character to the poster through your choice of a suitable type. Typefaces and type styles play important roles in attracting attention, and contribute to the poster's overall theme and clarity.

BOX 5.3 CHARACTERISTICS OF TYPEFACES AND TYPE STYLES

- typeface: the particular character of the letter forms, from which there are thousands to choose (e.g. **Helvetica**, Times, `Courier`)
- typeweight: the thickness of the letter stroke (e.g., regular, **bold**)
- type style: may be roman (upright), *italic* (slanted), condensed, or extended
- type size: may be 14 point, 16 point, or any size necessary
- type colour: even with only black printing, may be **black,** white, or shaded

---

For example, a computer or space-age typeface might be appropriate for a poster investigating some of the effects of space-adjusting technology on international trade practices and patterns, and a playbill typeface—first used in the Victorian era on posters advertising stage-productions—could be appropriate for a poster considering nineteenth-century Australian health care conditions.

Colour

Often one of the most striking and emotive elements of a completed poster is colour, a component which adds to or detracts from the overall impact of the project. Colour can command attention, bring pleasure, and clarify a point

Use type and colour that complement your poster.

(Larsgaard 1978, p. 193). It can highlight important dimensions of a poster or suppress less important facets.

Having said that colour is important, it is also helpful to realise that colour should be used judiciously. To avoid confusion and chaos in the poster use as few colours as possible. Pechenik (2004, p. 242) suggests that a single background colour should be used to unify the presentation. Take care too in your choice of combinations of text and background colours. There should always be enough contrast between text and background to allow the text to be read easily from a distance. For example, orange text on a yellow background can be difficult to read, as can red text on a green background.

Colour can add symbolic connotations and feelings to the message of a poster. You might find the following list, adapted from Sim (1981), useful. It summarises some colour-connotation connections from a white Anglo-American perspective.

BOX 5.4 SOME COLOUR CONNOTATIONS

- black — clear-cut and crisp, death, dignity, doom and gloom, financial credit, formality
- blue — calm, climatological, coastal, coolness, rivers, peace, sadness
- brown — dismal, dreary, earth, pollution, soils
- green — agriculture, conservation, coolness, envy, freshness, growth, nature, rural, safety, spring, vegetation, wealth
- orange — autumn, flames, healthiness, sunshine, warmth
- red — action, blood, danger, financial deficit, fire, hazards, health, heat, Marxism, noise, passion
- white — cleanliness, glory, iciness, purity, snow
- yellow — beaches, happiness, light-heartedness, sand, sunshine, weakness

Colour may also be used to add information to particular graphics. For example, the appropriate use of red and black conveys the message that financial results represent profit and loss statistics, not simply dollar figures.

In some circumstances and for particular audiences, shapes associated with a poster may help to convey information and meaning. For example, a poster on housing for a school-age audience might be set on backing card cut to the shape of a house. You need to be careful, however, to ensure that you do not reproduce stereotypes or imply particular 'norms' through such devices. Not all families live in detached homes with pitched roof and chimney (Vujakovic 1995, p. 253).

Tables, figures, and photos

Tables

Tables used on posters should generally be kept simple and clear. Readers are unlikely to spend much time trying to decipher complex data sets. In many cases it is better to summarise and depict tabular information in the form of histograms, pie charts, and other graphic devices (see Figure 5.5). These will usually communicate your messages faster and more memorably, and for some audiences may be the most appropriate communication device. Although tables are a very useful means of communicating precise numerical information, ask yourself whether the data could be transformed into a 'picture' as opposed to a table. For example, a table of population growth figures for Rarotonga since 1900 might be better presented as a **line graph**. Try to achieve a balance between the extent to which you use tables and figures in your poster.

> Consider summarising data for your poster as a figure.

Figure 5.5   Converting a numerical table into a poster-ready figure

	COMPANY EXPENDITURE		
YEAR	LOCALLY	OVERSEAS	TOTAL
1981	5,067,000	1,010,000	$6,077,000
1982	5,328,000	3,126,000	$8,454,000
1983	6,141,000	2,842,000	$8,983,000
1984	7,002,000	6,989,000	$13,991,000
1985	8,269,000	2,354,000	$10,623,000
1986	2,103,000	2,413,000	$4,516,000
1987	2,025,000	4,201,000	$6,226,000
1988	1,567,000	3,368,000	$4,835,000
1989	4,824,000	423,000	$5,247,000
1990	6,041,000	0	$6,041,000

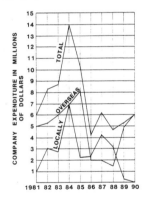

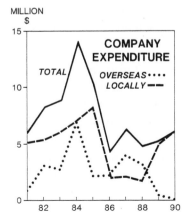

Figures and photos

Images are a particularly important part of a poster. For example, you can use photographs to show pasture before and after the eradication of rabbits, or to illustrate transformations in a city after a large industry closes local operations and moves overseas. You can use accompanying diagrams to explain the processes and procedures underlying those surface appearances (Vujakovic 1995, p. 253). The WWW can provide some useful images that might otherwise be difficult to obtain. For example, Google's Images search capability may turn up helpful illustrations and photographs that may be used subject to copyright restrictions. There are also growing numbers of specialist online image galleries that can prove helpful (e.g. University of Chicago Library's American Environmental Photographs Collection). Given its importance, it is vital that graphic material in your poster be bold and relevant. Avoid filling up your work with pleasing but unnecessary pictures. These are likely to detract from the central matters you wish to communicate.

> The WWW provides a vast array of images useful for posters.

In the process of considering the production of figures for a poster, you should address several questions. These include:

- What type of 'picture' will best illustrate the point? For example, would a pie chart be more effective than a bar chart?
- What symbols and colours can you employ to make a greater impression and to communicate the idea more clearly? For example, would it be effective to illustrate South Africa's balance of payments history in a **bar graph** depicting piles of coins shaded red or black depending on each year's deficit or surplus? The graphical devices you employ may be more readily understood, and may therefore be more effective, if they incorporate symbols and colours which have evolved through tradition, convention, and public recognition to be representative of their content.
- Are all the graphic conventions likely to be comprehensible to the audience? Maps, for example, should always have a legend/key explaining all the symbols used.

Figure 5.5 shows examples of statistics from the same research, which might be incorporated into a poster display in different forms. In general, it is advisable to find a simplified but graphically interesting way of displaying data when producing a poster. Whereas the table might provide the most accurate record of research data collected, it does not enable the viewer to absorb the major trends as quickly as a graphic depiction would. A detailed graph, which might be used in a written report, would enable the reader not only to obtain a picture of the relative trends quickly but also to make a reasonable interpretation of the data. However, a graph such as this is still unnecessarily detailed for a poster display. A simplified and more interesting portrayal, like the third item in Figure 5.5, enables the viewer to grasp the essential pattern quickly. In this example of a graph suitable for a poster display, interest and clarity are achieved by differentiating linework, type style, and size. The addition of colour might increase visual appeal.

If you use photographs in your poster, be sure they are of high quality (for example, in focus and with sharp contrast) and sufficiently large to be clearly visible from a distance of 1–2 metres. If the size of the photographed object would not be immediately clear to your audience, provide some idea of **scale** (Singleton 1984, p. 18). For example, include your camera lens cover or a ruler in the photograph. Do not forget to provide an appropriate title for the photograph (and for other figures on the poster).

You will work long and hard to prepare a good poster. Protect your investment. Use good-quality adhesives to affix text, photos, maps, and figures to the poster board. Detached images do not make a good impression. If you are feeling especially wealthy and motivated, consider getting your poster laminated. This will keep everything in place and protect the poster from the weather. Alternatively, a large bin liner will usually make a good carry-bag for your masterpiece. The bag's intended use should not be taken as a slight on your hard work!

> If you want to keep your poster, present it at a conference, or display it permanently, consider getting it laminated.

Acknowledging sources

As with any other form of academic communication, you must accurately acknowledge any information and ideas, figures and facts, or text and tables you have drawn from other sources. These should be cited in exactly the same way as they would be in an essay or report (see chapter 10 for a discussion of referencing conventions). In some cases, and particularly for formal academic posters, it is appropriate to include your reference list on the front of the poster. In other situations (e.g. community information posters) it may be more appropriate to firmly affix the list of references to the back of the poster, where they do not detract from the main message of your work. If you are at all uncertain about the correct location for references, speak to your lecturer.

A final note …
Throughout the production process of your poster, keep in mind the principles which were introduced earlier: attention-getting, brevity, coherence, direction, and careful use of evidence. Providing, of course, that the poster draws on

good research, careful application of these principles should contribute to the production of first-class work.

REFERENCES AND FURTHER READING

Brown, B.S. 1996, 'Communicate your science! ... Producing punchy posters', *Trends in Cell Biology*, vol. 6, pp. 37–9.

Day, R.A. 1989, *How to Write and Publish a Scientific Paper*, Cambridge University Press, Cambridge.

Hay, I. & Miller, R. 1992, 'Application of a poster exercise in an advanced undergraduate geography course', *Journal of Geography in Higher Education*, vol. 16, no. 2, pp. 199–215.
Essentially intended to be read by lecturers, this paper critically discusses a strategy for incorporating a poster exercise into an upper-level class. Special emphasis is given to the rationale for conducting the project and to the practical dimensions of poster production, much of which is elaborated upon in this book.

Hay, I. & Thomas, S. 1999, 'Making sense with posters in biological science education', *Journal of Biological Education*, vol. 33, no. 4, pp. 209–14.

Howenstine, E., Hay, I., Delaney, E., Bell, J., Norris, F., Whelan, A., Pirani, M., Chow, T. & Ross, A. 1988, 'Using a poster exercise in an introductory geography course', *Journal of Geography in Higher Education*, vol. 12, no. 2, pp. 139–47.

Jenkins, A. 1994, 'Conveying your message by a poster', in D. Saunders (ed.), *The Complete Student Handbook*, Blackwell, Oxford.
An easily read chapter which is written at a more general level than the one in this book. By comparison, Jenkins's discussion has less detail on preparing posters and a little more on techniques for presenting posters within a poster session (i.e. with other posters).

Knight, P. & Parsons, T. 2003, *How to Do Your Essays, Exams, and Coursework in Geography and Related Disciplines*, Nelson Thornes, Cheltenham.

Larsgaard, M. 1978, *Map Librarianship*, Libraries Unlimited, Littleton, Colorado.
Includes discussion of some useful design principles.

Lethbridge, R., 1991, *Techniques for Successful Seminars and Poster Presentations*, Longman Cheshire, Melbourne.
This short book briefly introduces poster design principles and goes on to provide a comprehensive review of technical aspects of preparing illustrations. Indeed, the book's title may be a little misleading given the volume's overall emphasis on graphic production techniques.

McMahon, N. 2003, *Making an Academic Poster Display* (online), Available: <http://student.dcu.ie/~mcmahon4/posteradvice.html> (15 July 2005).
Most useful for its links to helpful web sites on academic poster production.

Mills, V. 1967, *Making Posters*, Studio Vista, London.
This book approaches poster construction from a graphic arts perspective, but it does provide some useful information on colour, lettering, and design for those people preparing academic posters.

Mulnix, A. & Penhale, S.J. 1997, 'Modelling the activities of scientists: A literature review and poster presentation assignment', *The American Biology Teacher*, vol. 59, pp. 482–7.

Pechenik, J.A. 2004, *A short guide to writing about biology*, Pearson Longman, New York.
Chapter 11, 'Writing a poster presentation', offers a useful and detailed discussion on the process of converting a written paper into a good poster presentation.

Sim, R. 1981, *Lettering for Signs, Projects, Posters, Displays*, 2nd edn, Learning Publications, Balgowlah, Australia.

Simmonds, D. & Reynolds, L. 1989, *Computer Presentation of Data in Science*, Kluwer Academic, Dordrecht.
Includes a very short section on poster layout.

Singleton, A. 1984, *Poster Sessions. A Guide to Their Use at Meetings and Conferences for Presenters and Organisers*, Elsevier, Oxford.
A good, succinct discussion of posters, poster sessions, and their uses.

Vujakovic, P. 1995, 'Making posters', *Journal of Geography in Higher Education*, vol. 19, no. 2, pp. 251–6.
Readable and concise discussion of poster production.

6

Communicating with Figures and Tables

As Bertrand Russell once said, most of us can recognise a sparrow, but we'd be hard put to describe its characteristics clearly enough for someone else to recognise one. Far more sensible to show them a picture.

Rowntree 1990, p. 193

KEY TOPICS

- Why communicate graphically?
- General guidelines for clear graphic communication
- Different types of graphic
- Preparing a good table

WHY COMMUNICATE GRAPHICALLY?

In geography and environmental studies, words or numbers alone are often not sufficient to communicate information effectively. Graphic communication allows you to display a large amount of information succinctly and helps your audience absorb it readily. Effective illustrations can help a reader achieve a rapid understanding of an argument or issue.

Figures employ human powers of visual perception and pattern recognition, which are much better developed than our capacity to uncover meaningful relations in numerical lists (Krohn 1991, p. 188). Often we see things in graphic form which are not apparent in tables and text. Krohn argues that graphs reveal relationships that allow both the numbers upon which they are based and the concepts by which we understand those numbers to be reinterpreted. As such, graphs are critical interactive sites for comprehending the world around us.

> Graphic material can reveal relationships difficult to see in tables and text.

In addition to their intellectual functions, graphics can enhance various forms of technical writing in different ways (Eisenberg 1992, p. 81):

- *in essays and reports*: graphs and tables summarise quantitative information, freeing up text for comments on important features
- *in instructions*: graphics may help people to understand principles behind the operation of some process or the characteristics of a phenomenon
- *in oral presentations*: charts, tables, and figures relieve monotony, help guide the speaker, and aid the audience's understanding of data.

This chapter discusses the character and construction of different types of illustrative material. It is important first to introduce a few general guidelines.

GENERAL GUIDELINES FOR CLEAR GRAPHIC COMMUNICATION

Good graphics are concise, comprehensible, independent, and referenced.

1. Concise

Graphics should present only that information which is relevant to your work and required to make your point. Critically review the data you are going to portray to find out what they 'say' and then let them say it graphically with the minimum of embellishment (Wainer 1984, p. 147). If you reproduce an illustration or table you have found in your research you may need to redraw or rewrite it to remove irrelevant details.

2. Comprehensible

Your audience must understand what the graphic is about. Provide a clear and complete title which answers 'what', 'where', and 'when' questions, and effective labelling. Effective data labels and axis labels are:

- legible and easy to find
- easily associated with the axis/object depicted (they should be close together)
- readable from a single viewpoint. A reader looking at the graphic should be able to read the text without having to turn the page sideways (Gerber 1990–91, p. 28).

> A good graphic is stand-alone comprehensible.

Although you should fully label your graphics, do make sure that **data regions** are as clear of notes, axis markers, and keys as practicable. In short, the graphed information should be clear and easy to read.

If your graph displays two or more data sets, they must be easily distinguished from one another. Graphs should include no more than *four* simultaneous symbols, values, or lines (Cartography Specialty Group of the Association of American Geographers 1995, p. 5) and each line or symbol should be sufficiently different from the others to facilitate discrimination.

You can also make a graphic more comprehensible by making effective use of the data region (i.e. that part of the graph in which the data is displayed). Choose a range of axis scale marks which will allow the full range of data to be included while ensuring that the scale allows the data to fill up as much of the data region as possible. If you take photographs, this principle will be familiar to you. Just as good photos will usually 'fill the frame', so a good graph will typically fill the data region. Finally, tick marks on each axis should also be placed at sufficiently frequent intervals for a reader to work out accurately the value of each data point (Pechenik 2004, p. 162).

3. Independent

Graphics should stand alone. Someone who has not read the document associated with the graphic should be able to look at the table or illustration and understand what it means. Graphics should also be independent of one another.

4. Referenced

You must acknowledge sources. Use an accepted referencing system to note sources of data and graphics. Each graphic should be accompanied by summary bibliographic details (author, date, page, in the case of the **author–date system**) or a **note identifier** allowing the reader to find out where the graph or the data upon which it is based came from. A reference list at the end of your work should provide the full bibliographic details of all sources.

Make sure that references are to the source *you* used, and not that of the author of the text you are borrowing from. For example, imagine you are copying a penguin population graph you found in a book written by Dr Emperor and published in 2006. Emperor had, in turn, cited the source of her graphed data as the Argentine Penguin Research Foundation. Following the author–date system, the graph you present in your work would be referenced as (Argentine Penguin Research Foundation, in Emperor 2006, p. 12). The reference would not simply be to Emperor. Of course, there would also be a full reference to Emperor's work in the list at the end of your paper. See chapter 10 for further information.

DIFFERENT TYPES OF GRAPHIC

Various forms of graphic communication are described in this chapter, and some advice on their construction is given. In a deliberate strategy, all graphs in this book have been drawn using Microsoft Excel. While other, more powerful, software packages for producing graphics exist, Excel is a commonly available package which produces adequate figures for most undergraduate assignments. It is readily available in most universities, and students familiar with computers should be able to produce graphics comparable with (or better than) any of those shown in this chapter. Hand-drawn figures can easily be produced to the same standard. Table 6.1 provides a summary of the major forms of graphic discussed, together with their nature and function.

Table 6.1   Types of graphic and their nature/function

Type of Graphic	Nature/Function
Scattergram	Graphic of point data plotted by (x,y) co-ordinates. Usually created to provide visual impression of direction and strength of relationship between variables.
Line Graph	Values of observed phenomena are connected by lines. Used to illustrate change over time.
Bar Chart	Observed values are depicted by one or more horizontal or vertical bars whose *length* is proportional to value(s) represented.
Histogram	Similar to bar graph, but commonly used to depict distribution of a continuous variable. Bar *area* is proportional to value represented. Thus, if class intervals depicted are of different sizes, the column areas will reflect this.
Population Pyramid	Form of histogram showing the number or percentage of a population in different age groups of the total population.
Pie (Circle) Chart	Circular shaped graph in which proportions of some total sum (the whole 'pie') are depicted as 'slices'. The area of each 'slice' is directly proportional to the size of the variable portrayed.
Logarithmic Graph (log–log and semi-log)	Form of graph using logarithmic graph paper. Key intervals on logarithmic axes are exponents of ten. Log graphs allow depiction of wide data ranges.
Table	Systematically arranged list of facts or numbers, usually set out in rows and columns. Presents summary data or information in orderly, unified fashion.

Scattergrams

A scattergram is a graph of point data plotted by (x,y) coordinates (see Figure 6.1 for an example). Scattergrams are usually created to provide a visual impression of the direction and strength of a relationship between variables.

Figure 6.1   Example of a scattergram. *Life expectancy and total fertility rates, selected countries, 2000–05*

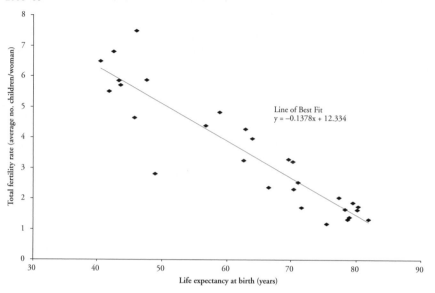

Data Source: United Nations (2004, pp. 67–77)

The *independent* variable (that is, the one which causes change) is depicted on the horizontal *x-axis* and the *dependent* variable (the variable which changes as a result of change in the independent variable) is plotted on the *y-axis*. To illustrate the difference between independent and dependent variables, consider the relationship between precipitation levels and costs associated with flooding. Damage costs associated with flooding will usually depend on the amount of rainfall. Thus, rainfall is the independent variable (x-axis) and damage costs are dependent (y-axis). Or, the severity of injuries associated with a motor vehicle accident (dependent variable, y-axis) tends to increase with motor vehicle speed (independent variable, x-axis).

> Be sure to put independent and dependent variables on the correct axes of your graph.

After points are located on the scattergram, you might draw a 'line of best fit' through the points by eye (i.e. your visual impression of the relationship expressed in the form of a line through the points). This line may be calculated mathematically and the regression equation expressed on the graph (see Figure 6.1).

Line graphs

Typically, line graphs are used to illustrate continuous changes in some phenomenon over time, with any trends being shown by the rise and fall of the line. Line graphs may also show the relationship between two sets of data. Figures 6.2, 6.3, and 6.4 are examples of line graphs.

Do not use a line graph if you are dealing with disconnected data (Eisenberg 1992, p. 97). For example, if you have air pollution data for every second year since 1945, the information should be graphed using a bar chart because a line graph would incorrectly suggest that you have data for each intervening year.

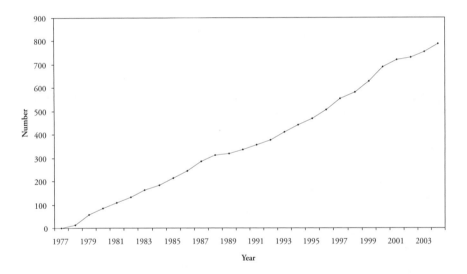

Figure 6.2   Example of a line graph. *Number of sites inscribed on the World Heritage List, 1977–2004*

Data Source: World Heritage Centre (2005, pp. 1–14)

Constructing a line graph

Plot each (x,y) data point for your data set(s). When all the data points are plotted, join the points associated with each data set to produce lines such as those shown in Figures 6.2, 6.3, and 6.4. In some cases however it is more appropriate to draw smooth curves than it is to 'join the dots' (Mohan, McGregor &

Figure 6.3 Example of a line graph. *Permanent arrivals and departures, Australia, September 2003–December 2004*

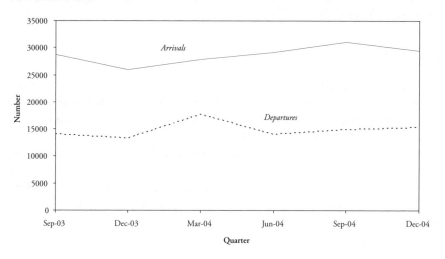

Data Source: ABS (2005b)

Figure 6.4 Example of a line graph. *Mean NVDI (Normalised Difference Vegetation Index)—a measure of vegetation 'vigour'—following application of three different herbicides. Figures calculated using Red and NIR (near-infrared) reflectance recordings from 3 x 1-metre-square test plots (10 plots for each herbicide)*

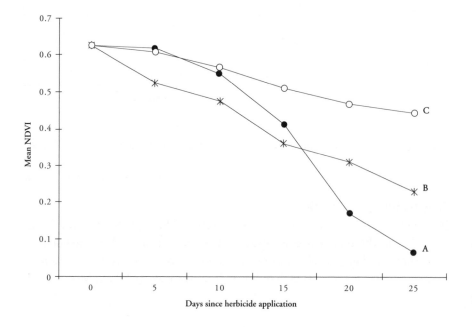

Strano 1992, p. 284; Pechenik 2004, p. 168) where, for example, a clear trend is disrupted by a single inconsistent data point. Make any such judgments very carefully.

If a number of lines are depicted in one graph, ensure that they can easily be distinguished from one another (see Figures 6.3 and 6.4) through use of colour, dotted lines, or labels.

If you are showing average (mean) values on your graph, you can usefully provide a visual summary of the variation within the data by, for example, depicting the data range or the standard deviation about the mean (Pechenik 2004, p. 171). An example is shown in Figure 6.5.

Figure 6.5 Example of a graph showing variation within data (mean and range). *Mean (including trendline) and range (minimum–maximum) of NVDI (Normalised Difference Vegetation Index)—a measure of vegetation 'vigour'—measurements. Figures calculated using Red and NIR (near-infrared) reflectance recordings from 3 x 1-metre-square test plots (10 plots for each herbicide)*

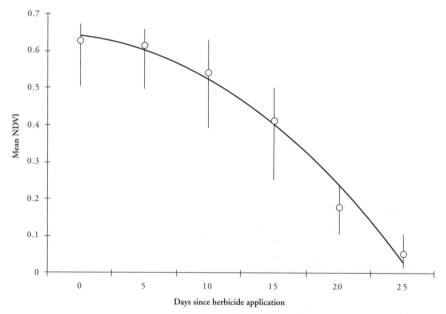

As Pechenik (2004, p. 172) points out 'Plots of standard deviations or standard errors are always symmetrical about the mean and so convey only partial information about the range of values obtained. If more of your individual values are above the mean than below the mean, the error bars will give a misleading impression about how the data are actually distributed. If your graph is fairly simple, you may be able to achieve the best of both worlds, indicating both the range and standard deviation (or standard error)'. An example is provided in Figure 6.6.

Figure 6.6   Example of a graph showing variation within data (data range, mean, and standard deviation). *Variations in NVDI (Normalised Difference Vegetation Index)—a measure of vegetation 'vigour'—measurements. Figures calculated using Red and NIR (near-infrared) reflectance recordings from 3 x 1-metre-square test plots (10 plots for each herbicide)*

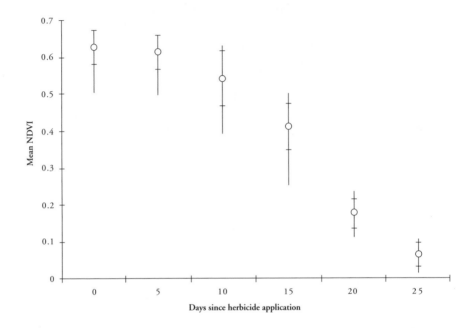

If you do include indicators of variation in your graph, make sure that you include in your caption of notes that accompany the figure details of what you have plotted, together with the number of measurements associated with each mean (Pechenik 2004, p. 173).

Line graphs will sometimes compare things that have different measurements. This can be done by using vertical axes on the left and right sides of the graph to depict the different scales. Figure 6.7 provides an illustration of the use of multiple vertical axis labels.

Bar charts

Bar charts are of two main types: *horizontal* and *vertical* (ABS 1994b, p. 108). Figures 6.8 and 6.9 show each type respectively. Horizontal bar graphs usually

Figure 6.7   Example of a graph using multiple vertical axis labels. *Darwin climate, average monthly rainfall, and daily maximum temperature, 1941–2004*

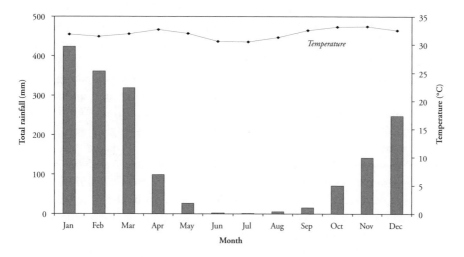

Data Source: Bureau of Meteorology (2004)

Figure 6.8   Example of a horizontal bar graph. *Percentages of the water used in Australian agriculture, by industry, 2000–01*

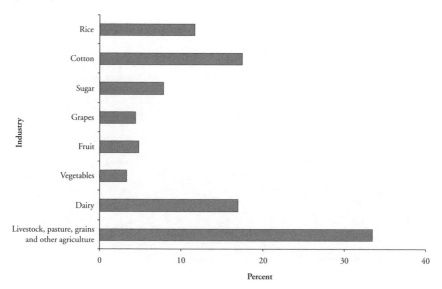

Data Source: ABS (2001a)

represent a single period of time, whereas column graphs may represent similar items at different times (Moorhouse 1974, p. 67).

In bar graphs the *length* of each bar is proportional to the value it represents (Coggins & Hefford 1973, p. 66). It is in this regard that bar graphs differ from histograms, with which they are sometimes confused. Histograms use bars whose *areas* are proportional to the value depicted.

Bar charts are a commonly used and easily understood way of taking a snapshot of variables at one point in time, depicting data in groups, and showing the size of each group (Moorhouse 1974, p. 64; Windschuttle & Windschuttle 1988, p. 278). Figure 6.10 achieves all of these ends in a single graph.

Bar charts can also be used to show the components of data as well as data totals. See Figure 6.11 for an example of such a *subdivided bar chart*. It is possible to go one step further and represent data in the form of a *subdivided 100% bar chart* (see Figure 6.12 for an example). These can be useful for depicting figures whose totals are so different that it would be almost impossible to chart them in absolute amounts (Moorhouse 1974, p. 66).

As Figure 6.13 illustrates, bar charts can be used to portray negative as well as positive quantities.

Figure 6.9   Example of a vertical bar graph. *Total dwelling units approved, South Australia, January–July 2004*

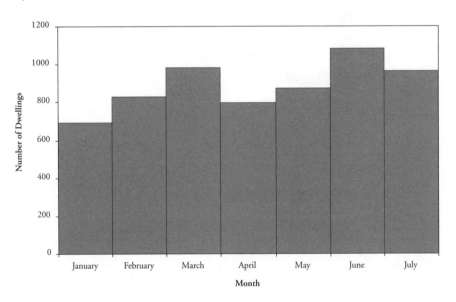

Data Source: ABS (2005a)

Figure 6.10   Example of a bar chart. *Male and female death rates from all cardiovascular diseases for Australian states and territories, 2002*

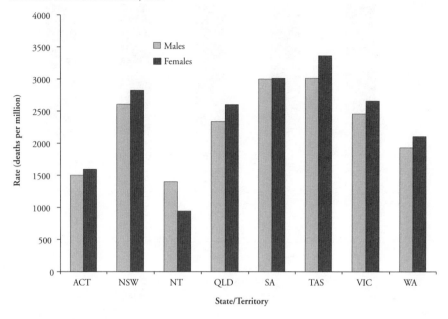

Data Source: Australian Institute of Health and Welfare (2004)

Figure 6.11   Example of a subdivided bar chart. *Comparison of part-time and full-time employment in Australia, 1985–2005*

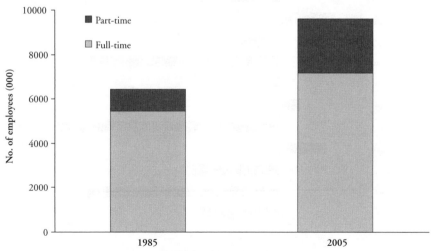

Data Source: ABS (2005c)

Figure 6.12 Example of a subdivided 100% bar chart. *Household type by major Australian cities, 2001*

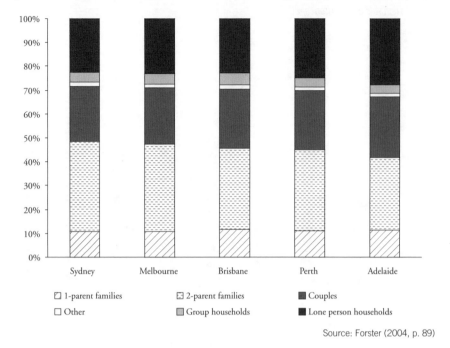

Source: Forster (2004, p. 89)

Figure 6.13 Example of a bar chart depicting positive and negative values. *Annual population growth rates for selected countries, 2000–05*

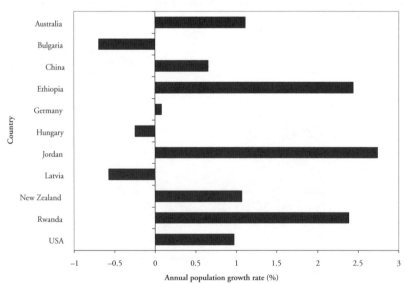

Data Source: United Nations (2004, pp. 45–50)

Constructing a bar chart

Examine the data which is to be graphed and select suitable scales for the graph's axes. In general, scales should commence at zero (Coggins & Hefford 1973, p. 66) although this is not critical. Label the axes.

When the chart is being designed, it is important to consider the sequence of items being depicted. In general, the items should be listed in order of importance to the viewer. However, in simple comparisons in a horizontal bar graph format it is best to arrange the bars in ascending order of length from bottom to top. Having said that, you must also be aware that some data sets are listed, by convention, in particular orders. For example, in Australia, Bureau of Statistics occupational groups are typically listed in the following order: Managers & Administrators, Professionals, Para-professionals, Tradespersons … Labourers & related workers, Inadequately described, Not stated. Similarly, industrial groups are usually listed in order through primary (e.g. farming), secondary (e.g. manufacturing), tertiary (e.g. retail), and quaternary (e.g. information transfer) divisions. Graphs should typically reflect such customary presentation forms. If you are not sure whether to set up a table in ascending order, speak to your lecturer.

The next step is to draw in the bars. Their width is a matter of choice, but should be constant within a graph. If you use different widths within the same graph, some readers may be led to believe that bar width, and hence area, is more important than lengths. Bars should be separated from one another, reflecting the discrete nature of the observed values (Jennings 1990, p. 18) and the space between the bars should be about one-half to three-quarters of their width. However, where the pattern of change is of greater importance than the individual values, no space between the observations is left at all (Coggins & Hefford 1973, p. 66). For example, compare Figures 6.9 and 6.10. In Figure 6.9 the pattern of change through the year is of more interest to the reader than is the specific value for each month. By contrast, the different, and therefore graphically differentiated, causes of death portrayed in Figure 6.10 are central to the chart's message.

Finally, add appropriate title, labels, key, and reference.

Make sure your graph is labelled fully and correctly.

Histograms

Histograms are mainly used to show the distribution of values of a continuous variable. A continuous variable is one which could have any conceivable value within an observed range (e.g. plant height, rainfall measurements, temperature) and may be contrasted therefore with **discrete data** in which no fractional numbers such as halves, quarters exist (e.g. plant and animal numbers). For examples of histograms, see Figure 6.14. This figure shows three histograms drawn using the same data set but different class intervals. Class intervals are explained shortly.

Histograms may be confused with vertical bar charts or column graphs, but there is a technical difference. Strictly speaking, histograms depict frequency through the area of the column, whereas in a column graph frequency is measured by column *height* (ABS 1994b, p. 120). Thus, while histograms usually have bars of equal width, if the class intervals are of different sizes the columns should reflect this. For example, if one class interval on a graph was $0 to $9 and the second was $10 to $29, the second should be drawn twice as wide as the first.

The phenomenon whose size is being depicted is plotted on the horizontal x-axis. Frequency of occurrence is plotted on the vertical y-axis. The frequency is the number of occurrences of the measured variable within a specific class interval (e.g. number of hotels with rooms available in a given price category).

Constructing a histogram

As Figure 6.14 illustrates, the method you choose to construct your histogram can have a significant effect on the appearance of the graph you finally produce. Figure 6.14(a), (b), and (c) were drawn using the same data (from Table 6.2). However, each was drawn using different methods of calculating class intervals and frequency distributions. Figure 6.14(a) splits the data range evenly on the basis of the *number* of x-axis classes desired. Figure 6.14(b) shows the data on the basis of the desired *size* of the x-axis classes (in this case $55) and figure 6.14(c) is the product of *minimising in-class variations* while maximising between-class variations.

Figure 6.14   Example of histograms drawn using the same data but different class intervals

(a) *Hotel accommodation costs, Wellington, 1994*

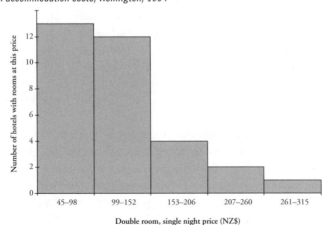

Double room, single night price (NZ$)

(b) *Hotel accommodation costs, Wellington, 1994*

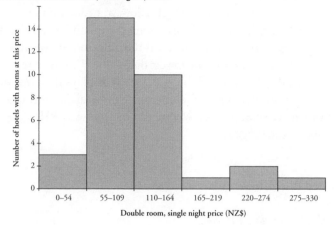

(c) *Hotel accommodation costs, Wellington, 1994*

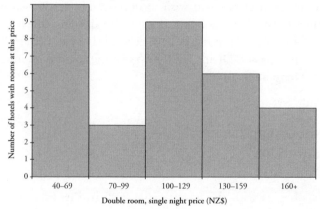

Data source: New Zealand Tourism Board (1995)

Table 6.2   Data set for histogram construction. *Single night, double room hotel accommodation rates (NZ$), Wellington, 1994*

109	253	118	56
112	124	60	45
95	162	90	59
45	198	100	50
136	156	315	50
156	105	144	65
253	118	101	55
105	152	50	80

Source: New Zealand Tourism Board (1995)

> **Range is the difference between the highest data value and the lowest.**

The first two methods of working out class intervals and frequency distributions which allow you to summarise the data to be depicted in your histogram require that you calculate the range of the data set. Range is the difference between the highest data value and the lowest data value. To illustrate, consider the data shown in Table 6.2, which displays the price of hotel accommodation in Wellington, New Zealand during 1994.

The most expensive room rate in Wellington in 1994 was $315, the lowest was $45. Therefore, the range is:

$$\$315 - \$45 = \$270$$

The next step is to calculate class intervals.

Methods of calculating class intervals

1   One common strategy for calculating class intervals is simply to divide the range by the number of classes you wish to portray. The result will be a number of even-size classes. For example, if we use the data in Table 6.2, the range is $315 – $45 = $270. You might have decided that you wish to have a histogram with five classes. Divide $270 by 5 and the result is an interval of $54. Thus, we have intervals of:

Class 1	$45–$98
Class 2	$99–$152
Class 3	$153–$206
Class 4	$207–$260
Class 5	$261–$315

The lowest class begins with the lowest value ($45 in this example). To find the *lower limit* of the *next* class we add $54, which produces a figure of $99. We then add $54 to $99 to produce the lower limit of the next class, $153, and so on. The *upper limit* of each class is found by subtracting 1 unit of the measurement form being used (e.g. $1, 1 cm, 1 m, 0.01 gram, 1 tonne) from the lower limit of the class above. The upper limit of the lowest class in the example is therefore $98. Repeat this procedure until the intervals for all classes are calculated. Note that *discrete class intervals* are used (e.g. $45–$98, $99–$152) rather than $55–$99, $99–$153). In this way there is no confusion about the class within which any data point is placed (e.g. in which class would you put a $99 room charge?).

2   An alternative, but closely related, strategy is the one followed in producing Figure 6.14b. Calculate the data range and then think about the character of the data set to be portrayed. Would it be useful to your audience to read the data on a graph which uses intervals of, for example, 10s or 50s rather

than the 13s, 77s, $54s and other odd numbers which might be achieved by the simple division of the range by the number of desired class intervals as described in the preceding strategy? Similarly, would it be useful to commence or end the class intervals at some points other than those fixed by the high and low points of the data set? With these thoughts in mind, I chose the following intervals for the data in Table 6.2.

Class 1 $0–$54
Class 2 $55–$109
Class 3 $110–$164
Class 4 $165–$219
Class 5 $220–$274
Class 6 $275–$330

> There are three common ways of working out class intervals in a data set. Choose the one that summarises the data most usefully.

The graph that resulted is Figure 6.14b. As you can see, class intervals that extended in value beyond the upper and lower limits of the data range were selected. The first class commences at $0 and the class interval is $55, which I thought useful when one is considering the matter of hotel accommodation costs in New Zealand.

3   Yet another technique of working out class intervals is to minimise in-class variations while simultaneously maximising between-class variations. Look for clusters of data points within the total data set and subdivide the data range using those natural breaks into equal size divisions which best discriminate between clusters. A useful tool in this process is the linear plot. Draw a horizontal line and affix to it a scale sufficient to embrace the maximum and minimum values of the data. Locate each of the data points on the scale with a short vertical line. If you are using the linear plot for presentation purposes, rather than for calculation only, you should also label each of the data points and provide a title and source. The plot will graphically portray the data distribution.

Figure 6.15   Example of a linear plot. *Accommodation rates (NZ$)*

40   100   150   200   250   300 320

In this example, the data is clustered quite heavily in the range $50–$150. It might be appropriate to produce a histogram which breaks the data into the following ranges (see Figure 6.14(c)):

Class 1 $40–$69
Class 2 $70–$99

Class 3 $100–$129
Class 4 $130–$159
Class 5 $160

There is no definite rule governing the number of classes in a frequency distribution. Choose too few and information could be lost through a large summarising effect. That is, the picture will be too general. With a lot of classes, too many minor details may be retained, thereby obscuring major features.

Once you have worked out class intervals, the next step in the construction of a histogram is the creation of a frequency table which will allow you to work out the total number of individual items of data that will occur in a particular class.

Constructing a frequency table
As shown in Table 6.3, constructing a frequency table is simply a matter of going through the set of data, placing a tally mark against the class into which each datum falls, then summing the tally to find the frequency with which values occur in each class. Table 6.3 uses the class intervals described in point 2 of the 'class intervals' discussion above.

Table 6.3   Frequency table of data from Table 6.2

Classes ($)	Tally of occurrence	Frequency
0–54	III	3
55–109	ʬʬ ʬʬ ʬʬ	15
110–164	ʬʬ ʬʬ	10
165–219	III	3
220–274	II	2
275–330	I	1

The observed frequency is then plotted on the y-axis of the histogram and the classes are plotted on the x-axis (see Figure 6.14b). The rectangles which result should touch each other, thus reflecting the continuous nature of the observations.

Population pyramids or age–sex pyramids

Population pyramids are a form of histogram used to show the number or, more commonly, the percentage of a population in different age groups of the total population. They also illustrate the female–male composition of that population. Figure 6.16 is an example of a population pyramid.

Figure 6.16   Example of a population pyramid. *Age–sex structure of Port Adelaide Enfield LGA, 2001 (total population = 98,255)*

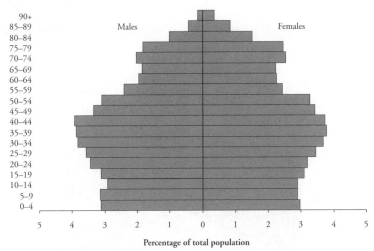

Constructing a population pyramid

Although a population pyramid is a form of histogram, a few peculiarities do bear noting. As Figure 6.16 illustrates, a population pyramid is drawn on one vertical axis and two horizontal axes. The vertical axis represents age and is usually subdivided into five-year age cohorts (e.g. 0–4, 5–9, 10–14 years). The size of those cohorts may be changed (e.g. to 0–9, 10–19, 0–14, 15–19) depending on the nature of the raw data and the purpose of your pyramid. Remember from the discussion of histograms, however, that if you depict different size cohorts in the same pyramid, the area of each bar must reflect that variability. For example, a 0–14 cohort would be half as wide as a 15–44 cohort on the same graph. On either side of the central vertical axis are the two horizontal axes. That on the left of the pyramid shows the percentage (or number) of males while that on the right shows the figures for females. You will also see from Figure 6.16 that the zero point for each of the horizontal axes is in the centre of the graph. As a final note, it may also be helpful for your reader if you include a statement within the graph of the total population depicted.

> By convention, a population pyramid shows males on the left and females on the right.

Circle or pie charts

Pie charts show how a whole is divided up into parts and what share or percentage belongs to each part. Pie charts are a dramatic way of illustrating the relative sizes of portions of some complete entity (Windschuttle & Windschuttle 1988, pp. 272–3). For example, a pie chart might show how a budget is divided up or who receives what share of some total. See Figure 6.17 for an example.

Figure 6.17 Example of a pie chart. *Primary land use in Murray–Darling Basin, 2000 (Total area = 1,056,420 km²)*

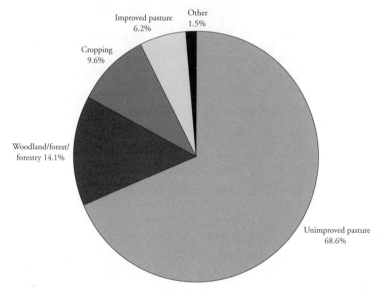

Data Source: Atech Group (2000, p. 61)

Constructing a pie chart

Constructing a pie chart usually requires a little arithmetic. It is necessary to match the 360° which make up the circumference of a circle with the percentage size of each of the variables to be graphed. Simply, this is achieved by multiplying the percentage size of each variable by 3.6 to find the number of degrees to which it equates. Obviously, if the values have not already been translated into percentages of the whole this will need to be done first.

For example, at the 1981 census there were 1,319,327 people in South Australia and 14,926,786 in the whole of Australia (i.e. the South Australian population was 8.8% of the national total). If a pie diagram of the Australian population by states and territories were to be drawn, the segment representing South Australia would have an angle of:

$$\frac{1,319,327}{14,926,786} \times 360 = 31.8°.$$

It is best not to have too many categories (or 'slices') in a pie chart as this creates visual confusion. Five or six segments would seem to be a fair maximum.

Generally, no segment should be smaller than 6°. This may require that some classes be grouped together.

The sectors in a pie chart normally run clockwise, with the largest sector occurring first (ABS 1994b, p. 117). The starting point for the first sector is created by drawing a vertical line from the centre of the circle to the 12 o'clock position on the circumference (Jennings 1990, p. 19).

Pie charts should also advise the reader of the *total value* of categories plotted, as shown, for example, by the statement in Figure 6.17 of the total land area. There is little point in letting a reader know percentages without allowing them the opportunity to determine exactly how much that percentage represents in absolute terms.

> A pie chart should always make clear the total value of all categories it illustrates.

Logarithmic graphs

Logarithmic graphs are used primarily when the range of data values to be plotted is too great to depict on a graph with arithmetic axes (commonly a scattergram or line graph). Comparative national Gross Domestic Product figures are good examples of such data, for national figures range from millions of dollars to billions and trillions of dollars. Similarly, historical population figures, which might grow from hundreds to thousands to millions, sometimes necessitate the use of a logarithmic graph. Figures 6.18a and 6.19 are examples of logarithmic graphs.

Figure 6.18 Comparison of data displayed on (a) semi-log and (b) arithmetic graph paper

(a) *South Australia's resident population, 1841–2001*

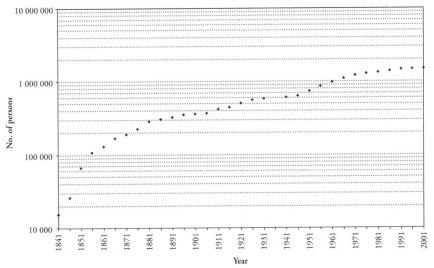

Figure 6.18 (*cont.*)

(b) *South Australia's resident population, 1841–2001*

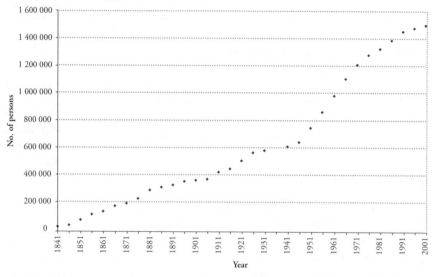

Data Source: ABS (2001c, p. 128)

Logarithmic graphs are sometimes also used to compare rates of change within and between data sets. Despite vast differences in numbers, if line *slopes* in a logarithmic graph are the same, then the *rate* of change is similar. This might be useful, for example, if one was illustrating historical rates of population change in a region and trying to argue that despite the fact that the population is now growing at millions of people per year the rate of change has not actually altered since the late 1800s, when the population was growing by thousands each year (see Figures 6.18a and 6.18b for example).

> Logarithmic graphs are good for depicting vast data ranges.

Before discussing this form of graph any further, it might be helpful to say a little about logarithms. The logarithm of a number is the power to which 10 must be raised to give that number. For example, the log of 100 is 2 because 10^2 = 100 (i.e. 10 raised to the power 2 = 100). Thus, the log of 10 is 1; the log of 100 is 2; the log of 1000 is 3 and so on.

Second, simple line graphs and scattergrams, as described earlier, typically use an *arithmetic* scale on their axes (e.g. 1, 2, 3, 4 or 0, 2, 4, 6 …) where a constant numerical difference is shown by an equal interval on the graph axes. In contrast, semi-logarithmic and log–logarithmic graphs use a *logarithmic* scale where the numerical value of each key interval on the graph increases *exponentially* (e.g. 10, 100, 1000, 10,000) and the lines in each cycle (each cycle is an exponent of ten) of the graph become progressively closer together (see Figures 6.18 and 6.19 for examples). Figure 6.18a is an example of a *semi-logarithmic* graph. It has a logarithmic y-axis and an arithmetic x-axis. (Histograms and bar graphs can also be drawn using semi-logarithmic paper if the variable to be depicted through the y-axis has a particularly large range.) Figure 6.19 is a *log–log* graph—both axes are logarithmic.

> **Semi-log graphs have one logarithmic axis; log–log graphs have two.**

Figure 6.19   Example of a graph with two logarithmic axes (a 'log–log' graph). *Relationship between GDP and passenger cars in use, selected countries, 1992*

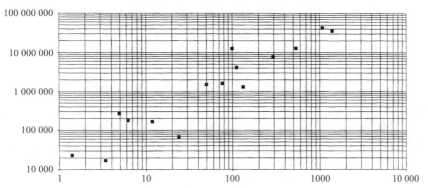

Zero is never used on a logarithmic scale because the logarithm of zero is not defined. Scales on log paper start with ... 0.001, 0.01, 0.1, 1, 10, 100, 1000, 10,000, 100,000 ... (or any other exponent of ten). If you look at figure 6.19 as an example, you will see that the x-axis commences at 1, whereas the y-axis commences at 10,000. The determination about the figure with which to start the axis is made on the basis of the smallest data point. For example, if the smallest figure for plotting was 35,000, you would start the axis at 10,000, not 1000 or 100,000.

> **Zero is never used on a logarithmic axis.**

Constructing a logarithmic graph

Consider the maximum and minimum values of the data sets to be plotted. In looking, for example, at the population of the state of South Australia over the period 1841–2001, we see that the population grew from 15,000 to 1.5 million people. To accommodate this range of data the graph will need to have three logarithmic cycles, with the first commencing at 10,000, the second at 100,000, and the third at 1,000,000. Because the years are plotted arithmetically, the graph will be drawn in semi-log format. Simply plot data points at their appropriate (x,y) co-ordinates. Add an appropriate title and indication of data source.

The same procedures apply for log–log graphs except, of course, that it is necessary to consider the number of cycles for both axes, not just one.

TABLES

Tables present related facts or observations in an orderly, unified manner. They are used most commonly for summarising results. Tables can be effective for organising and communicating large amounts of information, especially numerical data, although you should not make the mistake of trying to communicate too much information at once.

The main reasons for using tables are:

- to facilitate comparisons
- to reveal relationships
- to save space.

> A good table is
> stand-alone
> comprehensible.

Tables should be self-explanatory. This requires a comprehensive title and good labelling. Data in the table may be referred to and discussed in accompanying text, but should not be repeated extensively. Table 6.4 is an example of a correctly set-out table.

Table 6.4   Example of a table. *Major groundwater resources of Australian states/territories, 1987*

| State/Territory | Area of aquifers (km²) | Ground water resource (gigalitres) | | | | |
		Fresh	Marginal	Brackish	Saline	Total
New South Wales	595,900	881	564	431	304	2180
Victoria[1]	103,700	469	294	691	30	862
Queensland	1,174,800	1760	683	255	144	2840
South Australia	486,100	102	647	375	86	1210
Western Australia	2,622,000	578[2]	1240	652	261	2740
Tasmania	7240	47	69	8	—	124
Northern Territory	236,700	994	3380	43	10	4420
Australia	**5,226,440**	**4831**	**6877**	**1833**	**835**	**14,376**

Notes:
1. In case you had not noticed, I inserted a note identifier with the entry for Victoria simply to illustrate how a table footnote might look. See the discussion below to find out about the purpose of such notes.
2. Look, I did it again—this time beside the freshwater data entry for Western Australia.

Source: Australian Bureau of Statistics (1994, p. 18).

Elements of a table

Aside from the information being conveyed, the main elements of a table are:

1 *Table number*—each table should have a unique number (e.g. Table 1) allowing it to be easily identified in textual discussion.

2 *Table title*—the title, which is placed one line above the table itself, should be brief and allow any reader to fully comprehend the information presented without reference to other text. The title should answer 'what', 'where', and 'when' questions.

3 *Column headings*—headings are necessary to explain the meaning of data appearing in the columns. It is a good idea to specify the units of measurement (for example $, mm, litres) within the column headings (only a small amount of space is available for headings so they must be concise, however not so concise that they become ambiguous). Below the column headings a dividing line is placed to separate them from the data. The bottom of the table should be marked with a single horizontal line.

4 *Table notes*—notes appear below the table to provide supplementary information to the reader, such as restrictions that apply to some of the reported data. Table notes may also be used for explanation of any unusual abbreviations or symbols.

5 *Table source*—an indication of the source from which the data was derived or the place from which the table was reproduced should be provided. An accepted form of referencing must be used. See chapter 10 on referencing for more information.

In the end, always be sure that the way you present a table or figure helps your reader understand it completely and correctly. If you have any doubts, present the figure or table to a friend or your lecturer as a stand-alone document and ask them if it makes sense!

REFERENCES AND FURTHER READING

Anderson, J. & Poole, M. 2001, *Assignment and Thesis Writing*, 4th edn, John Wiley, Milton.
  Includes a useful and detailed discussion in chapter 12 on preparation and use of tables.

Atech Group 2000, *Aggregated Nutrient Emissions to the Murray–Darling Basin*, Prepared for the National Pollutant Inventory, Environment Australia, Canberra.

Australian Bureau of Statistics 1994, *Australia Yearbook*, Cat. No. 1301, AGPS, Canberra.

Australian Bureau of Statistics 2001a, *Water Account, Australia, 2000–01*, Cat. No. 4610.0, ABS, Canberra.

Australian Bureau of Statistics 2001b, *Census: Basic Community Profiles*, Cat no. BCP_LGA45890, ABS, Canberra.

Australian Bureau of Statistics 2001c, *South Australia: A Statistical Profile 2001*, Cat. No. 1368.4, ABS, Adelaide.

Australian Bureau of Statistics 2005a, *Dwelling Units Approved—South Australia(a)*, Cat no. 8731.0, ABS, Canberra.

Australian Bureau of Statistics 2005b, *Overseas Arrivals and Departures, Australia*, Cat. no. 3401.0, ABS, Canberra.

Australian Bureau of Statistics 2005c, *Labour Force Australia, Detailed: Electronic delivery* Cat: No. 6291.0.55.001, Table 08 Employed Persons by status in employment and Sex, ABS, Canberra.

Australian Institute of Health and Welfare 2004, *Deaths from all cardiovascular diseases in Australia*, Australian Institute of Health and Welfare National Mortality Database, (online), Available: <http://www.aihw.gov.au/pls/cvd/cvd_death.show_report> (20 April 2005).

Bureau of Meteorology 2004, *Climate averages for Darwin airport*, Commonwealth of Australia (online), Available: <http://www.bom.gov.au/climate/averages/tables/cw_014015.shtml> (20 April 2005).

Cartography Specialty Group of the Association of American Geographers 1995, 'Guidelines for effective visuals at professional meetings', *AAG Newsletter*, vol. 50, no. 7 (July), p. 5.

Coggins, R.S. & Hefford, R.K. 1973, *The Practical Geographer*, 2nd edn, Longman, Camberwell, Victoria.

Eisenberg, A. 1992, *Effective Technical Communication*, 2nd edn, McGraw-Hill, New York.

Forster, C.A. 2004, *Australian Cities: Continuity and Change*, 3rd edn, Oxford University Press, South Melbourne.

Gerber, R.V. 1997, 'Audio-visuals in geography', *Geographical Education*, vol. 3, pp. 25–42.

Hamblin, A. 1998, *Environmental Indicators for National State of the Environment Reporting—The Land*, Australia: State of the Environment (Environment Indicator Reports), Department of the Environment, Canberra.

Jennings, J.T. 1990, *Guidelines for the Preparation of Written Work*, 4th edn, University of Adelaide Roseworthy Campus, Roseworthy, South Australia.

Krohn, J. 1991, 'Why are graphs so central in science?', *Biology and Philosophy*, vol. 6, no. 2, pp. 181–203.
This paper critically questions the prominence, use, and significance of graphics in science.

Mohan, T., McGregor, H. & Strano, Z. 1992, *Communicating! Theory and Practice*, Harcourt Brace, Sydney.

Montgomery, S.L. 2003, *The Chicago Guide to Communicating Science*, The University of Chicago Press, Chicago.
Chapter 9 is a brief though advanced guide to using figures and tables in scientific communication.

Moorhouse, C.E. 1974, *Visual Messages*, Pitman, Carlton, Victoria.
Chapter 7 is a very handy piece on graphics. Well worth considering.

New Zealand Tourism Board 1995, *New Zealand Where to Stay Guide*, New Zealand Tourism Board, Wellington.

Pechenik, J.A. 2004, *A Short Guide to Writing About Biology*, Pearson Longman, New York.

Rowntree, D. 1990, *Teaching through self-instruction*, Kogan Page, London.

Schmid, C.E. 1983, *Statistical Graphics: Design Principles and Practices*, John Wiley, New York.

United Nations 2004, *World Population Prospects: The 2004 Revision, Highlights*, United Nations Department of Economic and Social Affairs, Population Division, New York (online), Available: <http://www.un.org/esa/population/publications/WPP2004/2004Highlights_finalrevised.pdf> (20 April 2005).

Wainer, H. 1984, 'How to display data badly', *The American Statistician*, vol. 38, no. 2, pp. 137–47.
A fascinating review of twelve techniques for displaying data badly! Well worth reading.

Windschuttle, K. & Windschuttle, E. 1988, *Writing, Researching, Communicating*, McGraw-Hill, Sydney.

World Heritage Centre 2005, *Properties inscribed on the World Heritage List*, UNESCO World Heritage Centre, Paris (online), Available: <http://whc.unesco.org/pg.cfm?cid=47> (20 April 2005).

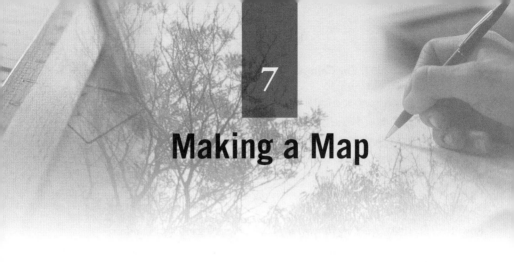

Making a Map

7

I have an existential map. It has 'You are here' written all over it.

Steven Wright

A map is often the heart, or better, the brain, of a scientific paper.

Paraphrase of Morgan, in Day (1989, p. 56)

KEY TOPICS

- Elements of a map
- Different types of map and how to make them

Geographers would be lost without maps! Put simply, 'A map is a graphic device to show where something is' (Moorhouse 1974, p. 86). In slightly more complex, though more informative, terms a map is 'a scaled, symbolic representation of part of any surface (usually the surface of the Earth) containing selective information and expressed using culturally-determined conventions' (Boyd & Taffs 2003, p. 47). Maps use labels, symbols, patterns, and colours to convey messages about spatial and other relationships. Maps are marvellous devices for exploring research questions and for pointing out relationships which might otherwise be difficult to see. Indeed, maps can provoke more research questions than they resolve! This chapter discusses the importance of maps and offers advice on ways of producing them.

ELEMENTS OF A MAP

Unless there are good reasons to the contrary, all maps should always include the following six critical components:

- *map number*: each map should have a unique number (e.g. Figure 4) allowing it to be identified in textual discussion.

> A good map is stand-alone comprehensible.

- *title*: the title, which is placed above the map itself, should be brief yet should allow any reader to understand the information presented without reference to other texts. The title should answer 'what', 'where', and 'when' questions.
- *northpoint*: an arrow indicating north allows the reader to orientate the map correctly. If possible, maps should also make clear the relationship between the area depicted and surrounding territories.
- *scale*: this is an indication of the relationship between distance on the map and distance on the ground. Scale is expressed in one of three ways. It may be expressed as a verbal statement (e.g. '1 cm represents 100 km'). It may be depicted graphically, as in Figure 7.1, where a short horizontal line provides an indication of a 10-km distance. Alternatively, scale may be expressed as a **representative fraction** (**RF**), such as 1:50 000 or 1:250 000. An RF of 1:50 000 means that any single unit of measurement, such as 1 cm, 1 m, or 1 inch, on the map represents 50,000 of those same units in reality. So, for example, if you are using a 1:50 000 scale map and find you have to hike a mapped distance of 40 cm, how far is the walk in reality? Multiply 50,000 by 40 to find out the distance in cm and then convert to a more comprehensible unit of measurement (such as km). Thus, $50,000 \times 40$ cm $= 2,000,000$ cm. This is 20,000 m or 20 km.
- *legend/key*: this is an explanation of the symbols, patterns, and colours used in a map or diagram.
- *data source*: an indication of the source of the mapped data should be provided. If you have copied the map from somewhere else, an accepted form of referencing must be used. See chapter 10 for more information on these two matters. In general, the acknowledgment might take the form of a 'Source: … ' statement on the map. However, if you are producing an original map, perhaps using a Geographical Information System (GIS), you may need to include an extensive array of information about the map, the data, and the sources on which you drew to produce it. Typically, the map should have the following details set out on it:
  - Produced by:
  - Data sources:
  - Projection:
  - Spheroid:
  - Datum:
  - Grid:
  - Completed:
  - Project:

Examples of the full array of information expected are set out below. The material on the left-hand side of the box is a full elaboration of all the details that might be expected. The material on the right is that which is more typically presented. As you will see, it is customary to abbreviate more commonly understood terms, such as Universal Transverse Mercator and Geodetic Datum of Australia.

BOX 7.1 EXAMPLE OF MAP PRODUCTION AND DATA DETAILS

Details		*Typically presented*	
Produced by:	A. Smith-Brown	Produced by:	A. Smith-Brown
Data sources:	Cadastre from DEHAA, SA, 2005	Data sources:	Cadastre from DEHAA, SA, 2005
	Roads from Transport SA, 2004		Roads from Transport SA, 2004
	Native vegetation from Planning SA, 2005		Native vegetation from Planning SA, 2005
Projection:	Universal Transverse Mercator (UTM)	Projection:	UTM
Spheroid:	GRS1980	Spheroid:	GRS1980
Datum:	Geodetic Datum of Australia (GDA94)	Datum:	GDA94
Grid:	Map Grid of Australia (MGA), Zone 54	Grid:	MGA, Zone 54
Completed:	3 June 2006	Completed:	3 June 2006
Project:	GEOG 3005, 'Introduction to GIS', Exercise 4, Vegetation Mapping	Project:	GEOG 3005, 'Introduction to GIS', Exercise 4, Vegetation Mapping

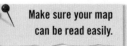

Make sure your map can be read easily.

Finally, it is worth noting that maps should, as far as possible, be sufficiently large to be read and interpreted easily and they should be readable from a single viewpoint. That is, a reader should be able to examine the text without having to turn the page sideways. Having said this, labels should also be aligned along linear features (for example, roads), extend over areal features, such as seas and suburbs, and should consistently locate point features (e.g. all point features labels might be placed at the four o'clock position relative to the item being labelled).

DIFFERENT TYPES OF MAP

There exist many different types or classes of map (see Robinson et al. 1994 for a discussion). Table 7.1 provides a summary of the nature and function of several common types of map. The rest of this chapter describes more fully the first three of these and offers some advice on their construction.

Table 7.1   Some common types of maps and their nature/function

Type of map	Nature/function
Dot map	Uses dots to illustrate spatial distribution of discrete data by unit of occurrence (e.g. one dot represents 1 person) or some multiple of those units (e.g. one dot represents 1000 sheep).
Choropleth map	A shaded or cross-hatched map used to display statistical distributions (e.g. rates, frequencies, ratios) on the basis of areal units such as nations, states, and regions.
Isoline map	Shows sets of lines connecting points of known, or estimated, equal values (e.g. elevation, barometric pressure, temperature).
Cadastral map	Specialised map showing surveyed land tenure (from *cadastre*, an official register or list of property owners and their holdings (Robinson et al. 1994, p. 11)).
Orthophoto map	Maps created from a mosaic of aerial photographs and overlain with information such as contours, transport routes, and place names. The Land Information New Zealand (LINZ) web site at <www.linz.govt.nz> provides some examples of these.
Topographic map	Common, general purpose map that typically depicts contours, physical (e.g., rivers, peaks), and cultural features (e.g., roads, churches, cemeteries). The Geoscience Australia web site at <http://www.ga.gov.au/map/images.jsp> offers online examples of topographic maps for Australia.

Dot maps

The dot map is a common way of showing both the spatial distribution and the quantity of a variable. Figure 7.1 is an example of a dot map. A dot representing every occurrence of a given characteristic is placed on the map (Toyne & Newby 1971, p. 91). Dots are useful for showing the distribution of discontinuous or discrete data sets (e.g. population, stock numbers). Dots may also represent some multiple of the individual units being depicted. For example, a single dot might represent 1000 people or 300 kangaroos.

Figure 7.1   Example of a dot map. *Distribution of Vietnamese-born people, Adelaide Statistical Division, 1996*

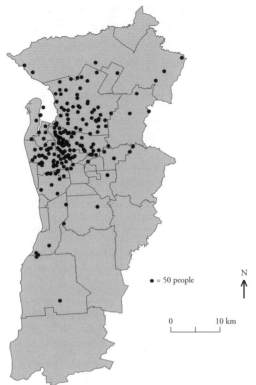

• = 50 people

N

0   10 km

Data Source: ABS (1996)

Constructing a dot map

1 Decide on the number of units each dot will represent. The scale of dots needs to be chosen carefully if it is to be effective. If the value of each dot is too large, sparsely populated districts may not be represented at all. If the value is too small, dots will join in densely populated districts (Garnier 1966, p. 16) and you are likely to go crazy drawing the map. The size of the actual dot is also important. If too large, it will make the map look messy and crude. If too small, it will fail to depict spatial variation. Try plotting the greatest and lowest densities to be shown on the map (see the next step for some help on that) using several different dot values to get some impression of the value that will be most effective.

2 Dot maps are generally divided into areas such as statistical divisions or administrative units, so for each division, calculate the number of dots to be shown and pencil in those numbers on your map.

3   Draw the appropriate number of dots, ensuring that they are spaced evenly (but not in lines). However, if variations are known to occur within the area, attempt to locate the dots in ways which best represent the spatial variations you know about. For instance, in drawing a dot map of the population distribution of Australia or New Zealand it would be inappropriate to distribute dots evenly across the entire country. Instead, dots would be placed in focal areas near major population centres.

4   Complete the map by adding a title, legend, scale, and source of data.

Proportional circle maps

Proportional circle maps are a variation on the dot map. Instead of using dots of identical size to represent numbers of some phenomenon, the size of each circle in a proportional circle map is, as the name suggests, directly related to the frequency or magnitude of the phenomenon represented. Figure 7.2 is an example of a proportional circle map.

Figure 7.2   Example of a proportional circle map. *Distribution of England-born people by Statistical Local Areas for Adelaide and Statistical Sub-division for South Australia, 1996*

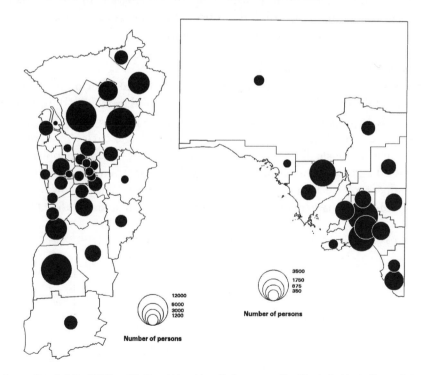

Source: Beer & Cutler (1999, p. 37). Copyright resides with Commonwealth of Australia. Used with permission.

Constructing proportional circles

Circles may illustrate quantities on maps by using a scale which is related to either:

1   the *diameter* of a circle, or
2   the *area of a circle*.

Both methods are discussed below. The area-based representation of quantities is to be preferred as it provides a more accurate visual portrayal of a quantity than the diameter-based approach.

Proportional circles—diameter-based

If the populations of two small towns (Port Gerard with 400 people and Susanville with 1600 people) are plotted using this form of proportional circle, the *diameter* of the circle representing Susanville should be four times as large as that of the circle representing Port Gerard. The diameter of the circle is directly proportional to the given value. Thus, if you have decided that each millimetre of circle radius will represent 100 people, the circle diameter for Port Gerard will be 4 mm while that of Susanville will be 16 mm (Garnier 1966, p. 18). This is a simpler method of drawing proportional circles than the area-based technique, but it overemphasises the visual impact of large values because circle areas grow exponentially with increases in radius.

Proportional circles—area-based

In this method, statistics are portrayed by circles whose *areas* are proportional to the size of the variables being depicted. This is achieved by making the diameter of the circle proportional to the square root of the number being illustrated. Taking the example discussed above, the area of the larger circle should be four times that of the smaller one. The square root of Port Gerard's population of 400 is 20 and the diameter of that circle will be proportional to that number. The square root of Susanville's population of 1600 is 40 and, following either the graphical or mathematical method of calculating circle size outlined below,

Figure 7.3   Example of a graphic scale for creating proportional circles

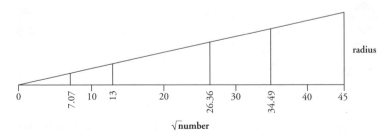

an appropriately sized circle will be drawn. Even though the square root of Susanville's population is only two times as large as that of Port Gerard, the circle area will be four times greater thanks to the magic of mathematics. The end result will be two circles whose areas give an accurate visual representation of the fact that one town has four times as many people as the other.

> Area-based proportional circles show quantity more accurately than diameter-based circles.

To create area-based proportional circles using a graphic method, follow the steps listed below.

1 Decide on the radius of the biggest circle that can be used on your map or figure. This will depend on the scale of the map and the number of proportional circles to be shown. Aim for a result which is a happy medium between a small number of insignificant circles and something that looks like a bubble-bath.

2 Calculate the square root of each of the quantities to be illustrated.

3 Construct a continuous scale of circle size from which you can read off the radius of any of the circles to be drawn. (It may be useful to consult Figure 7.3 as you read this section and the next.) To make this scale, find yourself a spare sheet of paper and create a horizontal arithmetic scale which:
   a is divided into equal units;
   b begins at zero; and
   c embraces the whole range of the square roots you calculated in the first step.

4 In step 1 you decided what the maximum circle radius should be. Now draw a vertical line of that length upwards from your horizontal arithmetic scale at the point corresponding with the largest square root value you calculated in step 2. Join the top of that vertical line to the zero point on the horizontal axis. Believe it or not, the result should be a triangle which will allow you to read off required radii from the horizontal axis without any further calculations. See Figure 7.3 for an example.

5 To use the scale you have created, place the point of your compass on that part of the horizontal axis which corresponds to the square root of the value to be represented. Open the other leg of the compass to reach that point of the diagonal line directly above the square root value to be plotted. With the compass set at this radius, draw a circle on the map (or illustration) centred on the location of the area being plotted.

6 A circular scale must be shown on the finished map. A neat and simple way of doing this is to draw circles corresponding to rounded representative figures in the data (not the square root values). See Figure 7.4 for an example.

> Include both a circular scale and a linear scale on a proportional circle map.

Figure 7.4 Example of a completed proportional circle scale

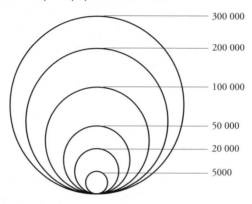

- 300 000
- 200 000
- 100 000
- 50 000
- 20 000
- 5000

Do *not* use the triangular scale you created to construct the proportional circles as the scale in your illustration.

Following International Cartographic Association (1984, p. 106) advice, proportional circle areas can also be calculated mathematically. This is a relatively straightforward procedure.

Say,

N = maximum value to be represented
n = one of the other values in the data series
S = the area of the circle representing N
s = the area of the circle representing n
R = the radius of the circle representing N
r = the radius of the circle representing n

$$\text{then} \quad \frac{s}{S} = \frac{n}{N} \quad \text{or} \quad \frac{\pi r^2}{\pi R^2} = \frac{n}{N} \quad \text{thus} \quad r = \frac{R\sqrt{n}}{\sqrt{N}}$$

You will see that this procedure still requires you to take steps 1 and 2 outlined in the graphic method of calculation. Of course, you will also need to prepare a scale to put on the completed map (step 6 above).

The technique of using proportional circles may be usefully extended to represent two quantities (e.g. freight tonnages in and out of a region) in the form of a *split proportional circle*. To achieve this, follow the instructions above, but draw two semi-circles at each point. Figure 7.5 provides an example.

The semi-circle on one side might, for example, represent freight into a region or births in a place, whereas the semi-circle on the other side would represent freight exports or deaths. The circles are made proportional to the figures being illustrated in exactly the same way as discussed above, but only half of the circle is actually drawn. The same scale must be used for the quantities in each half or comparison would be impossible.

Figure 7.5   Example of a split proportional circle

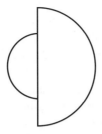

Another way of displaying information on maps is as a *proportional pie diagram*, where the size of the circle will show the magnitude of a given value. However the circle is then subdivided into different size segments, each of which represents some percentage of the total value (see the discussion on pie charts in chapter 6 for more information). For example, a map of housing availability in Darwin might show proportional circles indicating the number of homes in each suburb, and these in turn might be internally subdivided to show the proportions of government housing, owner-occupied housing, rental dwellings, and so on in each of the mapped suburbs.

> Proportional pie charts are a useful way of showing magnitudes and proportions simultaneously.

Choropleth maps

A choropleth map displays spatial distributions by means of cross-hatching or shading. Figure 7.6 is an example. Choropleth maps are commonly used to display rates, frequencies, and ratios such as marriage and divorce rates, population densities, birth and death rates, percentage of total population classified according to sex, age, ethnicity, and per capita income. Choropleth maps may also be used to show non-statistical data such as soil types and vegetation types (Moorhouse 1974, p. 92).

Constructing a choropleth map

The description that follows outlines the preparation of a choropleth map depicting statistical information. Non-statistical maps require completion of only the last three steps.

Preparing a choropleth map involves a number of basic steps (Sullivan 1993, pp. 69–71).

1   Calculate the range of the data to be mapped. Remember, the range is the difference between the highest and lowest value. For example, if the highest value is 250 mm and the lowest is 72 mm then the range is 178 mm (i.e. 250 – 72 = 178).

2   Decide on the number of classes into which the data will be grouped. This
will depend on the purpose of the map and the nature of the

> Try to use four to six
> data classes on a
> choropleth map.

data. If there are too many classes the values for specific areas
may be difficult to identify. Four to six classes is generally sufficient to identify spatial patterns without making the map too
detailed.

3   Determine the interval or range of values within a single class. To do this,
follow the directions outlined in the earlier discussions on class intervals and
frequency distributions under 'Constructing a histogram'. In general, the
outcome should be one in which there are approximately equal size classes
(in terms of class interval or number of observations in each class) and there
should be no vacant classes (Toyne & Newby 1971, p. 86).

4   Create a cartographic pattern (grey tones or colour) to represent each of
the class intervals you have selected. This will be your *legend*. Low values
are typically represented by light colours or shading and high values by
darker colours or shading. An easy method is to use a single colour changing
progressively from light to dark. Use colours that match the phenomenon

Figure 7.6   Example of a choropleth map. *Unemployment rate, Melbourne Statistical Division, 1996*

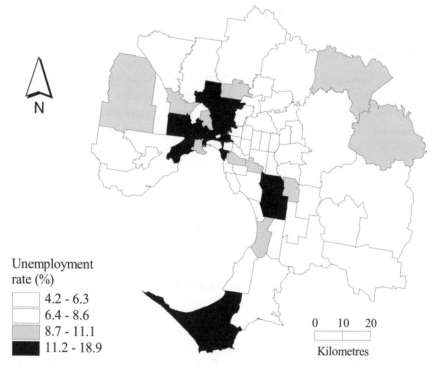

Unemployment
rate (%)

☐ 4.2 - 6.3
☐ 6.4 - 8.6
▨ 8.7 - 11.1
■ 11.2 - 18.9

0   10   20

Kilometres

Date source: ABS (1996)

being mapped. For example, greens for vegetation, browns for soils. See a good atlas for examples.

5 Transfer the cartographic patterns of the legend to the map. For every geographic unit such as a nation, state, region, or shire, shade or colour that unit according to the pattern in the legend. Avoid having blank areas, which do not provide any information.

6 Complete the map by adding a title, scale, northpoint, etc.

Isoline maps

Most of us see one form of isoline map every day when we look at newspaper and television weather reports. In common with other forms of isoline map, weather maps show sets of lines (isolines) connecting points known, or estimated to have, equal value (atmospheric pressure is usually portrayed in weather maps). See Figure 7.7 for an example. The topographic map, depicting contours of equal elevation, is another frequently encountered form of isoline map.

Isoline maps always use data with continuous distributions (e.g. rainfall, temperature). Table 7.2 lists common types of isoline and the variables they depict.

Isoline maps depict continuous data.

Table 7.2   Some common isolines and the variables they depict

Isoline	Connecting Places of Equal
Isobar	Atmospheric pressure
Isotherm	Temperature
Isohyet	Rainfall
Contour line	Elevation
Isobath	Water depth

Constructing an isoline map

The following steps are required to prepare an isoline map (based on Garnier 1966).

1 On a base map of the area being represented, locate all points for which precise figures for the phenomenon being mapped are available. See Figure 7.8(a).

2 Calculate the range of the values being mapped and, taking that figure into consideration, decide on a suitable value for the interval between each isoline (i.e. for a contour map, should it be 5 metres, 10 metres, or 100 metres …?). In making this decision, it is helpful to consider the number of known observations upon which you are basing the map. Toyne and Newby (1971, p. 99) suggest that the number of isolines (classes) be no more than

five times the logarithm of the number of observations. Thus, for example, if your map has 100 observed points on it, one might expect a map with ten isoline classes. A map with 23 known points would have about seven isoline classes. So, if you are drawing a topographic map on the basis of 100 observed points with a data range of 900 metres (say from 800 m to 1700 m), it would seem appropriate to aim for an interval between each isoline of about 100 metres (e.g. 800 m, 900 m, 1000 m …). Remember, however, that the interval you choose should be set at a value that will show the detail of the distribution without overcrowding the map. It may be help-ful to do several trial plots of the data to determine the best interval to use.

3   Draw the isolines. This is the most difficult part. Disappointing as it may be, the process is not a case of just joining dots. Most point data will not correspond exactly to the contour values decided in the preceding step.

Figure 7.7   Example of an isoline map. *Average annual rainfall, South Australia (isohyets in millimetres)*

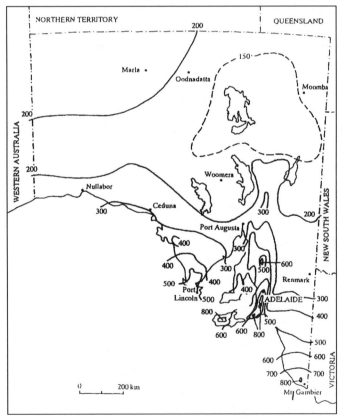

Figure 7.8   Three steps to creating an isoline map

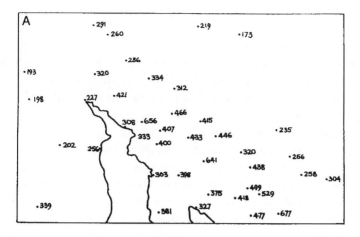

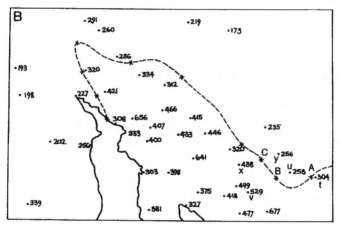

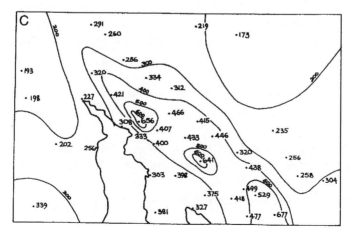

The position of isolines between point data of different values is worked out by the technique of interpolation. Figure 7.8(b) shows how this is done for a map of precipitation in South Australia. Assume that the rate of change between one known point and another is constant, unless information you have suggests otherwise. Point A, which depicts isohyet value 300, is between point u (258 mm) and point t (304 mm); point B lies about one-quarter of the way between points u (258 mm) and v (529 mm); and point C is somewhat closer to point y (256 mm) than it is to point x (438 mm).

4   The appropriate points are then joined by smooth lines as shown in Figure 7.8(c). Make sure that your map has enough isolines to show the data pattern accurately without creating visual confusion. If you have too many isolines, or if the data pattern is not depicted as well as you would like it to be, rethink your selection of isoline interval and redraft the map.

5   Label enough of the isolines with their values to enable readers to understand the map quickly. Place the isoline values so they can be read without turning the map.

6   Complete the map by adding a title, scale, northpoint, etc.

REFERENCES AND FURTHER READING

Australian Bureau of Statistics 1996, Census.

Beer, A. & Cutler, C. 1999, *Atlas of the Australian People. 1996 Census. South Australia*, Department of Immigration and Multicultural Affairs, Canberra.

Boyd, B. & Taffs, K. 2003, *Mapping the Environment: A Professional Development Manual*, Southern Cross University Press, Lismore.

Day, R.A. 1989, *How to Write and Publish a Scientific Paper*, Cambridge University Press, Cambridge.

Garnier, B.J. 1966, *Practical Work in Geography*, Edward Arnold, London.

International Cartographic Association 1984, *Basic Cartography for Students and Technicians*, vol. 1, International Cartographic Association, Great Britain.

Map and Chart-Making updated (online): <http//www.ruf.rice.edu/~feegi/carto.html> (1 February 2006).
A helpful portal to a range of cartographic resources available on the Internet.

Monmonier, M. 1993, *Mapping It Out: Expository Cartography for the Humanities and Social Sciences*, University of Chicago Press, Chicago.

—— 1996, *How to Lie With Maps*, 2nd edn, University of Chicago Press, Chicago.
As the title suggests, this is a fascinating and informative book. By focusing on how to lie with maps, it makes good mapping practice clear.

Moorhouse, C.E. 1974, *Visual Messages*, Pitman, Carlton, Victoria.

Muehrcke, P.C. & Muehrcke, J.O. 1998, *Map Use*, 4th edn, J.P. Publications, Madison, Wisconsin.
This marvellous, comprehensive book covers a wide range of material on maps and map use. A 'must read'.

Robinson, A.H., Morrison, J.L., Muehrcke, P.C., Guptill, S.C., & Kimerling, A.J. 1994, *Elements of Cartography*, 6th edn, John Wiley, New York.

Sullivan, M.E. 1993, 'Choropleth mapping in secondary geography: An application for the study of middle America', *Journal of Geography*, vol. 92, no. 2, pp. 69–74.

Toyne P. & Newby, P.T. 1971, *Techniques in Human Geography*, Macmillan, London.

Wood, D. & Fels, J. 1992, *The Power of Maps*, Guilford Press, New York.

8

Preparing and Delivering a Talk

All the great speakers were bad speakers at first.

Emerson in Mohan, McGregor & Strano (1992, p. 331)

It is not okay to be boring.

An orator is someone who says what he thinks and feels what he says.

William Jennings Bryan

KEY TOPICS

- Why are public-speaking skills important?
- Preparing to give a talk
- How to deliver a successful talk
- Coping with questions

WHY ARE PUBLIC-SPEAKING SKILLS IMPORTANT?

Although talking comes naturally to most of us, public speaking remains one of the most frightening things many people can imagine. And believe it or not, lecturers do appreciate the fact that public speaking is intimidating. While some lecturers have grown accustomed to speaking before a large audience, many still feel some trepidation about speaking to an unknown class, a professional gathering, a community meeting, or even a wedding party. They do understand the sleepless nights, sweaty palms, pounding heart, cotton mouth, and jelly-legs that sometimes precede a talk. So, when you are asked by your lecturer to give a prepared talk in class, it is unlikely that the assignment has been set lightly. Lecturers usually have three fundamental objectives in mind when they ask you to give a talk in your geography or environmental studies class.

> Public speaking serves valuable intellectual, vocational, and professional functions.

First, preparing for and delivering a talk encourages you to organise your ideas, to construct logical arguments, and to otherwise fulfil the objectives of a university education (for a discussion, see Jenkins & Pepper 1988, p. 69).

Second, your lecturers also have your vocational interests in mind. Many of the jobs in which university-educated geographers, environmental managers, and social scientists find themselves require them to make public presentations. While business and educational leaders acknowledge oral communication and public-speaking skills to be among the most important abilities a university graduate can have (see, for example, Hay 1994a), a number of international surveys indicate that these skills are also among the most poorly developed. Consequently, your future employers are likely to be impressed if you can point out to them that, through your degree, you have given twenty multimedia talks to audiences ranging in size from five to fifty people, particularly if you can explain that you have used each of those opportunities to refine your presentation skills.

Third, developing the ability to speak effectively at conferences and other professional or community gatherings is a critical component of effective geographical or environmental practice. If we are to make contributions to our significant work in areas such as environmental justice, global warming, and indigenous peoples' land rights, it is vital that we be able to share the results of our work in such fora (Hay, Dunn & Street 2005, p. 159). Given the importance of these skills, it would appear that, despite any fears of speaking you might have, you will probably not be spared from having to give one or several 'public talks' of, say, 10 to 20 minutes duration throughout your degree. The 'mechanics' of giving such a talk are outlined in this chapter which is subdivided into three main parts. The first deals with the essentials of preparing for the talk; the second with delivering the talk; the third with coping with post-talk questions. Throughout the chapter, reference is made to the use of Microsoft's PowerPoint software. This widely used aid to spoken presentations may help you to produce high-quality graphics and handouts for your talk.

The discussion which follows is not intended to be a 'prescription' for a perfect talk. Instead, it offers guidelines to help you prepare for and deliver your first few 'speeches'. With experience you will develop your own 'style'—a form of presentation which may be very effective and yet may transgress some of the guidelines discussed here. Practice will help you to develop your own approach, but you may also want to keep a critical eye on your lecturers and on

Try to develop your own style of public speaking but remember the expectations of your audiences.

other people who give talks which you attend. Pay attention to the form and manner of their delivery. Try to identify those devices, techniques, and mannerisms which you believe add to, or detract from, a presentation. Apply what you learn to your own talks. You might also find it helpful to look over Figure 8.1 to get some idea of the sort of criteria which are important for giving a successful talk.

Figure 8.1 Assessment schedule for a talk

Student Name: Grade: Assessed by:

The following is an itemised rating scale of various aspects of a formal talk. Sections left blank are not relevant to the talk assessed. Some aspects are more important than others, so there is no formula connecting the scatter of ticks with the final percentage for the talk. A tick in the left-hand box means that the criterion has been met satisfactorily. A tick in the right-hand box means it has not. If you have any questions about the individual scales, comment, final grade, or other aspects of this assignment, please see the assessor indicated above.

First impressions

	✓	✗
Speaker appeared confident and purposeful before starting to speak	☐	☐
Speaker's personal grooming and dress standards of high quality	☐	☐
Speaker attracted audience's attention from the outset	☐	☐

Presentation Structure

Introduction

Title/topic made clear	☐	☐
Purpose of the presentation made clear	☐	☐
Organisational framework made known to audience	☐	☐
Unusual terms defined adequately	☐	☐

Body of presentation

Main points stated clearly	☐	☐
Sufficient information and detail provided	☐	☐
Appropriate and adequate use of examples/anecdotes	☐	☐
Discussion flowed logically	☐	☐

Conclusion	✓	✗
Ending of presentation signalled adequately	☐	☐
Main points summarised adequately/ideas brought to fruition	☐	☐
Final message clear and easy to remember	☐	☐

Coping with questions

	✓	✗
Whole audience searched for questions	☐	☐
Questions addressed in order	☐	☐
Questions handled adeptly	☐	☐
Full audience addressed with answers	☐	☐
Speaker maintained control of discussion	☐	☐

Delivery

	✓	✗
Speech clear and audible to entire audience	☐	☐
Talk given with impulsion (engagement and enthusiasm)	☐	☐
Presentation directed to all parts of audience	☐	☐
Eye contact with audience throughout presentation	☐	☐
Speaker kept to time limit	☐	☐
Good use of time without rushing at end	☐	☐
Pace neither too fast nor too slow	☐	☐

Visual aids and handouts—if appropriate

	✓	✗
Visual aids well prepared	☐	☐
Visual aids visible to entire audience	☐	☐
Speaker familiar with own visual aids (for example, OHTs, PowerPoint images, blackboard diagrams)	☐	☐
Effective use made of handouts and visual aids	☐	☐
Handouts well prepared and useful	☐	☐

Assessor's comments: was this an effective talk?

PREPARING TO GIVE A TALK

You cannot expect to talk competently off-the-cuff on any but the most familiar topics. Effective preparation is critical to any successful presentation. Preparation for a talk should begin some days (at least) in advance of the actual event and certainly not just the night before. Give yourself plenty of time to revise and rehearse. But before you can prepare your talk, several things must first be done.

Establishing the context and goals

* *Who is your audience?* Target the presentation to the audience's characteristics, needs, and abilities. The ways in which a topic might be developed will be critically influenced by the background and expertise of your listeners (Eisenberg 1992, p. 333). Find out how big the audience will be as this may affect the style of presentation. For example, a large crowd will make an interactive presentation somewhat difficult.
* *Where are you speaking?* If possible, visit the venue in which the talk is to be held. Room and layout characteristics can have an effect on the formality of the presentation, the speed of the talk, attentiveness of the audience, and the types of audio-visual aids that can be employed. Check, for example, to see if the talk is to be given in a large room, from a lectern, with a microphone, to an audience seated in rows … The boxed section below confirms the need for such reconnaissance by even experienced academics at major professional gatherings!

BOX 8.1 EXAMPLE OF RECONNAISSANCE BEFORE A TALK

At some point in your career you will arrive to present a paper in a theatre or other space that is clearly unsatisfactory, and you will definitely experience technical failures that are beyond your control. In 2003, the Royal Geographical Society and Institute of British Geographers decided to hold the annual geography conference in the Society's august premises located next to the Albert Hall in London. I was to present a paper in a theme session of what was overtly intended as an international conference. Emails from conference organisers had indicated that my paper was to be delivered in Basement Room 1. After a 22-hour flight and a taxi ride, I arrived at the statue of Livingstone outside the Society's premises. It was clear that major renovations were underway, and most of the 'presentation spaces' had been very recently emptied and painted. My journey to locate Basement Room 1 took me downstairs; curiously I then had to take a small stairwell upwards and to the left, to eventually find my presentation space. If not for the fresh white paint, the stairwell had a distinct Hogwart's feel to it. Basement Room 1 was a horror. A claustrophobic broom cupboard! There was not a single screen or piece of technology to be seen. The 15 tightly packed chairs were unable to accommodate delegate demand the next morning when I presented. The sad-looking overhead projector that had appeared was permanently and excessively out-of-focus. Not a scrap of usable technology! I handed out copies of the written paper, which fortunately had the tables and graphics as an attachment, and I presented my paper. Other presenters were not so lucky as to have hard copy, the ultimate back-up for a conference presentation. (Hay, Dunn & Street 2005, p. 167)

- *How long will you speak?* Confirm how much of the time available is for the talk and how much is intended for audience questions. Avoid the embarrassment of being asked to conclude the talk before it is finished or of ending well short of the deadline.
- *Why are you speaking?* The style of presentation may differ depending on your purpose. The purpose may be to present information; to stimulate discussion; to present a solution to a problem; or, perhaps, to persuade a group of the value of a particular view or course of action. Depending on the purpose of the talk, you may have to alter the style and content of your presentation.

> To give a successful talk make sure you know why you are speaking, where, to whom, and for how long but, above all, work out what your central message is.

- *Who else is speaking?* This may influence the audience's reaction to you (Eisenberg 1992, p. 332). It may also require that you take steps to avoid repeating things someone else might say.
- *What is your subject?* Be sure that your subject matches the reason for the presentation. A mismatch may upset, bore, or alienate your audience. A clear sense of purpose will also allow you to focus your talk more clearly.
- *Do your research.* Keeping in mind the purpose of your talk, gather and interpret appropriate and accurate information. Make a point of collecting anecdotes, cartoons, or up-to-date statistics, which might make your presentation more appealing, colourful, and convincing.
- *Eliminate the dross.* If you have already written a paper upon which your presentation is to be based, be aware that you will not be able to communicate everything you have written. Carefully select the main points and devote attention to the strategies by which those points can be communicated as clearly and effectively as possible. Courtenay (1992, p. 220) makes the following suggestions.
  - ○ List all the things you know or have found out about your subject.

- ○ Eliminate all those items you think the audience might already know about.
- ○ Eliminate anything that is not important for your audience to know. Keep doing this until you are left with one or two new and dynamic points. These should not already be known to your audience and they should be interesting and useful to them. These points should form the basis of your presentation. Similarly, Stettner (1992, p. 226) makes a very good argument for organising a talk around no more than, and no fewer than, three main points.

Organising the material for presentation

- *Give your talk a clear and relevant title.* An audience will be attracted to, and informed by, a good title. Be sure that your title clearly illustrates the subject matter of the talk.
- *Choose the right framework.* Ensure that the framework used is appropriate and that the organisational framework helps make the point of your presentation clear. For example, if your main aim is to discuss potential solutions to male homelessness in Dunedin, it would probably be less useful to spend most of the time discussing the historical development of social security policies in New Zealand as a prelude to that.

BOX 8.2 SOME ORGANISATIONAL FRAMEWORKS FOR A TALK

Most presentations seem to adopt one of the following five organisational frameworks:

- *chronological*—e.g. the history of geographic thought from the nineteenth century
- *scale*—e.g. overview of national responses to desertification followed by detailed examination of responses in a particular area
- *spatial*—e.g. a description of Japan's trading relations with other countries of the Pacific
- *causal*—e.g. implications of financial deregulation for the New Zealand insurance market
- *order of importance*—e.g. ranked list of solutions to the problem of male homelessness in Perth.

Structuring your talk

In summary, a great talk will:

- Start with a clear, memorable statement
- Focus material on a small number of key points
- Be concise, with an even balance of material from one point to another
- Be 'signposted'
- End with a clear, memorable statement, consistent with the start! (Knight & Parsons 2003, p. 164).

Let us look at a great talk's structure in more detail. In most cases a talk will have an introduction, a discussion, and a conclusion. The introductory and concluding sections of oral presentations are very important. About 25% of your presentation ought to be devoted to the 'beginning' and 'end'. The remaining time should be spent on the discussion.

Introduction
- *Make your rationale for talking and your conceptual framework clear.* This gives the audience a basis for understanding the ideas which follow. In short, let listeners know what you are going to tell them. The box below explains how to do this effectively.
- *Capture the audience's attention from the outset.* Do this with a rhetorical question, relevant and interesting quotes, amazing facts, an anecdote, startling statements ... Avoid jokes unless you have a real gift for humour.
- *Make the introduction clear and lively.* First impressions are very important.

Try to win your audience's attention from the very start of your talk.

BOX 8.3 INTRODUCING A TALK EFFECTIVELY

- *State the topic*—'Today I am going to talk about ... ' Do this in a way which will attract the audience's attention.
- *State the aims or purpose*—Why is this talk being given? Why have you chosen this topic? For what reasons should the audience listen?
- *Outline the scope of the talk*—Let the audience know something about the spatial, temporal, and intellectual boundaries of the presentation. For example, are you discussing Australian attitudes to the environment from a Maori perspective; or offering a geographer's view of British financial services in the 2000s? Some people love to point out gaps in your work's coverage, so head them off by making clear what you are and are not covering.
- *Provide a plan of the discussion*—Let the audience know the steps through which you will lead them in your presentation and the relationship of each step to the others. It is useful to prepare a written plan for the audience (e.g. on an overhead transparency or PowerPoint slide) which outlines your intended progression.

Discussion

- *Construct a convincing argument supported with examples.* Remember, you are trying to present as compelling a case in support of your findings as possible.
- Ensure there is a 'fluid logic between your main points' (Montgomery 2003, p. 172).

> Limit your talk to discussion of key points and make clear the relationship of each to the overall trajectory.

- *Limit discussion to a few main points.* Lindsay (1984, p. 48) observes that a rule of broadcasting is that it takes about three minutes to put across each *new* idea. Do not make the mistake of trying to cover too much material.
- *Present your argument logically, precisely, and in an orderly fashion.* Try producing a small diagram which summarises the main points you wish to discuss. Use this as a basis for constructing your talk. It might also make a useful handout, overhead transparency, or PowerPoint slide for your audience.
- *Accompany points of argument with carefully chosen, colourful, and correct examples and analogies.* It is helpful to use examples built upon the experience of the audience at which they are directed. Analogies and examples clarify unfamiliar ideas and bring your argument to life.
- *Connect the points of your discussion with the overall direction of the talk.* Remind the audience of the trajectory you are following by relating the points you make to the overall framework you outlined in the introduction. For example, 'the third of the three points I have identified as explaining ... '
- *Restate important points.*
- *Personalise the presentation.* This can add authenticity, impact, and humour. For example, in discussing problems associated with administering a household questionnaire survey, you might recount an experience of being chased down dark suburban streets by a large, ferocious dog. Avoid overstepping the line between personalising and being self-centred by ensuring that the tales you tell help the audience understand your message.

Conclusion

> When you tell your audience you are about to finish, you get their attention!

- *Cue the conclusion.* Phrases like 'To conclude ... ' or 'In summary ... ' have a remarkable capacity to stimulate audience attention.
- *Bring ideas to fruition.* Let the audience know exactly what the take-home message is! Restate the main points in words other than those used earlier in the discussion, develop some conclusions, and review implications. Connect your talk with its wider context.

- *Tie the conclusion neatly together with the introduction.* The introduction noted where the talk is going. The conclusion reminds the audience of the content and dramatically observes the arrival at the foreshadowed destination.
- *Make the conclusion emphatic.* Do not end with a whimper! A good conclusion is very important to an effective presentation, reinforcing the main idea or motivating the audience (Eisenberg 1992, p. 340). Use the conclusion to reinforce your main ideas or to motivate the audience. For instance, if you have been stressing the need for community involvement in reducing greenhouse gas emissions, try to 'fire up' the members of the audience so that they feel motivated to take some action of their own.
- *Terminate the presentation clearly.* Saying 'Thank you', for example, makes it clear to the audience that your talk is over. Try to avoid giggling self-consciously and saying things like 'Well, that's the end'.

Preparing your text and aids to delivery

Different people have different preferences when it comes to preparing a presentation 'script'. Some opt for a full script; others for brief notes; and others for graphic images such as a flow diagram. The same model is not appropriate for everyone, so heed Montgomery's (2003, p. 171) advice to 'design and write out your talk in a manner you feel comfortable with'. Having said this, there are a few points worth considering.

Preparing notes

- *Prepare well in advance.* Mark Twain is reported to have said 'It usually takes more than three weeks to prepare a good impromptu speech' (in Windschuttle & Elliott 1994, p. 341). Twain may have overstated the case a little, but it is fair to consider the talk as the tip of the iceberg and the preparation the much larger submerged section.
- *Prepare a talk, not a speech.* In general, you should avoid preparing a full text to be read aloud. A presentation which is simply read aloud is often boring and lifeless. If you must prepare a text to be read, remember that a talk needs to be kept simple and logical. Because your talk will go past your listener only once, it must also 'be very well organized, developed logically, stripped of details that divert the listener's attention from the essential points of the presentation …' (Pechenik 2004, p. 252).
- *Write for talking, not reading.* Most people speak at between 125 and 175 words per minute (Dixon 2004, p. 100), though a good speed for formal presentation delivery is about 100 words per minute (Montgomery 2003, p. 171). So, if you feel absolutely compelled to write a script you

> If you use a script for a talk, make sure it is written for speaking, not reading.

will know that a 10-minute talk will require you to prepare about 1000 words. Keep sentences short and simple. Major points need to be restated. Language should be informal, but should not employ slang and other conventions of café conversation and barroom banter.

- *Prepare personal memory prompts.* These might take the form of clearly legible notes, key words, phrases, or diagrams to serve as the summary outline of your talk. Put prompts on cards, on the cardboard borders of overhead transparencies, or on note paper, ensuring that all pages are numbered sequentially—just in case you drop them! If you are using PowerPoint for your talk, consider using the 'View Notes Page' option. This useful option allows you to prepare and print out a set of speaker notes associated with each slide in your show.

- *Revise your script.* Put your talk away overnight or for a few days after you think you have finished writing it. Come back to the script later, asking yourself how the talk might be sharpened.

Preparing handouts and visual aids

- *Consider preparing a written summary for the audience.* In general, an oral presentation should be used to present the essence of some body of material. You might imagine the talk to be like a trailer for a forthcoming movie which presents highlights and captures the imagination. If members of the audience want to know more, they should come along to the full screening of the film (i.e. read the full paper). Depending on the circumstances, it may be helpful, therefore, to prepare a full copy or summary of the paper on which the presentation is based to be distributed to the audience. Microsoft PowerPoint can be a very helpful tool for preparing a summary of a talk. PowerPoint includes among its print options a function that allows you to prepare handout copies of images you plan to use during your talk. With the aid of such a document, the audience is better able to keep track of the presentation and you are freer to highlight the central ideas and findings instead of spending valuable time covering explanatory detail.

- *Prepare visual aids.* Slide projections, PowerPoint projections, models, blackboard sketches, overhead transparencies, video tapes, maps, and charts help to clarify ideas which the audience may have difficulty understanding; hold the audience's attention; and promote interaction with the audience. Table 8.1 sets out a variety of visual aids and some of their advantages and disadvantages. Do remember, however, not to prepare too many aids as they may defeat these purposes. The Google web site (<www.google.com>) offers access to many images that may be judiciously incorporated into your presentation or handouts—subject to copyright regulations and with appropriate acknowledgment of course.

Table 8.1   Advantages and disadvantages of various visual aids

Type	Advantages	Disadvantages
Whiteboard	• Reinforces main points • Allows for use of colour • Good for building up a series of connected ideas • Easy to organise, and can be used outdoors	• Not good for large and/or complicated diagrams • Not useful for large audiences • You usually have to turn your back to the audience • Requires clear handwriting
Flipchart or paper pad stand	• Inexpensive and easily transported • Important material can be prepared in advance • Prompts can be pencilled in beforehand	• Suitable only for small groups • You usually have to turn your back to the audience • Needs a stable easel for support • Requires clear handwriting
Prepared poster	• Provides a brief striking message • Can include complex colour and design elements	• Can be large and awkward to carry • Can be costly to design well
Overhead transparency projector (OHP)	• Images can be seen by everyone • Good for prepared material using colours or diagrams • Can be prepared from computer-generated slides • No need to turn away from audience • Can use overlays • Can be masked so you can reveal information gradually • Can be stored and reused	• Needs a power source • Needs to be correctly aligned • Projector bulbs can fail without warning • Material can be too small to be read • Transparencies can be awkward to manage
Slides (consider saving slides to a CD or computer as an alternative way of using these images)	• Images are of better quality than with OHP • Better at displaying pictures and photographs than OHP • Can be stored and reused	• Projector needs a power source and a darkened room • Needs careful slide alignment, projector focus ... Projectors are notoriously unreliable • Expensive to produce
Computer-generated visual with data projector	• Relatively easy to combine text, graphics, audio, and video • Can generate a sophisticated project relatively cheaply	• Needs a power source • Needs a computer and projector • Technical difficulties in usage are common
Real object	• May be readily available and convenient to display • Audience can see how object works and looks, and it can be used	• May not be suitable for large groups • Potential for damage to object • Not appropriate for large objects
Model	• Works well for large objects • Gives audience sense of scale and of relationships between elements of the object	• May not be to scale • Detail may not be seen by audience • Potential for damage to model • Potentially costly to produce

Source: Street, Hay & Sefton (2005, pp. 177–8)

- *Make visual aids neat, concise, and simple.* Simple and clearly drawn overhead transparencies (OHTs) and other illustrations are more easily interpreted and recalled than are complex versions. Sloppily produced visual aids suggest a lack of care, knowledge, and interest. Visual aids ought to be consistent in their style but should not be boring.
- *Consider producing a title slide.* This might set out your name, the title of your talk, your contact details, and perhaps an outline of the talk to follow.
- *Make no more than five or six points on an OHT or PowerPoint projection.* Make each point in as few words as possible (say, about six words per point).
- *Do not include unnecessary text on OHTs and other projections.*
- *Produce large and boldly drawn visual aids.* Visuals that can be seen from about 20 metres should be adequate in most cases.

> Visual aids must be large, clear, and in highly visible colours.

- *Information shown on OHTs should be typed (or printed neatly).* Type and then photocopy onto OHT acetate. The type size of the original document must be sufficiently large (or should be enlarged with a photocopier) to allow the transparencies to be read easily. Use 18- or 24-point type for the text sections of OHTs and PowerPoint slides. If you handwrite OHTs, print the text. *Do not write cursively as this is difficult for some people to read.* Use upper and lower case text because IT IS MUCH EASIER TO READ THAN BLOCK CAPITALS.
- *Use line graphs, histograms, pie charts (and cartoons).* Graphic depictions of information are usually more effective and more easily understood than tables. However, tables can be useful if they are easy to read. Well-chosen cartoons can very effectively communicate a message and help to lighten the atmosphere.
- *Avoid taking graphs or tables directly from a written paper.* These often contain more information and detail than can be comprehended readily. Redraw graphs and redesign tables to make the small number of points you wish to convey.
- *Use a limited range of colours on OHTs and other projected images.* Up to three colours should be employed. Judicious use of colour on complex illustrative material can help clarify the message. Remember that some colours may evoke certain feelings which add to or detract from the case you are arguing. For example, black can be symbolic of death, green of envy, and white of purity. (This is explained more fully in chapter 5.) You should also take care to use dark colours on OHTs. Light colours such as yellow and orange cannot be seen clearly. For the sake of colour-blind members of your audience, avoid using red and green together, black on red, and black with blue.

- *Ensure that all of your OHT will be displayed through the projector.* Leave some space around the margins of each sheet of acetate to avoid the problem of text overlapping the edge of the projector unit.
- *Number your OHTs.* If you drop your OHT collection in the middle of your talk, it is much easier to recover if the slides are numbered!
- *Plan to leave a good impression.* If you are using PowerPoint, consider preparing an attractive and relevant final image that can be left on the screen when you have finished speaking and are answering audience questions. It is sometimes useful to restate the title of your talk and your name in this final slide.

Rehearsing

With public speaking, practice makes perfect.

Few people, if any, are naturally gifted public speakers. It is a skill developed through experience. People new to public speaking often speak very quickly or too slowly; they belabour minor points; fail to engage with their audience through eye contact, for example; or do not know how to operate audio-visual equipment correctly. You can overcome such problems through practice and useful feedback from other students or family members.

Rehearse until there is almost no need to consult prepared notes for guidance—about ten times ought to do it. The intent is not to commit the talk to memory. Instead, rehearsing helps to ensure that you have all the points in the right order and that you have a crystal-clear sense of your talk's key message and its trajectory. This is vital to success. Rehearsing also enables you to practise the pacing and timing of your talk so you don't, for example, spend 90% of your allotted presentation time discussing 20% of your talk's content! It may also allow you to work out whether you sound boring or arrogant. Importantly, it also allows you to manage your spoken material, handouts, and audio-visual resources within the time available (Hay, Dunn & Street 2005, p. 166).

- *Speak your material out loud!* Not only may you begin to hear problems of logic in your presentation but you will also have the opportunity to practise pronouncing some of those complicated disciplinary terms, such as 'existentialist' or 'distanciation', that you might have to employ.
- *Time rehearsals.* Most novice speakers are stunned to find out how much longer their presentation takes to deliver than they had expected, than it took to read quietly, or than they felt had elapsed while they were talking. Match the time available for the talk with the amount of material for presentation. Allow for a few extra minutes to compensate for impromptu comments, technical problems, pauses to gather thoughts, or the breathtaking realisation that the audience is not following the tale! If your talk is

too long, decide what material can be removed without affecting the main points. It is better to do the pruning beforehand than to be forced to stop your talk, or make the revisions in midstream.

- *Make full use of the visual aids to be used in the talk.* Visual aids can consume time rapidly as you move from one medium, say the overhead projector, to another, the blackboard. Consequently, pay careful attention to the use of time in the delivery of multimedia presentations.

- *Record one or two rehearsals.* It is often useful to make a video recording of a trial presentation. Video cameras do not 'pull punches' in the same way that an audience of friends and family, sensitive to your feelings, might. If that option is unavailable to you, try an audio recording. Find out if you enliven your talk through variations in pitch, tone, and pace or if you use those annoying saboteurs of a good talk: 'umm', 'err', 'you know', 'like', and 'ah' …

> Rehearse your talk using all the prompts and props you plan to employ.

Final points of preparation

- *Are you dressed and groomed for the occasion?* Although the audience's emphasis should be placed on the intellectual merits of your argument, your appearance may affect some people's perceptions of what you have to say. Looking rough suggests that you have no respect for your audience and even less for yourself. You might not have to go as far as what Reece (1999) suggests and wear business attire, but you should look as if you have taken some care about your appearance.

- *Take water.* No matter how well prepared you are, there is a possibility that you will suffer from 'cotton mouth' during your talk. This unpleasant affliction causes your mouth to dry out and your tongue to swell to such a size that you can scarcely speak. Water consumed during the talk seems to help!

- *How do the visual aids work?* Be familiar with the function of any aid that you will be using. Do not be so unprepared that you must exasperate your audience with stupid questions like: 'How do I switch this projector on?' or 'Can anyone work the video player?' You should have checked before your presentation. It is your talk!

> When it is your turn to speak, take control: of technology, timekeeping, volume, and vision …

- *Be prepared for technical problems.* Ensure that you have a strategy for dealing with computer, overhead projector, and slide projector glitches. For instance, if you plan on using PowerPoint, take along OHT or hardcopy copies of your slides in case there are problems with your computer or the data-show projector.

- *Can the audience see you and your visual aids?* Before your talk, sit in a few strategically placed chairs around the room to see whether the audience will be able to see you and your visual aids. Consider where you will stand while talking and take care to avoid the problem of your silhouette obstructing the audience's view of OHTs or the blackboard.

* *Is there a clock in the room?* If not, make sure you can see your watch or have some other way of checking the time.
* *Is everything else ready?* Are summaries ready for distribution; are note cards in order … ?
* *Make absolutely clear in your mind the central message you wish to convey. This is critical to a good presentation.* Knowing your message will give you the confidence your audience will need if they are to have faith in what you are telling them. It also means that if for some unforeseen reason something goes wrong, or you 'stall' and lose the plot momentarily, you can take a breath, reflect on your central message, and resume your talk with the minimum of fuss. Importantly too, if you do not have the message of your talk firmly established in your own mind, you are unlikely to be able to let anyone else know what that message is.

DELIVERY

> ### BOX 8.4 DIRECTIVE FOR LULLING AN AUDIENCE TO SLEEP
>
> Wear a dark suit and conventional tie; turn down the lights; close the curtains, display a crowded slide and leave it in place; stand still, read your paper without looking up; read steadily with no marked changes in cadence; show no pictures, use grandiloquent words and long sentences.
>
> Booth (1993, p. 42)

People in your audience *want you to do well.* They want to listen to you giving a good talk and they will be supportive and grateful if you are well prepared, even if you do stumble in your presentation or blush and stammer. The guidelines outlined here are a target at which you can aim. No one expects you to give a flawless presentation.

> Audiences support speakers who try to do well.

It will make your presentation more convincing and credible if you remember and act on the fact that the audience comprises *individuals*, each of whom is listening to you. You are not talking to some large, amorphous body. Imagine that you are telling your story to one or two people and not to a larger group. If you can allow yourself to perform this difficult task, you will find that voice inflection, facial expressions, and other elements important to an effective delivery will fall into place.

- *Be confident and enthusiastic.* One of the most important keys to a successful presentation is your enthusiasm. You have a well-researched and well-prepared talk to deliver. Most audiences are friendly. All you have to do is tell a small group of interested people what you have to say. Try to instil confidence in your abilities and your message. Do not start by apologising for your presentation. If it is so bad, why are you giving it?
- *Look interested—or no one else will be!*
- *Talk naturally, using simple language and short sentences.* Try to relax, but be aware that the presentation is not a conversation in a public bar. Some degree of formality is expected. Do not use slang or colloquial language unless you have a specific reason for doing so.
- *Speak clearly.* Try not to mumble and hesitate. This may suggest to the audience that you do not know your material thoroughly. You can sometimes make your speech clearer by slowing the rate of delivery.
- *Project your voice.* Be sure that the most distant member of the audience can hear you clearly.
- *Engage your audience.* Vary your volume, tone of voice, and pace of presentation. Involve the audience through use of the word 'you' e.g. 'You may wonder why we used … ' (Lindsay 1984, p. 55).
- *Use appropriate gestures and movement.* Step out from behind the computer monitor or lectern and move around a little, engaging with different parts of your audience.
- *Try to avoid nervous habits.* Be conscious of distracting behaviour, such as jangling money in your pocket, swaying, pacing back and forth, or saying things like 'umm' a lot, which you may have detected in your rehearsals. Find alternative, good speaking habits.
- *Make eye contact with your audience.* Although this may be rather intimidating, eye contact is very important. It also allows you to gauge audience response.
- *Face the entire audience.* Do not talk to walls, windows, floor, ceiling, blackboard, or projector screen. It is the audience—the entire audience—with which you are concerned. If you are using an overhead projector, remember that you can see your OHTs on the glass in front of you. If you are using PowerPoint, you should have a print-out or the screen image of your slides in front of you. Avoid turning your back on your audience to look at the projection screen.
- *Pay attention to audience reaction.* If the audience does not seem to understand what you are saying, rephrase your point or clarify it with an example.

Pay attention to your audience: Can they hear? Can they see? Are they bored? Do they understand? …

- *Direct your attention to the less attentive members of the audience.* This may not be as reassuring as focusing your presentation on those whose attention you already have, but it will help you to convey your message to as large a part of the audience as possible.
- *Write key words and unusual words on the whiteboard.*
- *Avoid writing or drawing on whiteboards or overhead acetate for more than a few seconds at a time.* Long periods devoted to the production of diagrams may destroy any rapport you have developed with your audience.
- *Stop talking when a diagram/slide/map is first shown.* This is to allow the audience time to study the display. Then, take a moment to familiarise your audience with elements of the visual aid (e.g. axis labels), remembering that they have never seen the image before. There is no point in telling people what the image means before they have had a chance to work out what it is about (Pechenik 2004, p. 255).
- *Point to the audience's screen, not yours.* Some speakers new to PowerPoint will point with their finger to images on the monitor in front of them believing perhaps that the audience can see what they mean. Others insist on shaking the mouse about and hence the cursor in ways that can best be described as nauseating for the audience. Other problems confront users of overhead projectors. These projectors magnify the barely noticeable shaking hands of almost any speaker into a splendid and captivating tremble. All of these problems can be overcome by pointing with a hand or ruler to the audience's screen. Take care using laser pointers. They too can take a slight hand tremble and increase its amplitude significantly (Pechenik 2004, pp. 255–6).
- *Do not obstruct the audience's view of completed diagrams.*
- *Be sure that overhead and other light projections are sufficiently high for all the audience to see.* As a rule of thumb, make sure the projection is screened higher than the heads of people in the front row of your audience.
- *When you have finished with an illustration, remove it.* The audience's attention will be directed back at you (where it belongs) and will not be distracted. Do not talk about a topic which is different to the one on your visual display.
- *Switch off overhead projectors and other noisy machines when they are not being used.* If this is impossible, it may be necessary to speak more loudly than usual in order to compensate for the whirring of electric cooling fans.
- *Keep to your time limit.* Audiences do not like being delayed, but you should take care not to rush at the end. Last-minute haste may leave the audience with a poor impression of your talk. Watch the time as you proceed. If it is apparent that you will run out of time let the audience know the key headings you planned to cover and then jump straight to the conclusion. This is likely to be the fastest, most effective, and polished way of summarising the

balance of your talk. Of course, if you have rehearsed properly, this problem should rarely occur!

COPING WITH QUESTIONS

The post-presentation discussion which typically follows a talk allows the audience to ask questions and to offer points of criticism. It is an important part of the overall presentation which can completely change an audience's response to you and your work. Take care to be thorough and courteous in your response to comments and questions.

- *Let the audience know whether you will accept questions in the course of the presentation or after the talk is completed.* Be aware that questions addressed during a presentation may disturb the flow of the talk, may upset any rapport developed with the audience, and may anticipate points addressed at some later stage within the presentation.
- *Stay at or near the rostrum throughout the question period.* Question-time is still a formal part of the presentation. Act accordingly.
- *Be in control of the question and answer period.* However, if there is a chairperson, moderation of question-time is their responsibility.
- *Address the entire audience, not just the person who asked the question.*
- *Recognise questions in order.* Take care to receive inquiries from everyone before returning to any member of the audience who has a second question.
- *Search the whole audience for questions.* Compensate for blind spots caused by building piles, the rostrum, and other barriers.
- *Always be succinct and polite in replies.* You should be courteous even to those who appear to be attacking rather than honestly questioning, for two reasons. First, if the intent of the question has been misinterpreted—with an affront being seen where none was intended—embarrassment is avoided. Second, one of the best ways of defusing inappropriate criticism is through politeness. If, however, there is no doubt that someone is being hostile, keep your cool and, if possible, move closer to the critic. This reduction of distance is a powerful way of subduing argumentative members of an audience.

> Treat question-time as seriously as the main part of your talk.

- *Repeat aloud those questions which are difficult to hear.* This ensures that you heard the question correctly. Repetition is also for the sake of the audience who may not have heard the question either.
- *Clarify the meaning of any questions you do not understand.*
- *Avoid concluding an answer by asking the questioner if their query has been dealt with satisfactorily.* Argumentative questioners may take this opportunity to steal the limelight, thereby limiting the discussion time available to other members of the audience.

- *Deal with particularly complex questions or those requiring an unusually long answer after the presentation.* If possible, provide a brief answer when the question is first raised.
- *If you do not know the answer to a question, say so.* Do not try to bluff your way through a problem, as any errors and inaccuracies may call the content of the rest of the talk into question.
- *Difficult questions may be answered by making use of the abilities of the audience.* For example, an inquiry might require more knowledge in a particular field than you possess. Rather than admitting defeat, it is sometimes possible to seek out the known expertise of a specific member of the audience. This avoids personal embarrassment, ensures that the question is answered, and may endear you to that member of the audience whose advice was sought. It also lets other members of the audience know of additional expertise in the area.
- *Smile.* It is over!

REFERENCES AND FURTHER READING

Barnacoat, M. 1993, 'Presentation skills: the psycho-social approach', in *Communication for Scientific, Technical and Medical Professionals*, eds V. Hoogstad & J. Hughes, MacMillan, South Melbourne.
A helpful chapter which discusses presentation strategies and ways of overcoming speaker fear.

Beer, D.F. (ed.) 1992, *Writing and Speaking in the Technology Professions: A Practical Guide*, IEEE Publications, New York.
Part 7 of this edited collection contains a number of good, short papers on speaking effectively to groups.

Booth, V. 1993, *Communicating in Science: Writing a Scientific Paper and Speaking at Scientific Meetings*, 2nd edn, Cambridge University Press, Cambridge.
Chapter 2 is an entertaining and informative exhortation to speak well at professional gatherings.

Bowman, L. 2001, *High Impact Presentations: The Most Effective Way to Communicate with Virtually Any Audience Anywhere*, Bene Factum, London.

Burdess, N. 1998, *Handbook of Student Skills*, Prentice Hall, New York.

Calnan, J. & Barabas, A. 1972, *Speaking at Medical Meetings: A Practical Guide*, Heinemann, London.
A marvellous little book. Although some of the material applies only to specific fields within the medical profession, most of the content of this easily read, humorous volume is applicable to speakers in other domains.

Campbell, J. 1990, *Speak for Yourself: A Practical Guide to Giving Successful Presentations, Speeches and Talks*, BBC Books, London.
At about 150 pages, this is the most comprehensive review on preparing and presenting a talk I have found. The book accompanies a BBC video of the same title.

Carle, G. 1992, 'Handling a hostile audience with your eyes', in *Writing and Speaking in the Technology Professions: A Practical Guide*, ed. D.F. Beer, IEEE Publications, New York, pp. 229–31.
Carle's paper outlines an interesting three-step strategy for dealing with hostile audiences.

Clerehan, R. 1991, *Study Skills Handbook for Tertiary Students*, Language and Learning Services, Monash University, Melbourne.

Committee on Scientific Writing RMIT. 1993, *Manual on Scientific Writing*, TAFE Publications, Collingwood, Victoria.
Chapter 4 includes a helpful and short discussion on a talk-planning strategy called clustering.

Courtenay, B. 1992, *The Pitch*, Margaret Gee, McMahons Point, NSW.
This book comprises a series of short articles written by Courtenay—acclaimed author of *The Power of One, Tandia, April Fool's Day*, etc.—for *The Australian* newspaper. A number of the articles discuss the business of making an oral presentation.

Daniel, P.A. 1991, 'Assessing student-led seminars through a process of negotiation', *Journal of Geography in Higher Education*, vol. 15, no. 1, pp. 57–62.
Includes an assessment schedule for student seminar (interactive) presentations.

Dixon, T. 2004, *How to Get a First: The essential guide to academic success*, Routledge, London.

Dudley, H. 1977, *The Presentation of Original Work in Medicine and Biology*, Churchill Livingstone, Edinburgh.
See chapter 5 for a discussion on giving talks and a helpful section on coping with questions.

Eisenberg, A. 1992, *Effective Technical Communication*, 2nd edn, McGraw-Hill, New York.
Chapter 15 is a lengthy discussion on preparing and giving a talk. Some useful notes on aspects of body language and on writing out a talk are included.

Harwell, G.C. 1960, *Technical Communication*, MacMillan, New York.
Chapter 9 covers oral communication and includes a discussion of body language.

Hay, I. 1994a, 'Justifying and applying oral presentations in geographical education', *Journal of Geography in Higher Education*, vol. 18, no. 1, pp. 43–55.

Hay, I. 1994b, 'Notes of guidance for prospective speakers', *Journal of Geography in Higher Education*, vol. 18, no. 1, pp. 57–65.
Hay (1994a) and (1994b) are earlier versions of the chapter presented in this book.

Hay, I., Dunn, K. & Street, A. 2005, 'Making the most of your conference journey', *Journal of Geography in Higher Education*, vol. 29, no. 1, pp. 159–71.
Extends this chapter's discussion to look further at effective delivery and ways of taking advantage of a conference experience to forge valuable professional relationships.

Hughes, J. 1993, 'Oral communication: preparation, planning and performance', in *Communication for Scientific, Technical and Medical Professionals*, eds V. Hoogstad & J. Hughes, Macmillan, South Melbourne.
A pithy chapter discussing a variety of matters including speech organisation and delivery (including dress, body language, and grammar).

Jenkins, A. & Pepper, D. 1988, 'Enhancing students' employability and self-expression: How to teach oral and groupwork skills in geography', *Journal of Geography in Higher Education*, vol. 12, no. 1, pp. 67–83.
Includes an extensive discussion of the academic and vocational rationale for teaching and learning oral communication skills.

Jones, M. & Parker, D. 1989, 'Research report development of student verbal skills: The use of the student-led seminar', *The Vocational Aspect of Education*, vol. 41, no. 108, pp. 15–19.
In its introduction this paper outlines some of the vocational reasons for learning to speak effectively.

Kenny, P. 1982, *A Handbook of Public Speaking for Scientists and Engineers*, Adam Hilger, Bristol.

Knight, P. & Parsons, T. 2003, *How to Do Your Essays, Exams, and Coursework in Geography and Related Disciplines*, Nelson Thornes, Cheltenham.

Lindsay, D. 1984, *A Guide to Scientific Writing*, Longman Cheshire, Melbourne.
Chapter 3 includes a useful example of an aide-mémoire.

Mohan, T., McGregor, H. & Strano, Z. 1992, *Communicating! Theory and Practice*, Harcourt Brace, Sydney.

Montgomery, S.L. 2003, *The Chicago Guide to Communicating Science*, The University of Chicago Press, Chicago.
Chapter 13 provides a very helpful guide to scientists on giving high-quality talks to both professional and lay audiences.

Pechenik, J.A. 2004, *A Short Guide to Writing About Biology*, Pearson Longman, New York.

Reece, P. 1999, 'The number one fear: Public speaking and the university student', in *Teaching in the Disciplines/Learning in Context* (online), eds K. Martin, N. Stanley & N. Davison, Proceedings of the 8th Annual Teaching Learning Forum, University of Western Australia, Available: <http//cleo.murdoch.edu.au/asu/pubs/tlf/tlf99/ns/reece.html> (12 July 2001).

Richards, I. 1988, *How to Give a Successful Presentation*, Graham and Trotman, London.

Stettner, M. 1992, 'How to speak so facts come to life', in *Writing and Speaking in the Technology Professions. A Practical Guide*, ed. D.F. Beer, IEEE Publications, New York, pp. 225–8.
Includes a helpful discussion on why a talk should cover no more than or no fewer than three main points.

Street, A., Hay, I. & Sefton, A. 2005, 'Giving talks in class', in *Communicating in the Health and Social Sciences*, eds J. Higgs, A. Sefton, A. Street, L. McAllister & I. Hay, Oxford University Press, Melbourne, pp. 176–83.

Windschuttle, K. & Elliott, E. 1999, *Writing, Researching, Communicating*, 3rd edn, McGraw-Hill, Sydney.

Young, C. 1998, 'Giving oral presentations', *Journal of Geography in Higher Education*, vol. 22, no. 2, pp. 263–8.

9

Coping with Exams

Examinations are formidable even to the best prepared, for the greatest fool may ask more than the wisest man can answer.

Charles Caleb Colton, 1820

KEY TOPICS

- Why have exams?
- Types of exam
- Preparing for an exam
- Techniques for passing different types of exam

Some people flourish in exams, completing their best work under conditions that others might find highly stressful. In part, good performance may be a consequence of a person's particular response to stress, but it is more likely the result of good exam technique. This chapter discusses exams, their types, and strategies for test success.

WHY HAVE EXAMS?

Exams serve three main educational purposes. These are to test:

- your level of factual knowledge
- your ability to **synthesise** material learned throughout a teaching session, and
- your ability to explain and justify your informed opinion on some specific topic.

These reasons provide some indication of the sorts of things an examiner is likely to be looking for when marking a test. Some tests may seek to fulfil only one of these objectives (e.g. some short answer and multiple choice tests may only be examining your ability to recall information) while others will be looking for all of them (e.g. essay questions or oral exam of a thesis).

TYPES OF EXAM

Exams in geography and the environmental sciences usually fall into one of four categories (or combinations thereof). These types are set out in Table 9.1.

Table 9.1   Types of exam and their characteristics

	Closed book
Characteristics	Requires that you answer questions on the strength of your wits and ability to recall information. Consulting any material in the exam room other than that provided by the examiner for the purposes of the test is not permitted.
Sub-types	• Multiple-choice • Short answer • Essay answer
	Open book
Characteristics	You may consult reference materials such as lecture notes, textbooks, and journals during the exam. Sometimes the sources you are allowed to consult will be limited by your examiner.
Sub-types	• Exam room • Take home
	Oral exam **(viva voce***)*
Characteristics	Used most commonly as a supplement to written exams, or to explore issues emerging from an Honours, Masters, or PhD thesis. You may have to give a brief presentation before participating in a critical but congenial discussion with examiners about your written work.
	Online exam
Characteristics	Requires that you complete and submit your exam while online (i.e. at a computer). Usually takes place under secure conditions in a computer laboratory. Still relatively uncommon in geography and environmental studies but used increasingly in distance-education and 'flexible' delivery. May embrace each of the exam types set out above—with the exception of the *viva voce*.

Of these forms of exam, the closed book model is most common. Consequently, the following discussion will focus on that model. Nevertheless, a good deal of the general advice will apply to the other exam types. Some specific guidance on other exam forms is provided at the end of the chapter.

An important component of success in exams is good 'exam technique'. Technique can be broken into two parts: (1) preparation and (2) sitting the exam.

PREPARING FOR AN EXAM

Review throughout the teaching term

This is one of the most difficult things to do in preparing for an exam. It is also very important. Try to review course material as the teaching session progresses, beginning on the very first day of classes. You might review by rewriting lecture notes or keeping up-to-date with notes from assigned readings. Not only will this help you remember material when the time comes to sit the exam, but it will also make it easier to understand lecture material as it is presented throughout the teaching session. That can be a major benefit when it is time to complete the examination. Chapters 1 and 2 of Orr's (1984) book offer detailed guidance for organising in-term revision. It is perhaps useful to remember Dixon's (2004, pp. 152–3) sage counsel that if 'you have worked out what the key questions are in each course you are taking; have looked at old exam papers and paid attention to the course documentation; have attended and paid attention to your lectures and seminars; have made useful and well-organised notes; and have read around the subject and thought carefully about what your line is on the central issues; then you do not have too much to worry about'.

Find out about the exam

> Reduce anxiety by finding out as much as possible about the exam.

Ask teaching staff to let you know what you can expect in the exam in terms of the types of question you may be asked, the time allowed, the materials needed, and so forth.

BOX 9.1 QUESTIONS TO ASK ABOUT YOUR EXAM

- How long will I have to complete the exam? (Am I allowed extra time because I come from a non-English speaking background or for some other reason?)
- Do I have to pass the exam to pass the entire course?
- What is the pass mark?
- How much does the exam contribute to the final grade?
- How many questions are in the exam?
- How many questions do I have to answer? Are any questions compulsory?
- What kind of questions are they (e.g., essay, multiple-choice, short answer)? Are there either/or options available?
- How are the marks divided among the questions?
- Is there any information provided in addition to the exam (e.g. mathematical tables)?

- Will I be examined on material not covered in lectures and tutorials?
- Can I use a calculator or dictionary?
- Am I allowed to bring in any notes or books?
- Where is the exam and when is it being held?
- What happens if I am sick on the day of the exam?

Adapted from Hamilton (1999, p. 19)

Seek some direction about how you might focus your supplementary reading. Listen for clues from your lecturer about content. Sometimes lecturers will make thinly disguised hints about the content of an exam throughout the teaching term.

If past exam papers are available to you, look at them to get a sense of the likely format of the exam you will sit and the main topics it might cover. Be aware, however, that the style and content of exams may change from year to year.

Friedman and Steinberg (1989, p. 175) suggest that you should try to anticipate questions and areas which might be in the exam. Although this can be helpful, it can also be a dangerous game for the inexperienced. Unless you have been told that the exam will concentrate on specific topics it is usually better to have a good overview of all the material covered in a class. Broad comprehension means that you should be able to tackle competently any question you encounter. If you narrow the scope of your revisions, you are gambling with your grade.

Revising for a limited range of topics covered in a class is a risky strategy.

Be quite sure that you know exactly *when* and *where* the exam is to be held. This is your responsibility and not that of academic staff.

Find a suitable study space

Arrange a comfortable, quiet, well-lit, and ventilated place where you can study undisturbed. If possible, make sure it is a place where you can lay out papers and books without risk of them being moved. Try to avoid studying at the dining-room table unless everyone plans to eat from plates balanced on their knees for the weeks you are studying.

Keep to a study schedule

Once you have found out the dates and times of your exams, prepare a study calendar. This calendar should allocate specific days or parts of days to the revision of each topic. When you make up your study timetable think about those times when you work best and schedule your study periods accordingly. Avoid doing something else then like playing squash or working at the supermarket. If possible, set up the timetable so you can be doing those sorts of thing when you are feeling mentally flat or slow.

An example of an exam study calendar is shown in Table 9.2. In the example, the fortunate student has only two exams. Each exam contributes the same proportion to the final grade in a subject and the student is performing equally well in both subjects. Reflecting this balance, the student has allocated twelve study periods to environmental management and eleven to geography. Some blocks of time for relaxation, exercise, and other day-to-day activities are also set aside. In your own timetable you might also find it helpful to schedule a short break every one or two hours. During these times you can make coffee, listen to a piece of music, or do something else which refreshes you for the next study period.

Make a personal study timetable and keep to it.

Table 9.2   Example of an exam study calendar

Date	A.M. activity	P.M. activity	Evening
20 November	End of classes	Relax, buy groceries etc.	Get notes in order
21 November	Get notes in order	Environmental Management	Environmental Management (play squash)
22 November	Environmental Management	Environmental Management	Environmental Management
23 November	Geography	Geography	Relax (swim)
24 November	Geography	Geography	Geography
25 November	Environmental Management (yoga)	Environmental Management	Environmental Management
26 November	Environmental Management (run)	Environmental Management	Environmental Management
27 November	Environmental Management	**Environmental Management Exam**	Relax
28 November	Geography	Geography	Geography (play squash)
29 November	Geography	Geography (swim)	Geography
30 November	**Geography Exam**	Celebrate!	Continue celebrating

If the exams outlined in Table 9.2 were weighted differently from one another or if the student were performing better in one topic than another, it would be advisable to devote extra time to specific topics as appropriate. Be sure to stick to your revision schedule.

Concentrate on understanding, not memorising

In most written exams, you will be required to demonstrate an understanding of the subject material rather than to regurgitate recalled information. In consequence, your revision should focus on comprehension first and fact second. Be sure you understand what the course was about and the relationships between content and overall objectives.

When you have a grasp of course objectives, you will be in a better position to make sense of content. Possession of a 'conceptual framework' upon which you can hang substantive material will also allow you to respond in a critical and informed manner to exam questions. To develop this understanding, check course syllabuses, lecture notes, essay questions, practical exercises, and textbooks. Try to draw a concept map which indicates the key ideas and relationships between them. You may also find it helpful to condense your notes from, say, thirty pages to six pages and then to one page. Then expand them out again without referring to the original notes. This process of condensing and elaborating on material should help you to develop a good understanding of the subject matter.

> Usually it is better to study for meaning than for detail.

Vary your revision practices

To add depth and to consolidate your understanding of course material, use various means of studying for a topic (Barass 1984, p. 147). Set yourself questions, solve problems, organise material, make notes, prepare simple summary diagrams, and read notes thoughtfully.

Practise answering exam questions

Have a go at answering past exam questions under exam conditions. Be sure you understand some of the key phrases and instructions which might appear (e.g. 'discuss critically', 'evaluate', 'compare and contrast'). The Glossary at the end of this book may help you to clarify some of these terms. You may also find it helpful to take your trial exam answers to your lecturer to confirm that you are on the right track.

One good reason for practising exams under exam conditions has to do with changing technology. You probably do most of your in-term writing on a computer. In an exam you are likely to be asked to write manually for three hours. Can you do that? What happens to your fingers? Further, word-processors allow you to move paragraphs around and make revisions quickly. Paper and pen do not offer that liberty and you have to plan your writing much more carefully.

Seek help if you need it

If there is topic matter you do not understand, ask your lecturer. If you are experiencing emotional or other difficulties which affect your study, speak to the lecturer or a university counsellor. You will not be the only person facing such problems.

Maintain your regular diet, sleep, and exercise patterns

Do not make the mistake of popping caffeine tablets and staying up into the early hours of the morning cramming information into your overtired brain—unless you already make a habit of that! You run the risk of falling asleep during the exam. Radical changes to your lifestyle are likely to increase levels of stress and may adversely affect your exam performance. If you are in the habit of exercising regularly, keep doing that. Most people find that exercise perks them up, makes learning easier, and enhances exam performance. Exercise a little common sense too. Do not let exam revision time coincide with your conversion from couch potato to trainee marathon runner, for example. You might also consider telling your partner, friends, and family that you may be a little more difficult to live with while you are studying!

Good exam preparation includes looking after yourself.

Avoid cramming late into the night immediately before an exam. That is rather like preparing for a 10-kilometre 'fun run' (one of the world's great oxymorons!) by going for a long run the day before. Instead, if your preparation has gone according to schedule you should be ready to sit the exam. Spend the night before catching up on a few key revision issues, making sure you have all you need for the exam, relaxing, and getting some sleep.

On the day of your exam—if the exam is in the morning—it is vital that you consume something to raise blood-sugar levels. It is better that you try to eat something like muesli that is slowly digested than something that will give you a momentary buzz (e.g. a chocolate bar) before dumping you on a post-sugar low. If you do not think you can eat anything substantial, try several small, healthy snacks (e.g. dried fruit and nuts). Do not face an exam on an empty stomach.

Dress appropriately

For a typical closed book exam in a lecture hall or university gymnasium the key is to dress comfortably. Be sure that you will be warm enough or cool enough to function at your optimum level. Feel good about how you look. Your performance may match that feeling.

Pack your bag

Make sure you have your student identification card (in most universities you are required to present your ID in order to sit the exam), pencils/pens, ruler, paper, eraser, watch, lucky charms, and a calculator (if required). Exam booklets and scribbling paper will usually be provided. If the weather is hot, you might also want to pack a drink. This is particularly important for summer exams in some poorly insulated exam venues. Take extra warm clothing if it is possible that the venue will be cold.

Get to the right exam in the right place at the right time

Be sure that you know whether the exam is held in the morning, the afternoon, or the evening. You should also double-check the location of the exam. Every year, some people turn up in the afternoon for a morning exam or arrive at the wrong place. If you do miss the exam for some reason, see your lecturer *immediately*. You will usually find them in their office for the duration of the exam.

Arrive in good time—not too early, not too late. When you are planning your departure for the exam, allow for the possibility of traffic delays, late buses, and bad weather.

SITTING EXAMS: TECHNIQUES FOR PASSING EXAMS

Before an exam almost everyone feels tense and keyed up. However, if you have studied effectively and know about the type of exam you will be sitting, the anxiety you feel will probably help you perform at a higher level than if you were quite blasé about the whole affair. Breathe deeply and stride into the exam room with a sense of purpose. You know your stuff and you know what the course was about. Here is the opportunity to prove it!

Check that you have all pages, questions, and answer sheets. On rare occasions, printing or instructional errors may occur. If you believe this may have happened, check with the invigilator. Confirm too that you have all the materials you need to complete the exam. Look on the reverse side of every page of the exam to see if there are extra questions hiding there.

Always make sure you have the entire exam.

Read the instructions carefully before beginning

Check to see how long you have to complete the exam, which questions need to be answered, and the mark value of each question. It is wise to *repeat* this process after answering the first question (or several in the case of a multiple-choice/short answer exam) to confirm that you are doing things correctly. Lecturers find it most disheartening to mark an exam paper by a capable student who has not followed instructions. It is even more upsetting to be that student.

Work out a timetable

Calculate the amount of time you should devote to each question. Time allocations can be calculated on the basis of marks per question.

The table below provides an example.

Table 9.3 Exam answering timetable—three-hour exam (180 minutes)

Question 1	5 marks	9 minutes
Question 2	10 marks	18 minutes
Question 3	15 marks	27 minutes
Question 4	20 marks	36 minutes
Question 5	50 marks	90 minutes
Total	**100 marks**	**180 minutes**

This time-budget could be modified usefully by allowing about 10 minutes at the end of the exam to proofread answers. This can be a valuable use of time.

It is most important that you not only allocate time carefully but that you *adhere to your timetable.* It would be stupid, in the example above, for example, to spend 30 minutes on Question 1. To help with this, write down the time you need to start each question or section of the exam soon after you get into the exam room. Keep this timetable handy and stick to it. The point is obvious but worth stating: a small amount of extra time spent on any question deprives you of time on others. Time discipline may be difficult, but it is undeniably a key to exam success.

Read the questions carefully before beginning

In closed book essay examinations, you will usually be given some preparatory time (commonly 10 minutes) in which to read the questions and to make notes on scrap paper. Use this time effectively. Carefully choose the questions you will answer and think critically about their meaning. Take note of significant words and phrases and underline key words. Jot down ideas that spring to mind as you look over the questions. Use the time as a brainstorming session and record your thoughts immediately. Do not rely on your memory. After several hours of answering an exam paper, you may have completely forgotten the brilliant ideas you had for that last question. Your notes will trigger your memory.

 Plan your exam.

Plan your answers

Do not make the mistake of rushing into your answers like the proverbial bull at a gate. Essay questions in an exam need to be approached in much the same way as essay questions in term time (see chapter 1). Work out a strategy for approaching your answer to each question. Once the exam has begun, use the ideas you jotted down during reading time as the basis of an essay plan for each answer. Make a rough plan of each answer before you begin writing. This might all be done on separate pages in your examination answer booklet. Not only is a plan likely to give a coherent structure to your answers but, if you do run out of time, the marker *may* refer to the plan to gain some impression of the case you were making. However, take care to distinguish essay plans from final answers in your answer booklet (e.g. put a pen stroke through the plan).

Begin with the answers you know best

There is usually no requirement for you to answer questions in any particular order. It is often helpful to tackle the easiest questions first to build up confidence and momentum. Further, if you have the misfortune to run out of time, you will have shown your best work.

Answer the questions asked

Surprisingly, the most common mistake people make in exams is not answering the question that was asked, sometimes opting to spew forth a prepared answer on a related topic (Barass 1984, p. 156; Friedman & Steinberg 1989, p. 175). Markers want to know what you think and what you have learned about a *specified* topic. As you will appreciate, the right answer to the wrong question will not get you very far!

> Examiners prefer focused, concise, and careful answers—not pages of waffle.

Examiners are assessing your level of understanding of particular subjects. Do not try to trick them; do not try using the 'shotgun technique', by which you tell all that you know about the topic irrespective of its relevance to the question; do not try to write lots of pages in the hope that you might fool someone into believing that you know more than you do. Concentrate instead on producing focused, well-structured answers. *That* will impress an examiner.

Attempt all required questions

It is usually easier to get the first 30–50% of the marks for any written question than it is to get the last 30–50%. In consequence, it is foolish to leave any questions unanswered. In the worst case, make an informed guess. If you find that you are running out of time, write an introduction, outline your argument in note form, and write a conclusion. This will provide the marker with some sense of your depth of understanding and may see you rewarded appropriately.

Grab the marker's attention

People marking written exam papers usually have many scripts to assess. They do not want to see the exam question rephrased as the introduction to an essay answer. They probably do not want to read long rambling introductions. Instead, they will want you to capture their attention with clear, concise, and coherent answers. Spare the padding. Get to the point.

Emphasise important points

You can emphasise key points by underlining words and by using phrases which give those points emphasis (e.g. 'The most important matter is … ', 'A leading cause of … '). You might also find it useful to use headings in essay answers to draw attention to your progression through an argument. Your examiner will certainly find headings useful. If used judiciously, bullet/numbered lists and correctly labelled diagrams can also be helpful.

Support generalisations

Use examples and other forms of evidence to support the general claims you make (Dixon 2004, p. 161; Friedman & Steinberg 1989, p. 177). Your answers will be more compelling and will signal your understanding of course material more effectively if they are supported by appropriate examples drawn from lectures, reading, and your own experience than if they rest solely on bald generalisations.

Write legibly and comprehensibly

Examiners hate scripts that are hard to read. It is very difficult to follow someone's argument if frequent pauses have to be made to decipher hieroglyphics masquerading as the conventional symbols of written English. Try to write legibly. If you have problems writing in a form that can be easily read, write on alternate lines or print to ensure the examiner is able to interpret your work. Keep your English expression clear too. Errors of punctuation and grammar may divert the examiner's attention from the positive qualities of your work. Many problems of expression can be overcome by using short sentences. These also tend to have greater impact than long sentences.

> Especially if you are accustomed to word processing, practise handwriting (legibly) before a long exam.

Leave space for additions

Begin answers on new pages so that you can add material if time allows. This is particularly important if you have been prudent enough to leave yourself some time for proofreading. Often, people find that they recall material about one question while they are answering another. It is useful to have the time and space to add those insights.

Keep calm

If you find that you are beginning to panic or that your memory has gone blank, stop writing, breathe deeply, and relax for a minute or two. A few moments spent this way should help to put you back on track. Do not give up in frustration and storm out of the exam room. Why run the risk of working out a

way through a problem *after* you have left the exam room but
while the exam is still on?

> Don't leave an exam early in despair. Stay and think.

Whatever you do, do not cheat! Exams are carefully super-
vised. Copying and other forms of academic dishonesty in
examinations do not go unnoticed.

Proofread completed answers

Allow yourself time to proofread your answers. Check for grammatical errors,
spelling mistakes, and unnecessary jargon. You may also find time and opportunity to add important matters you missed in the first attempt at the question.

Sensible exam technique is critical to success. If you follow the advice outlined above, you will have taken some major steps towards a distinguished exam
performance.

Multiple-choice exams

Aside from familiarity with the test material, good results in multiple-choice
exams depend, in part, on being conversant with some of the peculiarities of
this form of exam. As the following points suggest, there is much more to success in a multiple-choice exam than simply selecting (a), (b), or (c).

- Go quickly through the exam answering all those questions you can complete easily. If there is a question you find difficult, move on and return to it
  later if you have time.
- Multiple-choice options usually include a number of completely unrealistic alternatives, sometimes added by the
  examiner for comic relief. Delete those options which are
  clearly incorrect. Consider humorous responses for dele-
  tion, as they are likely to have been included as distracters.
  This will help you narrow down your choices.

> Make yourself familiar with the quirks of multiple-choice exams.

- Read all the answer options before selecting one.
- Avoid extreme answers. For example, if you were asked to state the correct
  population of New Zealand in 2006 and the options were: (a) 1.1 million
  (b) 4.1 million (c) 7.6 million (d) 23 million, you would be well advised to
  avoid option (d) as it is distinctly larger than the other three options.
- Avoid answers that include absolutes (Burdess 1991, p. 57; Northey &
  Knight 1992, p. 117). In the world in which we live, 'never', 'always', and
  'no one' are rarely true.
- Avoid answers that incorporate unfamiliar terms (Burdess 1991, p. 57;
  Northey & Knight 1992, p. 117). Examiners will sometimes use technical
  words as sirens luring you into shallow waters.

- Do not be intimidated or led astray by an emerging pattern of answers. If, for example, every answer in the first ten questions of the test appears to have been 'b' that does not mean that the next answer ought to be a 'b'. Nor, of course, does it mean that the next answer is not 'b'!
- If there appears to be no correct answer among the options provided, choose the option you judge closest to correct.
- If in real doubt about the correct answer, select the longest option. It is often more difficult for an examiner to express a correct idea in few words than it is to express an incorrect one.
- Unless you have been advised that penalties are imposed for giving incorrect answers, answer every question. If you do not know the answer, make an informed guess. If the question has four options, you have a 25% chance of getting the answer right.
- Do not 'overanalyse' a question. If you have completed a multiple-choice test and are proofreading your answers, be cautious about revising your initial response. If you are hesitant about changing your original answer to a different response, leave things alone. You probably got it right the first time. Have faith in yourself.

In the interests of the mental balance of other people sitting the exam and perhaps for your own well-being, try to avoid behaving in a way which might distract them (e.g. shaking your leg, tapping a pencil, or drumming your fingers on the desk). Depending on how stressed others in the class are, you may not survive the exam!

Oral exams

Formal oral exams are quite rare in geography and the environmental sciences and hence most people do not get the opportunity to practise them as they might a written or multiple-choice test. Partly as a result of this, the oral exam, or *viva voce*, can be quite intimidating. But if you think about it, the oral examination is simply a formalised extension of the sort of discussion you might have had with colleagues, friends, and supervisors about the subject you are studying. As such, it should not be too daunting a prospect. Remember, the examiners are real people too. In some instances, they may be quite nervous about the entire process themselves and particularly about their ability to put you at ease so that a genuine, thoughtful discussion can take place.

To prepare yourself for an oral exam, think about its likely aims. If you do not know the aims of the exam, ask your lecturer/supervisor. Generally, the examiners/discussants will want you to fill in detail which you might not have had the opportunity to include in a written paper or in your thesis. The discussants might also wish to use the *viva voce* as a teaching and learning forum. They may want to encourage you to think about alternative ways in which you might have approached your topic and to discuss those alternatives with them. If you can, try to look forward to a *viva voce* as a potentially rewarding opportunity to explore a subject about which *you* may be the best informed.

As specific advice for completing an oral examination, some of the following points may be useful.

- If the *viva voce* is about a thesis or some other work you have written, read through that work taking a few notes on its key points and otherwise refreshing your memory about it. Think about critical matters from each section that you would like to discuss. You will then be better positioned to make the *viva voce* run as you would like should the opportunity arise.
- As the date of your *viva voce* approaches, conduct a search of recent journals to see if any relevant papers have been published. Your examiners may not yet have read those papers and this will provide you with an opportunity to impress them! (Beynon 1993, p. 94)
- Enlist the help of a friend or family member who is well versed in the topic of the exam. Try to think of the sorts of things the examiner might ask you to demonstrate, and practise some brief, clear answers. The boxed section later in this chapter sets out some questions commonly asked in oral exams. In trying to make your answers to these questions clear to your learned friend or relative, you may discover areas which need further revision.
- At the exam itself, present yourself in a way which is both comfortable and suitable to the formality of the occasion. As a rule of thumb, think about the type of clothing your examiners are likely to be wearing and dress slightly more formally than they will. Your examiners will also appreciate it if you take your sunglasses off and switch off your mobile phone.
- Try to display relaxed confidence. To do this, maintain eye contact with your examiners, sit comfortably in an alert position, and do not fidget. Remember to speak clearly. Try to formulate brief but clear answers. To this end, it is useful to have considered some of the questions you might be asked before the exam begins.
- If you do not understand a question, say so. Ask to have the question rephrased. It may not be you who has the problem; it is quite possible that the question does not make sense.
- Take time to think about your answers. Do not feel obliged to rush a response.
- To give yourself a few extra moments to think about a question, you may find it helpful to repeat the question aloud—but not every time!

- In most exams, as in a discussion, you should feel free to challenge the examiners' arguments and logic, but be prepared to give consideration to their views.
- If it appears to you that the examiners have wrongly interpreted something you have said or written, let them know precisely what you meant.

BOX 9.2 COMMON QUESTIONS IN ORAL EXAMS

A number of questions appear regularly in oral exams. Give them some careful thought before the exam.

- Why did you select your research question?
- How does your work connect with existing studies? Does it say anything different? Does it confirm other work?
- How does your work fit into geography or environmental studies/management? What makes it a distinguishable part of the literature in the discipline?
- Why did you select your methodology? Are there any weaknesses in the approach you adopted?
- What are some of the sources of error in your data?
- What practical problems did you encounter? How did you overcome them?
- Are any of the findings unexpected?
- What avenues for future research does your work suggest?
- What are the particular strengths or weaknesses of your research?
- What have you learned from your research experience? What would you do differently if you had your time again?

> Before a *viva voce*, prepare your answers to questions you are most likely to be asked.

'Open book' exams

The 'open book' exam is deceptive. At first, you might think, 'What could be easier than a test into which I can take the answers'? Later—perhaps as late as during the exam itself—you may come to realise that these exams can be a trap for young players. The key lies in the fact that to deal with 'open book' exam questions as quickly and effectively as possible, you must know your subject. The 'open book' exam simply allows you access to specific examples, references, and other material which might support *your* answers to questions. You still have to interpret the question and devise an answer. *You* must produce the intellectual skeleton upon which your answer is constructed, and then place upon that the flesh of personal knowledge, example, and argument drawn from reference material. If you do not understand the background material from which the questions are drawn, you may not be able to perform as well as you should.

The following may be useful additional advice in preparing for an 'open book' exam:

> 'Take-home' and 'open book' exams require careful preparation.

• Study as you would for a 'closed book' exam.
• Prepare easily understood and accessible notes for ready reference.
• Become familiar with the texts you are planning to use. If appropriate, mark sections of texts in a way which will allow you to identify them easily (e.g. highlighter pen, sticky-paper notes). Do not mark books belonging to other people or libraries!

'Take-home' exams

While a 'take-home' exam may appear to offer you the luxury of time, preparation remains a key to success. Do not make the mistake of squandering your time trying to get organised *after* you have been given the exam paper! Not only will you be 'burning daylight' but also the preparation is likely to be hurried and inadequate. Here are some suggestions to help you prepare for a take-home exam.

Be sure to have at your disposal appropriate reference material with which you are familiar. In short, you should have read through, taken notes from, and highlighted a sufficiently large range of reference materials to allow you to complete the exam satisfactorily. Arrange all the reference material in a way which allows you to find specific items quickly (e.g. arrange materials alphabetically by author, under subject headings, by date of publication, or by some other method you find useful).

Keep to a timetable such as that shown in Table 9.4. The student in this example has used an eight-hour working day (e.g. 8 a.m.–noon, 1 p.m.–5 p.m.) to calculate the amount of time available for each exam question. Evenings might be spent proofreading answers.

Table 9.4   Example of a two-day, take-home exam time budget (i.e. about 16 working hours)

Question 1	20 marks	@ 3 hours
Question 2	30 marks	@ 4 hours
Question 3	50 marks	@ 8 hours
Total	**100 marks**	**16 hours**

If you are given 48 hours to complete an exam, you do not have to work on the questions that long. Your aim should be to produce concise, carefully considered, well-argued answers, supported with examples where appropriate. You are not meant to be writing for the entire time. Instead, think carefully and focus clearly on the questions asked.

> Set limits on the time and resources you will use in a 'take-home' exam.

If you will be writing the exam on a computer, be sure that there are sufficient supplies of paper and toner to allow you to print the paper when you finish late at night and all the shops are closed!

Take-home exams present opportunities and challenges. They provide an opportunity to write very good answers to questions. They also offer the challenge of knowing when to stop. It can be very tempting to spend too much time on the exam, gnawing on it as a dog would a bone.

Online exams

Although they are still fairly uncommon, online exams seem destined to be used more widely in geography and environmental studies. Much of the advice about preparing for and completing exams that has been set out earlier in this chapter applies to this form of exam, but there are a few peculiarities and key points that need to be considered:

* *Become familiar with your computing and testing environment.* As with any other exam, it is helpful to feel as comfortable as possible with the medium or context in which the exam will be conducted. An unfamiliar computing environment can distract you enough that you perform poorly in an exam. It might be argued too that there are more opportunities for things to go wrong in a computer-based exam than in other forms of exam. Although many of these problems are beyond your control, you can prepare yourself to respond to difficult situations. This begins by becoming familiar with the computing environment you will be using. If you are not using your own home computer, check to see if the machines you will be using are organised in ways with which you are not familiar. If they are, spend some time getting acquainted with the hardware and software. It may also be

> Make yourself comfortable with online exam environments— the computers, the passwords, the malfunctions …

possible to find a computer in a location that is quiet enough to allow you to concentrate on the exam. If practice exams are available, try them. This experience will allow you to check and confirm your access to the machine and the exam itself. It will also help you uncover and then resolve any problems that may arise before the exam. If no practice exam is available, ask if one can be made available.

* *Deal with special needs.* If you have any special needs, related perhaps to visual impairment or seating requirements, make these known to your lecturer or tutor well before the exam. It can be very difficult, if not impossible, for staff to try to accommodate individuals' specific needs as the exam is commencing.

At the very least, having these things organised ahead of time will minimise distractions and problems that might prevent you from performing well.

• *Know your user-name and password.* Most student computing facilities require that you use an account to gain access to the online exam. These accounts can be specific to each student or they can be generic, allowing each student to use the same account to log on. Be sure that you know your current and correct user-name and password. Do not assume that the account you used last year will work this year. Make sure it does. Make sure too that you enter your personal identification and password details correctly when you begin the exam. An error here might identify your answers as those of another student.

• *Know how to deal with malfunctions.* The best way to prevent a computer or software malfunction is to make sure your computer is restarted before you begin the exam. To do this you may need to arrive at the exam room early, power down the machine, wait 30 seconds and then restart the computer. Once the machine has started, it is best to not use the computer for anything until you are allowed to start the exam. If you experience a malfunction with software or hardware, record the time of receipt and content of any error messages you see on the screen and report the problem to the invigilator. If possible, do not dismiss the error message. Computer personnel will need to see the messages to resolve the problem.

• *Read instructions carefully.* It is important that you read all the instructions provided by staff and presented to you by the software. If you do not under-stand what something means, ask.

• *Disregard your neighbours' progress.* In many online exams the order in which questions are presented to students may vary. This is sometimes used as a means to prevent cheating. Do not be discouraged then if any or all of your neighbours are moving much more quickly through the exam than you. It is possible that the software has presented them with different and perhaps less difficult sections of the exam from those which you are completing.

• *Work locally. Save frequently.* When answering a free response exam question (i.e. essays or short answers), and whenever possible, it is a good idea to compose your answer using a word-processing program and to save it on your hard drive. You can then 'copy and paste' answers into the exam format/software. Avoid working from a floppy disk for this purpose. Actively editing a file from a floppy disk is very slow, and floppy disks have a notoriously high failure rate—commonly because there is not enough space on the disk for the software to store the information you want to preserve. By saving your work on your hard drive or the network, you will still have a copy of your work should the exam software fail for some reason. You must also save your work frequently. Make sure that you save about every five minutes if you are actively working on a document. Save more frequently if what you are writing is complex and difficult to reproduce; less frequently if you are not actively writing. If you are required to submit your exam answers on a floppy disk, copy them from your network or hard-drive storage space to the floppy, taking care to leave a version on the network or your hard drive—even if it means emailing a copy of your answers to yourself.

* *Keep records and submit your answers.* It is a good idea to record the number of each question you have not answered or questions you are not sure about so that you can easily go back to them. This is particularly important in multiple-choice and true–false exams. Most students complete these exams well within the allocated time and often feel impatient about searching through each exam question looking for questions that should be checked. Most exam software allows you to edit and change answers to questions until you choose to submit them for assessment. It is not unknown for students to answer all exam questions and log off without formally submitting their answers for assessment. Make sure you submit your answers!

When you finish your exam, be sure you have saved a copy of your answers (as noted above), get a printout of your work if possible, and receive some acknowledgment of your submission. This might take the form of a receipt. Finally, if the software provides you with a score, record it and keep it so that you can compare it with the final grade you receive.

Good luck!

REFERENCES AND FURTHER READING

Barass, R. 1984, *Study! A Guide to Effective Study, Revision and Examination Techniques*, Chapman & Hall, London.
Chapters 12 and 13 of this book comprehensively review steps in preparing for and completing various types of examination. Barass's book is a very helpful reference.

Beynon, R.J. 1993, *Postgraduate Study in the Biological Sciences: A Researcher's Companion*, Portland Press, London.

Burdess, N. 1991, *The Handbook of Student Skills for the Social Sciences and Humanities*, Prentice Hall, New York.
Includes two dozen useful pages on exam preparation, conduct, and review.

Clanchy, J. & Ballard, B. 1997, *Essay Writing for Students: A Practical Guide*, 3rd edn, Longman Cheshire, Melbourne.
Their chapter on exam essays includes a short discussion on ways of revising for examinations.

Committee on Scientific Writing RMIT. 1993, *Manual on Scientific Writing*, TAFE Publications, Collingwood, Victoria.
Short review of examination preparation and completion strategies included as an appendix to the main volume.

Dixon, T. 2004, *How to get a first: The essential guide to academic success*, Routledge, London.

Exams and Assessment (Study Skills series) 1992, Video Education Australia.
A 15-minute video on how to prepare for an exam, dealing with stress, and coping with the results.

Friedman, S. & Steinberg, S. 1989, *Writing and Thinking in the Social Sciences*, Prentice-Hall, Englewood Cliffs, New Jersey.
Chapter 13 discusses, in some detail, ten handy hints to help improve performance in written exams.

Hamilton, D. 1999, *Passing Exams: A Guide for Maximum Success and Minimum Stress*, Cassell, London.

Hay, I. 1996a, 'Examinations I. Preparing for an exam', *Journal of Geography in Higher Education*, vol. 20, no. 1, pp. 133–8.

Hay, I. 1996b, 'Examinations II. Completing an exam', *Journal of Geography in Higher Education*, vol. 20, no. 2, pp. 259–64.
Hay (1996a) and (1996b) are versions of the chapter presented in this book.

Hay, I. & Bull, J. 2002, 'Passing online exams', *Journal of Geography in Higher Education*, vol. 26, no. 2, pp. 239–44.
Offers an extended discussion of the material presented in this chapter on ways of succeeding in online exams.

Kneale, P. 1997, 'Maximising play time: Time management for geography students', *Journal of Geography in Higher Education*, vol. 21, no. 2, pp. 293–301.

Northey, M. & Knight, D.B. 1992, *Making Sense in Geography and Environmental Studies*, Oxford University Press, Toronto.
A short section on preparing for different types of examination is provided in chapter 12.

Orr, F. 1984, *How to Pass Exams*, George Allen & Unwin, North Sydney.
A comprehensive book on exam preparation and performance. Most emphasis is given to effective intellectual, physical, and psychological means of preparing for examinations.

Referencing and Language Matters

If the English language made any sense, a catastrophe would be an apostrophe with fur.

Doug Larson

A man will turn over half a library to make one book.

Samuel Johnson

KEY TOPICS

- What are references and why do we need them?
- The author–date (Harvard) system
- The note system
- Plagiarism, academic dishonesty, and direct quotations
- Sexism and racism in language
- Some key points on punctuation

One important convention and courtesy of academic communication is citing or acknowledging the work of those people whose ideas and phrases you have borrowed. Although this business of referencing is relatively straightforward, many people encounter difficulties with it. This chapter provides an outline of the form and practice of the two styles of referencing used most commonly in geography and environmental disciplines. The chapter also discusses the serious matters of plagiarism, and sexist and racist language before concluding with some comments on common punctuation problems.

WHAT ARE REFERENCES? WHY DO WE NEED THEM?

When you use information which has originally appeared in someone else's work, you must acknowledge clearly where you got it from. You must always make the acknowledgment in a consistent and recognisable format. Such acknowledgments are called 'references'. In your academic work you are expected to draw on evidence from, and substantiate claims with, *up-to-date, relevant,* and *reputable* sources. The *number* and *range of references* used for your work are also important.

You must cite all references to:

- acknowledge previous work conducted by other scholars
- allow the reader to verify your data
- provide information so that the reader can consult your sources independently.

You *must* clearly acknowledge your references when you *quote* (use the original source's exact words), ***paraphrase*** (express a source's ideas in different words), or *summarise* (outline the main points) information, ideas, text, data, tables, figures, or any other material which originally appeared in someone else's work. References may be to sources, such as books, journals, newspapers, maps, films, photographs, reports, electronic sites, or personal communications (e.g. letters or conversations). References must provide enough bibliographic information for your reader to be able to find your source easily. 'Bibliographic' refers to the key descriptive elements of a publication such as a book, journal article, video, or online resource. These elements include details such as author, date of publication, title, volume number, and page numbers.

There are three principal systems of referencing: the *author–date* system (sometimes called Harvard, in-text, or scientific system); the **note system** (sometimes called the **endnote** or footnote system); and the *Vancouver* system. Of the three systems, the author–date (and variants of it) is the most widely used in geography and the environmental sciences. Although it is less common, some geography lecturers and journals employ the note system. For this reason, the note system is also discussed in the pages that follow. However, because the Vancouver system is confined largely to medicine and other health-related disciplines it is not discussed here. If you need to employ this approach to acknowledging sources, consult the International Committee of Medical Journal Editors' 'Uniform requirements for manuscripts submitted to biomedical journals' (2004) for advice. Use whichever system of referencing is recommended by your lecturer and no matter which system you adopt, be sure to employ the same style throughout any single piece of work.

Most geographers and environmental scientists use the author–date referencing system.

The advice which follows is based largely on the Australian Government Publishing Service's *Style Manual for Authors, Editors and Printers* (1994), which was updated in 2002 by Snooks & Co. You are advised to consult the Snooks book if you have detailed queries which are not addressed here.

> Use one system of referencing consistently throughout a piece of work.

Despite the frequency with which electronic sources (e.g. WWW, email) are now used, there are few comprehensive, consistent, and definitive guidelines for citing electronic sources (Library of Congress 2005). The sections below include some efforts to help remedy this by suggesting formats for a wide range of contemporary sources (e.g. satellite images, electronic journals, email, software). Should you have a type of source not included below, adhere to the same fundamental principles that are used in print media referencing. In short, make sure that you provide sufficient details for a reader to be able to track down for themselves the source you are citing. Present that information in a sequence that corresponds with the information you provide for your other sources.

THE AUTHOR–DATE (HARVARD) SYSTEM

The **Harvard system** comprises two essential components, brief *in-text* references noted throughout your work, and a comprehensive *list of references* cited at the end of the work.[1] The in-text reference gives the family name of the *author(s)*, the *date* of publication, and the *page(s)* where the information or quotation can be found. The list of references gives the author's family name and forename initials, year of publication, the title of the publication, the name of the publishing house, and place of publication. These are discussed more fully below.

In-text references

The in-text reference presents a summary of bibliographic details. Take particular note of the ways in which the various references are punctuated.

- If the reference is to *one page*:
  As Bloggs (2006, p. 50) has made so clear, a significant challenge confronting geography …

- If the reference is to *several following pages*:
  Environmental management is an area of growing employment opportunity (Jones 2005, pp. 506–7).

---

1. Footnotes may be used within the author–date system to provide an aside or information supplementary to the main text. Indeed, this is an example of such a footnote. Details on the use of footnotes are provided in the section on 'Notes and note identifiers' later in this chapter.

In order to avoid disruption in the flow of the sentence the citation of author, date, and pages used is generally placed at the end of the sentence, although (as in the first example) there are occasions when it is better placed within the sentence.

- If the reference is to a *number of authors*:
Several authors (Brown 2006, p. 9; Henare 2004, p. 16; Nguyen 2005, p. 52) agree …
Note that each reference is separated by a semicolon. It is common practice to set out such lists in chronological order, reverse chronological order, or alphabetically by author name. Whatever approach you adopt, use it consistently through your work.

- If the reference is to a single text written by *two or three people*:
A recent study (Chan & D'Ettorre 2002) has shown …
It has been made clear (Brown, White & Green 2006) that …
Chan and D'Ettorre (2002) have shown that …
Note that the names are linked within parentheses by an ampersand (&) but with an 'and' if the names are incorporated within the text.

> In-text references provide summary bibliographic details only. Full details of each reference should be included in a separate list of references at the end of your work.

- If the reference is to a single text written by *more than three people*:
Ninio et al. (2005, p. 16) argue that …
The abbreviation 'et al.' is short for *et alii* meaning 'and others'. The term may be written in italics though it need not be.

- If the reference is to an *anonymously written work*:
This is apparently not the case in Thailand (*Far Eastern Economic Review* 28 Jan. 2003, p. 12).
Poughkeepsie Yearning (1963) offers fine testament to this view.
The expressions 'Anonymous' and 'Anon.' should not be used. Instead, the work's title is given.

- If the reference is to a *map*:
Low levels of precipitation are evident through much of central Australia (Division of National Mapping 2002).

- If the reference is to work written by a *committee* or an *organisation*:
CSIRO (2004, p. 41) suggests that soil degradation is of major concern to the agricultural community in Australia.
Natural disasters may present significant difficulties for residents of New Zealand (Earthquake Commission 1995, p. 12).
Occasionally, a publication will have both individual and organisational authors listed. In such cases, it is common practice to treat the individual

as author. The organisation is mentioned when giving full details in the list of references cited.

- If the reference is to *one author referred to in the writings of another*:
Motor vehicles are a major cause of noise pollution in urban areas (Hassan, in Yeo 2005, p. 219).
  Avoid such references unless tracing the original source is impossible. You are expected to find the original source yourself to ensure that the information has not been misinterpreted or misquoted by the intermediate author.

- If reference is made to information gained by means of *personal communication*:
Aspects of the theory await investigation (Wotjusiak 2006, pers. comm., 2 May).
  References to personal communications should be incorporated more fluidly into the text than in the example above and, where appropriate, should include some indication of the quoted person's claim to authority or expertise in the relevant field. For example:
In an interview I conducted on 12 January 2006, Dr Melody Jones, Director of City Services, revealed that …
  Personal communications are not usually included in the list of references, but if you have cited a number of personal communications, it may be useful to provide a separate list which provides the reader with some indication of the credibility of the people cited (i.e. some indication of their authority in the context of your work).

- If the reference is to *electronic information*:
  The style of reference provided is the same as that for individual, group, organisational, and committee authors as outlined above. The in-text reference should indicate the author's name (which may be an institution) and provide details of the year in which the reference was created or last amended (for web sites this is usually noted towards the end of a page as 'Page last updated on …').
The National Aids Information Clearinghouse (2002) guidelines give clear advice on …
The full text of David Harvey's (1989) book, *The Condition of Postmodernity*, is now available on the **World Wide Web**.
  If there is no indication of a production date, you should record this as 'undated'. For example:
Genetic engineering seems likely to have a profound influence on Australian crop production figures (Witherspoon undated).
  The in-text reference for a WWW resource should *not* include the site or page's URL. This information is only included in the reference list.

List of references

This *alphabetically* ordered (by family name of author) list provides the complete bibliographic details of all sources actually referred to in the text. By convention it does not include those sources you consulted but have not cited (a full list of *all* references consulted is known as a *bibliography*).

The following examples of correctly formatted references may be useful when you prepare your own reference lists. The examples cover a range of commonly encountered sources. Look carefully at the examples and distinguish between the various kinds of work and how each is organised and punctuated. Note that:

- the second and subsequent lines of each reference are indented
- reference lists are single-spaced but with a blank line between each entry
- article titles are given minimal capitalisation but book and journal titles are capitalised
- book and journal titles are italicised or underlined. Article and chapter titles are *not*
- article and chapter titles appear in inverted commas.

Article in a journal
Journals are those **periodicals** typically intended for academic use (Snooks & Co. 2002, p. 204). Examples include *Area, New Zealand Geographer,* and *Australian Journal of Emergency Management.* Journals commonly give greater emphasis to volume and issue number details than to their day or week of publication (which is stressed with popular magazines).

Stokes, E. 1999, 'Tauponui a Tia: an interpretation of Maori landscape and land tenure', *Asia Pacific Viewpoint,* vol. 40, no. 2, pp. 137–58.

Article in a magazine
Magazines follow a similar style as journals but the volume and issue number are replaced by details of the publication date.

Brown, A. 2006, 'Muddied waters', *Gourmet Traveller Wine,* 16 January, pp. 23–6.

If the article runs on to additional pages later in the magazine, provide all page numbers. For instance:

Loi, V. 2006, 'Tales from Perth', *Australian Traveller,* 16 January, pp. 23–8, 68.

Complete book
Blunt, A. & Wills, J. 2000, *Dissident Geographies: An Introduction to Radical Ideas and Practice,* Pearson Education, Edinburgh Gate.

Bibliographic management software (e.g. EndNote, ProCite) now makes organising and setting out references easier than ever before.

Note that all authors' family names precede their initials in a list of references. When multiple authors are listed, no comma is placed between the ampersand (&) and the preceding initial. All authors should be identified in the reference list, even if you have used 'et al.' for works with more than three authors in your in-text reference.

Book, edition other than first

Mercer, D. 2000, *A Question of Balance: Natural Resources Conflict Issues in Australia*, 3rd edn, Federation Press, Leichhardt.

Edited volume

Pickles, J. (ed.) 1995, *Ground Truth: The Social Implications of Geographic Information Systems*, Guilford Press, New York.

Most references to edited collections will, in fact, be to specific chapters within the volume rather than to the volume as a whole. For that reason, it is more usual to see references set out in the form of a 'chapter in an edited volume' (shown below).

Chapter in an edited volume

Gill, N. 1999, 'The ambiguities of wilderness', in *Australian Cultural Geographies*, ed. E. Stratford, Oxford University Press, Melbourne, pp. 135–52.

Note that the editor's family name and initials are not inverted, and that the title of the book precedes the editor's name.

Government publication

Australian Bureau of Statistics 1999, *Household and Family Projections, 1996–2021*, Cat. no. 3236.0, ABS, Canberra.

Note that there is no full stop after the 'author's' name. Because Australian Bureau of Statistics is given as the author, it can be abbreviated when it appears as the publisher.

Book in a series

Sutton, P. 1995, *Country: Aboriginal Boundaries and Land Ownership in Australia*, Monograph 3, Aboriginal History, Canberra.

Paper in proceedings

Chapple, P., Tainish, J. & Book, J. 1999, 'Coast and clean seas initiative', *Proceedings of the 9th Annual NSW Coastal Conference*, Great Lakes Shire Council, Forster, pp. 205–14.

Douglas, F. 1999, 'Sun moths in back paddock', *Balancing Conservation and Production in Grassy Landscapes, Proceedings of the Bushcare Grassy Landscapes Conference, Clare, South Australia*, 19–21 August 1999, Environment Australia, Canberra, pp. 12–21.

Note that spans of page numbers can be abbreviated, as illustrated in the first example above, but not spans of dates.

> Be sure your references are punctuated and set out correctly. Many markers (and editors) are very picky about this.

Paper in working paper series

Kitchin, R.M. 1997, 'A geography of, for, with or by disabled people: reconceptualising the position of geographer as expert', *SARU Working Paper 1*, School of Geosciences, Queen's University of Belfast, Belfast.

Thesis

Marshall, D. 1996, Putting pokies in place. A consideration of the costs and benefits of pokies since their introduction to South Australia: the case of Peterborough, BA(Hons) thesis, Flinders University, Adelaide.

Stephenson, W.J. 1999, Development of shore platforms on Kaikoura Peninsula, South Island, New Zealand, PhD thesis, University of Canterbury, Christchurch.

Note that, as a thesis is an unpublished work, its title is not put into inverted commas or italics.

Unpublished paper

Bezuijen, M.R. & Carr, G.W. 1999, Canberra nature conservation management study, Unpublished report prepared for Canberra Urban Parks and Places by Ecology Australia, Fairfield.

Fergie, D. 1992, State of racism and racism of the state, Unpublished paper presented to the Annual Conference of Museum Anthropologists, in possession of Adelaide University Library, Adelaide.

Unpublished materials come in a variety of forms (for example, letters, papers presented at meetings). Provide, in a concise way consistent with the style of other references, sufficient details for your reader to be able to gain access to the material cited.

Newspaper

Kitney, G. 1998, 'Australia to gain from nuclear shutdown', *Sydney Morning Herald*, 14–15 Nov., p. 29.

McKinley, J. 1997, 'Poor ask what they have done to deserve disasters', *Sydney Morning Herald*, 3 Dec., p. 14.

If the article has no obvious author, provide all the details in the in-text citation; there is then no requirement to put the entry in the full reference list. (Note: this applies only to newspaper articles!)

(the *Age* 28 January 2006, p. 2)

… in the *Waikato Times* (14 February 2006, p. 12)

Media release

Dunn, K. 2000, *The geography of racism*, media release, University of New South Wales, 16 October.

Drifter, A. (Minister for Marine Affairs) 2004, *Coastwatch initiative not at sea*, media release, Parliament House, Wellington, 19 March.

Thwaites, J. (Minister for the Environment, Victoria) 2005, *Wild dog management group members appointed*, media release, 30 July.

Video/television broadcast/movie

Vietnam: Impact of Aid on a Developing Nation (video recording) 2005, Classroom Video and AusAID, French's Forest, NSW.

Shaking the Tree (motion picture) 2006, Big Picture Releases, Sydney.

Television programs are identified in much the same way as video recordings. It is helpful to include the precise date of broadcast and the name of the broadcasting network.

The Tree Man from Hamilton (video recording) 1999, Landline, broadcast 21 September 1999, ABC Television, Canberra.

Map

References to maps are usually set out in the following format:

Mapping organisation and Date, *Map title*, Edition number (if appropriate), Scale, Series.

For example:

Department of Lands, New South Wales 1996, *Wollongong*, 5th edn, 1:50 000, Topographic series.

Aerial photograph

An incorrectly formatted reference list reflects poorly on your work.

Aerial photographs can follow a similar referencing pattern to maps, although it is helpful to include a 'medium of the source' statement that makes it clear that the reference is to aerial photography. In some cases the photograph will not have a formal title describing its location. If this is the case, describe the general location as best you can and present that as the photograph's title. The general format for a reference to an aerial photograph is:

Custodian, State and Year of Photography, *Title* (may be described by photograph's general location), Scale, (medium of the source), Survey number, Frame number.

For example:

DEHAA (Department of Environment, Heritage and Aboriginal Affairs), South Australia 1982, *Robe*, 1:40 000, (aerial photography), Survey 2814, Frame 187.

Satellite imagery

The form of reference is usefully set out as:

Custodian and Year of imagery, *Title* (may include or be made up of a reference to platform, sensor type, and location), (medium of the source), Date, Path, Row.

For example:

ACRES (Australian Centre for Remote Sensing) 2000, *Landsat, 7 ETM+ image of South Australia* (satellite imagery), 19 January, Path 97, Row 83.

Airborne imagery

References to airborne images can be set out in the following form:

Custodian and Year of imagery, *Title* (may include sensor type and location), (medium of the source), Date of imagery, Image centre co-ordinates.

For example:

HyVista Corporation, Australia 2000, *HyMap image of Brookfield, South Australia*, (airborne imagery), 3 February, 34° 46′ S, 139° 45′ E.

Electronic journal article (from a fulltext database, journal collection, or WWW)[2]

A fulltext database is one that provides the complete text of a document. References to these and to electronic journal articles are usefully set out in the following format:

Author's family name, Initial(s). Document or article date, 'Title of document or article', *Title of Complete Work* (medium of the source), vol. [if available], no. [if available], Available: <name of database producer/name of database and/or protocol> (date of access).

Below are some examples:

---

2. There are no commonly accepted protocols for acknowledging electronic sources. The guidance that follows sets out some preliminary ideas that ought to cover most referencing situations. If you find yourself in 'uncharted territory', provide as much information as you believe someone else might require to gain access to the reference you are using. Set the citation out in a way that follows the general pattern of the author–date system.

Arlinghaus, S.L. 2001, 'Maps and decisions: Allen's Creek Flood Plain, Opportunity or Disaster', *Solstice: An Electronic Journal of Geography and Mathematics* (online), vol. 12, no. 1, Available: <http://www-personal.umich.edu/~sarhaus/solstice/sum01/flyer.html> (24 August 2005).

Monmonier, M. 2001, 'Where should map history end?', *Mercator's World* (online), vol. 6, no. 3, Available: Gale Group/Expanded ASAP (9 July 2001).

Delph-Janiurek, T. 1999, 'Sounding gender(ed): Vocal performances in English university teaching spaces', *Gender, Place and Culture* (online), vol. 6, no. 2, pp. 137–53, Available: Bell + Howell/Proquest (10 July 2001).

Page numbers are included in the Delph-Janiurek example, as the article is available in PDF format (i.e. a photographic image of the original document).

Richards, N. 1999, 'Maps: are they instruments of power?', *GEOView The Journal of GEOS* (online), Available: <http://www.ssn.flinders.edu.au/geog/geos/RICHARDS.htm> (18 August 2005).

Other WWW documents

References to WWW documents will typically be set out in the following format:

Author's family name, Initial(s) [or name of organisation responsible for the WWW page] and Document date, *Title of Document*, Name of publishing agency [if appropriate and if it does not repeat author's name], (medium of the source), Available: <Protocol and address> (date of access).

Here are some specific examples:

Australian Conservation Foundation 2001, *Anti-Nuclear Campaign* (online), Available: <http://www.acfonline.org.au/campaigns/antinuc/antinucintro.htm> (4 June 2001).

Bureau of Meteorology 2004, *Climate Averages for Darwin Airport*, Commonwealth of Australia (online), Available: <http://www.bom.gov.au/climate/averages/tables/cw_014015.shtml> (24 August 2005).

Smith, J. 2005, *John Smith's Home Page* (online), Available: <http://www.unibase.com/local/wmtk/template/example2/homepage.htm> (24 August 2005).

Weathersite Inc. 2005, *International Time Conversion Table* (online), Available: <http://www.weathersite.com/convINTtime.html> (24 August 2005).

Electronic sources present some referencing challenges. Be sure to provide sufficient information about them to allow someone else to find the source.

If the page or site has no author or no date, set the reference out as follows:

The Cook Islands Undated (online), Available: <http://www.ck/> (7 July 2001).

You should be wary of sites with no acknowledged or clear author. Think critically about the bases you have for believing what you are reading. Is the source credible? Why? For guidance on assessing web sites and web pages, see Table 1.1 of this book.

CD-ROM
Material on a CD-ROM is dealt with in much the same way as that for comparable hardcopy publications such as books or journals, except that a CD-ROM statement is inserted after the CD's title. For example:

Pawson, E. 1999, 'Remaking places', in *Explorations in Human Geography: Encountering Place* (CD-ROM), eds R. Le Heron, L. Murphy, P. Forer & M. Goldstone, Oxford University Press, Auckland.

Email, discussion lists, and newsgroups
These can be set out in the following format:

Author's family name, Initial(s). <author's email address[3]> Message year, 'Subject line from message' (medium of the source), Description of message or statement of list name (if appropriate), <List or recipient address>, date of message.

Some examples are:

Thomson, K. <k.thomson@massive.com.au> 2005, 'Historical Geographies of South Australia' (email), IAG-list, <iag-list@ssn.flinders.edu.au>, 9 April.

Brown, T. <tim.brown@hellfire.com> 2006, 'Job opening here' (email), Personal email to Melanie Smith, <m.smith@monastic.com.au>, 3 April.

Software programs and video games
Try setting these out as follows:

Author's family name, Initial(s) (or corporate author) and Date, *Title of program*, Version, Publisher, City [if available].

Some examples are:

Adobe Systems 2001, *Acrobat*, v. 5.0, Adobe Systems, San Jose, California.

Electronic Arts 2000, *SimCity 3000 Unlimited*, Electronic Arts.

Multiple entries by same author
If you have cited two or more works written by the same author they should be listed in chronological order by date of publication. If they were written in the same year, add lower case letters to the year of publication in both the reference list *and* the text to distinguish one publication from another (for example, 1987a, 1987b). List the same-year publications alphabetically according to the initial letters of significant words in the reference's title, and assign letters

---
3. Email addresses need not be underlined, but you will find that many word-processing packages make this unavoidable.

accordingly. The following example illustrates both same-year publications and same-author publications.

Lam, R. 2005a, *A Digest of Water Weeds in South Australia*, Bastian Publishers, Adelaide.

—— 2005b, 'Water weeds in South Australia', *Journal of Water Science*, vol. 66, no. 4, pp. 6–18.

—— 2006, 'Water weed hazards in New Zealand', *Australian and New Zealand Journal of Water Resources*, vol. 13, no. 3, pp. 135–68.

As the example above illustrates, where more than one reference by an author is included, the author's name can be replaced by a two-em rule in subsequent references.

A completed reference list noting some of the sources listed above and prepared according to the Harvard system would look like this:

BOX 10.1 EXAMPLE OF A COMPLETED REFERENCE LIST (HARVARD)

References

Australian Bureau of Statistics 1999, *Household and Family Projections, 1996–2021*, Cat. no. 3236.0, ABS, Canberra.

Australian Conservation Foundation 2001, *Anti-Nuclear Campaign* (online), Available: <http://www.acfonline.org.au/campaigns/antinuc/antinucintro.htm> (4 June 2001).

Bezuijen, M.R. & Carr, G.W. 1999, Canberra Nature Conservation Management Study, Unpublished report prepared for Canberra Urban Parks and Places by Ecology Australia, Fairfield.

> Set your reference list out in alphabetical order by author.

Blunt, A. & Wills, J. 2000, *Dissident Geographies: An Introduction to Radical Ideas and Practice*, Pearson Education, Edinburgh Gate.

Chapple, P., Tainish, J. & Book, J. 1999, 'Coast and clean seas initiative', *Proceedings of the 9th Annual NSW Coastal Conference*, Great Lakes Shire Council, Forster, pp. 205–14.

Department of Lands, New South Wales 1996, *Wollongong*, 5th edn, 1:50 000, Topographic series.

Dunn, K. 2000, *The geography of racism*, media release, University of New South Wales, 16 October.

Electronic Arts 2000, *SimCity 3000 Unlimited*, Electronic Arts.

Gill, N. 1999, 'The ambiguities of wilderness', in *Australian Cultural Geographies*, ed. E. Stratford, Oxford University Press, Melbourne, pp. 135–52.

Kitchin, R.M. 1997, 'A geography of, for, with or by disabled people: reconceptualising the position of geographer as expert', *SARU Working Paper 1*, School of Geosciences, Queen's University of Belfast, Belfast.

Kitney, G. 2006, 'Australia to gain from nuclear shutdown', *Sydney Morning Herald*, 14 Jan., p. 29.

Lam, R. 2005a, *A Digest of Water Weeds in South Australia*, Bastian Publishers, Adelaide.

—— 2005b, 'Water weeds in South Australia', *Journal of Water Science*, vol. 66, no. 4, pp. 6–18.

—— 2006, 'Water weed hazards in New Zealand', *Australian and New Zealand Journal of Water Resources*, vol. 13, no. 3, pp. 135–68.

Marshall, D. 1996, Putting pokies in place. A consideration of the costs and benefits of pokies since their introduction to South Australia: the case of Peterborough, BA(Hons) thesis, Flinders University, Adelaide.

Mercer, D. 2000, *A Question of Balance: Natural Resources Conflict Issues in Australia*, 3rd edn, Federation Press, Leichhardt.

Monmonier, M. 2001, 'Where should map history end?', *Mercator's World* (online), vol. 6, no. 3, Available: Gale Group/Expanded ASAP (9 July 2001).

Pawson, E. 1999, 'Remaking places', in *Explorations in Human Geography: Encountering Place* (CD-ROM), eds R. Le Heron, L. Murphy, P. Forer & M. Goldstone, Oxford University Press, Auckland.

Richards, N. 1999, 'Maps: are they instruments of power?', *GEOView The Journal of GEOS* (online), Available: <http://www.ssn.flinders.edu.au/geog/geos/RICHARDS.htm> (18 August 2005).

Stokes, E. 1999, 'Tauponui a Tia: an interpretation of Maori landscape and land tenure', *Asia Pacific Viewpoint*, vol. 40, no. 2, pp. 137–58.

Sutton, P. 1995, *Country: Aboriginal Boundaries and Land Ownership in Australia*, Monograph 3, Aboriginal History, Canberra.

Thomson, K. <k.thomson@massive.com.au> 2005, 'Historical Geographies of South Australia' (email), IAG-list, <iag-list@ssn.flinders.edu.au>, 9 April.

Vietnam: Impact of Aid on a Developing Nation (video recording) 1995, Classroom Video and AusAID, French's Forest.

THE NOTE SYSTEM

This system of referencing provides your reader with note or numerical references to a series of footnotes or a list of endnotes. As described below, these notes set out the bibliographic details of each reference cited. For that reason, you (and your lecturer) may consider it unnecessary to include a consolidated list of references at the end of your work. Including a bibliography is a matter of choice in the note system. However, it is worth noting that for the reader of your work, a bibliography can certainly be helpful for locating specific references you have used.

In-text references, footnotes, and endnotes

At each point in the text where you have drawn upon someone else's work, or immediately following a direct quotation, place a superior or superscript numeral (e.g. ³). This refers the reader to full reference details provided either as a *footnote* (at the bottom of the page) or as an *endnote* (at the end of the document/chapter). If you refer to the same source seven times, there will be seven separate note identifiers within the text which relate to that source. You must also provide seven endnotes or footnotes. This practice is sometimes simplified by providing full bibliographic details in the first endnote/footnote and abbreviated details in the subsequent notes (AGPS 1994, p. 168).

The second and subsequent references to a source do not need to be as comprehensive as the first, but they should leave your reader in no doubt as to the precise identity of the reference (e.g. if there are two books by the same author, you will need to provide sufficient detail for the reader to work out which text you are noting). In some disciplines Latin abbreviations such as **ibid.** (from *ibidem*, meaning 'in the same place'), op. cit. (from *opere citato*, meaning 'in the work cited'), and loc. cit. (from *loco citato*, meaning 'in the place cited') are used as part of that abbreviation process, although this practice is far less common today than it was in the past. If your lecturer wishes you to use these Latin abbreviations within your references he or she will explain them to you. Alternatively, Snooks & Co. (2002, pp. 214–15) provide helpful guidance.

Note that:

• the first endnoted or footnoted reference to a work must provide your readers with all the bibliographic information they might need to find the work
• the reference is indented from the note number so that readers can quickly identify the note they are looking for
• article titles are given minimal capitalisation but book and journal titles are capitalised
• book and journal titles are italicised or underlined. Article and chapter titles are not
• article and chapter titles appear in inverted commas
• the appropriate page number(s) for the material being cited should be included in each note. The bibliography will record the full page range of any article or chapter drawn from a larger work (e.g. edited collection, journal).

Article in journal

1   E. Stokes, 'Tauponui a Tia: An interpretation of Maori landscape and land tenure', *Asia Pacific Viewpoint*, vol. 40, no. 2, 1999, p. 139.

Article in a magazine

2   A. Brown, 'Muddied waters', *Gourmet Traveller Wine*, 16 January 2005, pp. 23–6.

3   Loi, V. 2006, 'Tales from Perth', *Australian Traveller*, 16 January 2005, pp. 23–8, 68.

The second example shows what to do if the article runs on to later pages in the magazine.

Complete book

4   A. Blunt & J. Wills, *Dissident Geographies: An Introduction to Radical Ideas and Practice*, Pearson Education, Edinburgh Gate, 2000, p. 102.

Book, edition other than first

5   D. Mercer, *A Question of Balance: Natural Resources Conflicts in Australia*, 3rd edn, Federation Press, Leichhardt, 2000.

Edited volume

6   J. Pickles (ed.), *Ground Truth: The Social Implications of Geographic Information Systems*, Guilford Press, New York, 1995.

Most references to edited collections will, in fact, be to specific chapters within the volume rather than to the volume as a whole. For that reason, it is more usual to see references set out in the form of a 'chapter in an edited volume' (shown below).

Chapter in an edited volume

7   N. Gill, 'The ambiguities of wilderness', in *Australian Cultural Geographies*, ed. E. Stratford, Oxford University Press, Melbourne, 1999, p. 55.

Government publication

8   Australian Bureau of Statistics, *Household and Family Projections, 1996–2021*, Cat. no. 3236.0, ABS, Canberra, 1994.

Book in a series

9   P. Sutton, *Country: Aboriginal Boundaries and Land Ownership in Australia*, Monograph 3, Aboriginal History Monograph Series, Canberra, 1995, pp. 13–14.

> As you are preparing your work, keep full details of all the references you consult. This will make preparing a reference list easy.

Paper in proceedings

10   P. Chapple, J. Tainish & J. Book, 'Coast and clean seas initiative', *Proceedings of the 9th Annual NSW Coastal Conference*, Great Lakes Shire Council, Forster, 1999, pp. 205–14.

11   F. Douglas, 'Sun moths in back paddock', *Balancing Conservation and Production in Grassy Landscapes, Proceedings of the Bushcare Grassy Landscapes Conference*,

Clare, South Australia, 19–21 August 1999, Environment Australia, Canberra, 1999, p. 15.

Thesis

12   D. Marshall, Putting pokies in place. A consideration of the costs and benefits of pokies since their introduction to South Australia: The case of Peterborough, BA(Hons) thesis, Flinders University, Adelaide, 1996, p. 61.

13   W.J. Stephenson, Development of shore platforms on Kaikoura Peninsula, South Island, New Zealand, PhD thesis, University of Canterbury, Christchurch, 1999, pp. 213–15.

Unpublished paper

14   M.R. Bezuijen & G.W. Carr, Canberra nature conservation management study, Unpublished report prepared for Canberra Urban Parks and Places by Ecology Australia, Fairfield, 1999, p. 4.

15   D. Fergie, State of racism and racism of the state, Unpublished paper presented to the Annual Conference of Museum Anthropologists, in possession of Adelaide University Library, Adelaide, 1992, p. 1.

Newspaper

16   G. Kitney, 'Australia to gain from nuclear shutdown', *Sydney Morning Herald,* 14–15 Nov. 1998, p. 29.

17   J. McKinley, 'Poor ask what they have done to deserve disasters', *Sydney Morning Herald,* 3 Dec. 1997, p. 14.

If the article has no obvious author, provide full bibliographic details in the text only:

(the *Age* 28 January 2006, p. 2)

… in the *Waikato Times* (14 February 2006, p. 12)

Media release

Aside from the location of author initials and year of publication, media releases are presented in the same way as set out under the author–date system:

18   K. Dunn, *The geography of racism,* media release, University of New South Wales, 16 October 2000.

19   A. Drifter (Minister for Marine Affairs), *Coastwatch initiative not at sea,* media release, Parliament House, Wellington, 19 March 2004.

20   J. Thwaites (Minister for the Environment, Victoria), *Wild dog management group members appointed,* media release, 30 July 2005.

Video/movie

21 *Vietnam: Impact of Aid on a Developing Nation* (video recording) 1995, Classroom Video and AusAID, French's Forest, NSW.

22 *Shaking the Tree* (motion picture) 1997, Big Picture Releases, Sydney.

Television programs are identified in much the same way as video recordings, except that the precise date of broadcast and the name of the broadcasting network should be included:

23 *The Tree Man from Hamilton* (video recording) Landline, broadcast 21 September 1999, ABC Television, Canberra.

Map

References to maps are usually set out in the following format:

Mapping organisation, *Map title*, Edition number (if appropriate), Scale, Series, Date.

For example:

24 Department of Lands, New South Wales, *Wollongong*, 3rd edn, 1:50 000, Topographic series, 1996.

Aerial photograph

Aerial photographs can follow a similar referencing pattern to maps, although it can be helpful to include a medium of the source statement that makes it clear that the reference is to aerial photography. In some cases the photograph will not have a formal title describing its location. If this is the case, describe the general location as best you can and present that as the photograph's title:

Custodian, State, *Title* (may be described by photograph's general location), Scale, (medium of the source), Survey number, Frame number, Year of Photography.

For example:

25 DEHAA (Department of Environment, Heritage and Aboriginal Affairs), South Australia, *Robe*, 1:40 000, (aerial photography), Survey 2814, Frame 187, 1982.

Satellite imagery

The form of reference is usefully set out as:

Custodian, *Title* (may include or be made up of a reference to platform, sensor type, and location), (medium of the source), Date, Path, Row.

For example:

26 ACRES (Australian Centre for Remote Sensing), *Landsat, 7 ETM+ image of South Australia* (satellite imagery), 19 January 2000, Path 97, Row 83.

Airborne imagery

References to airborne images can be set out in the following form:

Custodian, *Title* (may include sensor type and location), (medium of the source), Date of imagery, Image centre co-ordinates.

For example:

27 HyVista Corporation, Australia, *HyMap image of Brookfield, South Australia* (airborne imagery), 3 February 2000, 34° 46′ S, 139° 45′ E.

Electronic journal article (from a fulltext database, journal collection, or WWW)[4]

A fulltext database is one that provides the complete text of a document. References to these and to electronic journal articles are usefully set out in the following format:

Author's initial(s) Family name, 'Title of document or article', *Title of complete work*, (medium of the source), vol. [if available], no. [if available], page numbers [if appropriate], Document or article date, Available: <name of database producer/ name of database and/or protocol> (date of access).

Below are some examples:

28 S.L. Arlinghaus, 'Maps and decisions: Allen's Creek Flood Plain, Opportunity or Disaster', *Solstice: An Electronic Journal of Geography and Mathematics* (online), vol. 12, no. 1, 2001, Available: <http://www-personal.umich.edu/~sarhaus/solstice/ sum01/flyer.html> (24 August 2005).

29 M. Monmonier, 'Where should map history end?', *Mercator's World* (online), vol. 6, no. 3, 2001, Available: Gale Group/Expanded ASAP (9 July 2001).

30 T. Delph-Janiurek, 'Sounding gender(ed): Vocal performances in English university teaching spaces', Gender, Place and Culture (online), vol. 6, no. 2, 1999, pp. 137–53, Available: Bell + Howell/Proquest (10 July 2001).

Page numbers are included in the example above, as the article is available in PDF format (i.e. a photographic image of the original document).

> Make sure all your references—and particularly WWW sources—are credible.

31 N. Richards, 'Maps: are they instruments of power?', *GEOView The Journal of GEOS* (online), 1999, Available: <http://www. ssn.flinders.edu.au/geog/geos/RICHARDS.htm> (18 August 2005).

---

4. As noted in an earlier footnote, there are no commonly accepted protocols for acknowledging electronic sources. The following guidance sets out some preliminary ideas that ought to cover most referencing situations. If you find yourself in 'uncharted territory' provide as much information as you believe someone else might require to gain access to the reference you are using. Set the citation out in a way that follows the general pattern of the note system.

Other WWW documents

References to WWW documents will typically be set out in the following format:

Author's initial(s) Family name [or name of organisation responsible for the WWW page], *Title of document*, Name of publishing agency [if appropriate and if it does not repeat author's name], (medium of the source), Document date, Available: <Protocol and address> (date of access).

Here are some specific examples:

32   Australian Conservation Foundation, *Anti-Nuclear Campaign* (online), 2001, Available: <http://www.acfonline.org.au/campaigns/antinuc/antinucintro.htm> (4 June 2001).

33   Bureau of Meteorology, *Climate Averages for Darwin Airport*, Commonwealth of Australia (online), 2005, Available: <http://www.bom.gov.au/climate/averages/ tables/cw_014015.shtml> (24 August 2005).

34   J. Smith, *John Smith's Home Page* (online), 2001, Available: <http://www.unibase. com/local/wmtk/template/example2/homepage.htm> (7 August 2001).

35   Weathersite Inc, *International Time Conversion Table* (online), 2001, Available: <http://www.weathersite.com/convINTtime.html> (9 July 2001).

If the page or site has no author or date, set the reference out as follows:

36   *The Cook Islands* (online). Undated, Available: <http://www.ck/> (9 July 2001).

You should be wary of sites with no acknowledged or clear author. Think critically about the bases you have for believing what you are reading. Is the source credible? Why?

CD-ROM

Material on a CD-ROM is dealt with in much the same way as that for comparable hardcopy publications, such as books or journals, except that a CD-ROM statement is inserted after the CD's title. For example:

37   E. Pawson, 'Remaking places', in *Explorations in Human Geography: Encountering Place* (CD-ROM), eds R. Le Heron, L. Murphy, P. Forer & M. Goldstone, Oxford University Press, Auckland, 1999.

Email, discussion lists, and newsgroups

These can be set out in the following format:

Author's initial(s) Family name, <author's email address>, 'Subject line from message' (medium of the source), List name (if appropriate), <List or recipient address>, date of message.

Some examples are:

38   K. Thomson, <k.thomson@massimo.com.au>, 'Historical Geographies of South Australia' (email), IAG-list, <iag-list@ssn.flinders.edu.au>, 9 April 2005.

39   T. Brown, <tim.brown@hellfire.com>, 'Job opening here' (email), Personal email to Melanie Smith, <m.smith@monastic.com.au>, 3 April 2006.

Software programs and video games

Try setting these out as follows:

Author's initial(s) Family name, (or corporate author), Date, *Title of program*, Version, Publisher, Place of publication [if available].

Some examples are:

40   Adobe Systems, *Acrobat*, v. 5.0, Adobe Systems, San Jose, California, 2001.

41   Electronic Arts, *SimCity 3000 Unlimited*, Electronic Arts, 2000.

Second and subsequent references to a source

Second and subsequent references to a source do not need to be as comprehensive as the initial reference. They must simply provide the reader with an unambiguous indication of the source of the material. For example:

1   P. Carter, *Environmental Management for Beginners*, Green Publishing, Darwin, 1995, p. 56.

2   *Age*, 19 Feb. 2002, p. 7.

3   *The Creature from the Black Lagoon* (motion picture) 1997, Scary Movie Releases, Los Angeles.

4   Carter, *Environmental Management for Beginners*, p. 12.

BIBLIOGRAPHY

The bibliography at the end of a work using the note system of referencing includes all the works consulted irrespective of whether they are cited within the text. The bibliography is traditionally set out in alphabetical order according to authors' family names to make it easier for the reader to find the full details of sources you have cited in the text. The bibliography contains the same information about the works cited as the footnotes or endnotes but it is customary to place the author's family name first (rather than their initials, which appear first in the notes).

A completed bibliography noting some of the sources listed above and prepared according to the note system would look like this:

BOX 10.2 EXAMPLE OF A COMPLETED BIBLIOGRAPHY (NOTE SYSTEM)

Bibliography

ACRES (Australian Centre for Remote Sensing), *Landsat, 7 ETM+ image of South Australia* (satellite imagery), 19 January 2000, Path 97, Row 83.

Adobe Systems, *Acrobat*, v. 5.0, Adobe Systems, San Jose, California, 2001.

Bezuijen, M.R. & Carr, G.W. Canberra nature conservation management study, Unpublished report prepared for Canberra Urban Parks and Places by Ecology Australia, Fairfield, 1999.

Brown, A. 'Muddied waters', *Gourmet Traveller Wine*, 16 January 2005, pp. 23-6.

Brown, T. <tim.brown@hellfire.com>, 'Job opening here' (email), Personal email to Melanie Smith, <m.smith@monastic.com.au>, 3 April 2006.

Department of Lands, New South Wales, *Wollongong*, 3rd edn, 1:50 000, Topographic series, 1996.

Douglas, F. 'Sun moths in back paddock', *Balancing Conservation and Production in Grassy Landscapes, Proceedings of the Bushcare Grassy Landscapes Conference, Clare, South Australia*, 19–21 August 1999, Environment Australia, Canberra, 1999, pp. 12–21.

Gill, N. 'The ambiguities of wilderness', in *Australian Cultural Geographies*, ed. E. Stratford, Oxford University Press, Melbourne, 1999, pp. 135–52.

Monmonier, M. 'Where should map history end', *Mercator's World* (online), vol. 6, no. 3, 2001, Available: Gale Group/Expanded ASAP (9 July 2001).

Pawson, E. 'Remaking places', in *Explorations in Human Geography: Encountering Place* (CD-ROM), eds R. Le Heron, L. Murphy, P. Forer & M. Goldstone, Oxford University Press, Auckland, 1999.

Stokes, E. 'Tauponui a Tia: An interpretation of Maori landscape and land tenure', *Asia Pacific Viewpoint*, vol. 40, no. 2, 1999, pp. 137–58.

Thomson, K. <k.thomson@massive.com.au>, 'Historical Geographies of South Australia' (email), IAG-list, <iag-list@ssn.flinders.edu.au>, 9 April 2005.

Weathersite Inc, *International Time Conversion Table* (online), 2001, Available: <http://www.weathersite.com/convINTtime.html> (9 July 2001).

NOTES AND NOTE IDENTIFIERS

Sometimes you may wish to let your reader know more about a matter discussed in your essay or report but believe that extra information is peripheral to the central message you are trying to convey. An indication to your reader that this supplementary information exists may be provided within the text through the use of note identifiers, such as symbols (e.g. *, §, ¶, ‡), or preferably superscript numbers (e.g. [5]). If you are using the numerical system of referencing, these notes should be incorporated into the sequence of your references and should not stand apart from it. If you are using the Harvard system, these notes will be either at the bottom of the relevant pages or at the end of the document (before the list of references) in a separate section headed 'Notes'.

PLAGIARISM AND ACADEMIC DISHONESTY

Correct referencing is an important academic and professional courtesy. Failure to fully acknowledge sources of ideas, phrases, text, data, diagrams, and other materials is regarded widely as a significant transgression of intellectual etiquette. It may lead to the imposition of severe penalties (e.g. expulsion from a subject or from university) for plagiarism.

Plagiarism (from the Latin word for 'kidnapper' (Mills 1994, p. 263)) is a form of academic dishonesty involving the use of someone else's words or ideas as if they are your own. Plagiarism may occur as a result of deliberate and deceptive misuse of another person's work or as the result of ignorance or inexperience about the correct way to acknowledge other work. Plagiarism can take a number of forms including:

> Plagiarism is regarded very seriously by all universities.

- presenting substantial extracts from books, articles, theses, other published or unpublished works (such as working papers, seminar or conference papers, internal reports, computer software, lecture notes or tapes, numerical calculations and data), or the work of other students, without clearly indicating the origin of those extracts by means of quotation marks and references
- using very close paraphrasing of sentences or whole paragraphs without due acknowledgment in the form of references to the original work
- quoting directly from a source and failing to indicate that the material is a direct quote.

Academic dishonesty takes other forms, too, and may include:

- fabricating or falsifying data, or the results of laboratory, field, or other work
- accepting assistance from another person in a piece of assessed individual work, except in accordance with approved study and assessment provisions
- giving assistance, including providing work to be copied, to a person undertaking a piece of assessed individual work, except in accordance with approved study and assessment provisions
- submitting the same piece of work for more than one topic unless the lecturers have indicated that this procedure is acceptable for the specific piece of work in question.

Burkill and Abbey (2004) suggest some useful ways to help avoid plagiarism in your work. First, make it a habit to record all bibliographic details on notes from your reading and on photocopied articles and chapters. Second, and similarly, keep full bibliographic details of all material you obtain from the World Wide Web—not just the URL. Third, ensure that you provide a full list of references at the end of your written work.

Universities regard academic dishonesty as a very serious matter and will usually impose severe penalties. New technologies to detect plagiarism are being refined (e.g. EVE, MOSS, Tunitin.com). Many universities do not regard ignorance of what constitutes plagiarism as an excuse. So do take the time to become familiar with referencing procedures.

BOX 10.3 THINKING ABOUT PLAGIARISM

Q:1 Michelle has found some really relevant information from the journal, *Geographical Research*. She copies out a couple of sentences word for word, includes quotation marks and the reference. Is this the work of a plagiarist?

Q:2 Phil is searching the Internet for inspiration for his essay on 'Flooding in New Zealand's Bay of Plenty'. He stumbles across a web site that contains essays written by other students, and finds an essay that is very similar to the title he's been given. He decides to use some of the main ideas in his essay without mentioning where they came from, implying that they are his own ideas. Do you think this is plagiarism?

Q:3 You are working in the Environmental Sciences lab. It's all going well but then some of the equipment breaks. It will now take ages to get the last batch of results. Your friend did the same experiment last week and offers to give you their results. Would just using their results constitute plagiarism?

Q:4 A group of four students has worked together on a fieldwork project and they have each been asked to submit an individual account of the work as an assignment. Three of the students submit work with whole sections that are almost identical. Is this plagiarism?

Q:5 Joe is in a mess. He waits until the very final week that a major assignment is due before he gets down to it. He rather manically grabs some books on planning and constructs a quite substantial amount of his project by piecing together sections from different sources. In-text references to the original sources are given and he uses his own words to link the sections together. Do you think this is plagiarism?

Q:6 A geography student discovers that two of her classmates who are international students are copying a chapter of a book to be submitted as a semester assignment. When she confronts them, she discovers they do not believe that they are doing anything wrong. They claim that in their home country copying (without attribution) for such assignments is acceptable. What do you think?

Adapted from: Burkill & Abbey (2004, p. 441) and Preston (2001, p. 102)

If you have any queries about plagiarism that are not resolved in this book, have a look at Burkill and Abbey's (2004) paper on avoiding plagiarism; consult a good reference style manual, such as Snook & Co. (2002); or ask your lecturer for advice.

SEXISM AND RACISM IN LANGUAGE

You may remember from the chapter on essays that through writing we can shape the world in which we live. By using sexist or racist language in our writing and speaking we may unwittingly be contributing to those unacceptable forms of discrimination in society. In consequence, as you prepare an essay, report, or talk, try to avoid sexist and racist terminology and ideas. When you have completed your work read through it, ensuring that your language does not unkindly or unfairly discriminate against people. In doing the exercise you may also learn a little about your own attitudes.

Sexist language

Language may be sexist in a number of ways (AGPS 1994, pp. 121–35; Eichler 1991, pp. 136–7; Miller & Swift 1981):

- *use of false generics*—using words which refer to one sex when both are being discussed, or which encompass women and men when reference is being made to one sex only, e.g. talking about 'parents' when only mothers are being considered
- *use of 'man'* in compounds, verbs, and idioms, e.g. workman, manhole, manning the ship, man and the environment
- *poor use of pronouns* e.g. the use of he, she, him, his, or her to refer to any unspecified person or thing which may be male, female, or neither (such as a ship, hurricane, or country)

Reflect critically on the language you are using to make sure it is neither sexist nor racist.

- *trivialisation*—usually sees women's activities denigrated and often implies that women behave more irrationally and emotionally than men, e.g. women 'bicker' whereas men 'disagree'; 'office girl' compared with 'filing clerk'

- *stereotyping*—characterising men or women in ways which emphasise stereotypical characteristics, e.g. men depicted as unemotional, uncaring, clumsy; women depicted as emotional, passive, and nimble
- *generalisation*—characterising both men and women on the basis of statements which apply to only women or men, e.g. an author writing satirically about the US South once said: 'Who are these people? What are they like? Do they have any pastimes besides fighting, hunting, drinking and writing novels? Do they really sleep with their sisters and bay at the moon?' The paragraph might have been repaired as: 'Do the men really sleep with their sisters and bay at the moon? Do the women wear crinolines and stash their whiskey behind the camellias?' (Miller & Swift 1980, p. 48)
- *parallel/nonparallel treatment* in nonparallel/parallel situations—this sometimes takes the form of women having their role defined through their relationship with a man, e.g. 'man and wife', 'Mrs Smith, wife of famous Formula 1 driver, George Smith'. Less commonly the reverse applies.

Racist language

Racism is the discriminatory treatment of people on the basis of their race, ethnicity, or nationality. It has its basis in a dichotomy between an 'in-group' and an 'out-group'. Language may be racist in a number of different ways (AGPS 1994, p. 135):

- *in-group as norm; out-group as deviation*—the ethnic status of the in-group is rarely mentioned whereas that of out-group members is. This often happens in news headlines, e.g. 'Greek takes Queensland political position'; 'Japanese gang threat'
- *in-group as individuals; out-group as group*—people in the in-group are often described in terms which reflect their individuality (e.g. educational status, age) whereas members of the out-group have their identity outlined only in terms of association with that group
- *in-group portrayed positively; out-group portrayed negatively*, e.g. 'whingeing Pom'; 'Kiwi ingenuity'; 'Aussie battler'
- *in-group uses euphemisms to express actions with regard to out-groups*, e.g. 'detainment' of Asian refugees in Australia when, in fact, they appear to have been imprisoned
- *out-groups described in stereotypical terms*, e.g. Vietnamese immigrants to Australia depicted as being nimble-fingered and therefore suited to some forms of clothing manufacture; Chinese immigrants viewed as having business acumen

- *ethnic and racial slurs*—these set the out-group apart from the in-group, e.g. derogatory names, slurs, and adjectives such as 'wog', 'coon', 'convict', 'nip'
- *illustrative language representing particular group*—usually, illustrations tend to depict people as white, middle-class, and of Anglo-Saxon heritage, e.g. 'Mr John Doe'; 'Miss Jane Citizen'.

Racism and sexism are offensive and divisive. Avoid language which contributes to those, and other, forms of discrimination.

SOME NOTES ON PUNCTUATION

One of the most important skills you should have by the time you have completed your university degree is the ability to communicate clearly. One of the keys to good written communication is correct punctuation. The following notes are intended to help rectify some of the most common problems of written English. Please take the time to read and absorb them.

Comma   ,
- breaks up long sentences—e.g. Now there was only standing room in Second Class, the battered yellow coaches were filled to overflowing, and on the curves I could see people on the roofs of the following carriages.
- shows a pause or natural separation of ideas—e.g. After the recommendations were implemented, further evaluations were conducted.
- brackets or separates information in a sentence—e.g. The most common, and most easily rectified, problems on essay writing emerge from incorrect acknowledgment of sources.
- precedes linking words, such as 'but', 'so', 'hence', and 'whereas'—e.g. The aim was to examine sustainability, but the experiment failed.
- separates information in a list—e.g. The equipment included one inflatable boat, one motor vehicle, and a helicopter.

Full stop   .
- ends a complete sentence—e.g. Geography has not always had a smooth ride.
- ends an abbreviation where the final letter of the abbreviation is not the last letter of the word—e.g. p. for page, ed. for editor.

Ellipsis   ...
- indicates that words have been left out of a quotation—e.g. As the report claims, 'There are many factors determining the state of the physical environment ... but the most important is human intervention'.

- in informal writing may indicate that there is more of what you are saying but that you are not setting it out on the page—e.g. She went on and on about the rate of inflation, share market movements, currency exchange rates … .

Semicolon   ;

- connects two sentences or main clauses which are closely connected, but are not joined with a linking word—e.g. The initial survey revealed a high interest; results showed that further action is appropriate.
- separates complex or wordy items in a list—e.g. The following factors are critical: the environmental impact statement; the government and union policies; the approval of business and council; and public opinion.

Colon   :

- introduces a list—e.g. The following factors are critical: precipitation, temperature, and population.
- introduces a quotation—e.g. According to Openshaw (1999, p. 81): 'The fundamental technical change that is underpinning the development of the new post-industrial society is the transformation of knowledge which can be exchanged, owned, manipulated and traded'.

Quotation marks (inverted commas)   ' ' or " "

- indicate a shorter quotation as part of a sentence—e.g. For our purposes, militarism can be broadly defined as 'a set of attitudes and social practices which regards war and the preparation for war as a normal and desirable social activity' (Mann 1988, p. 166).
- show the titles of journal articles etc.—e.g. Harvey's paper 'Between space and time' is an example of an important contribution to the field.

Apostrophe   '

- indicates contractions in verbs—e.g. I'm, we'll, can't. Note that abbreviations of this sort belong to the informal register and are not usually acceptable in academic writing.
- indicates possession, as follows:
  - place the apostrophe at the end of the owner-word, then add a possessive 's', e.g. The researcher's results (i.e. the results of one researcher); the researchers' results (i.e. the results of more than one researcher)
  - if the original word ends with an 's', place the apostrophe at the end of the owner-word without adding a possessive 's', e.g. The thesis' results (i.e. the results of a thesis).

> Apostrophes are one of the most commonly misused or neglected elements of punctuation.

- It is important to distinguish between it's (= it is) and its (= belonging to it, whether singular or plural).

Capital letters
- Use minimally, especially in titles and headings. Small words such as 'and', 'in', 'the', and 'by' should not be capitalised.
- Use only for a specific and formally named item (e.g. France, English, Aborigines).

Punctuating numerals
- Do not use figures at the beginning of a sentence—e.g. 900 workers were laid off. Sentences should always begin with a word. You should write: Nine hundred workers were laid off.
- Write numbers of ten or fewer in words, except when followed by units of measurement—e.g. 9 mm, 'nine field sites'.
- Place a thin space between the numeral and the unit of measurement, and do not use full stops with units of measurement.

REFERENCES AND FURTHER READING

Australian Government Publishing Service. 1994, *Style Guide*, 5th edn, AGPS, Canberra.
    A very detailed and well-laid out volume which has formed the basis for some of the material discussed in this chapter. An important reference text. Recently updated by Snooks & Co. (2002).

Betts, K. & Seitz, A. 1994, *Writing Essays and Research Reports in the Social Sciences*, 2nd edn, Nelson, Melbourne.
    A broad review of referencing and the logic for it is contained in chapter 4.

Burkill, S. & Abbey, C. 2004, 'Avoiding plagiarism', *Journal of Geography in Higher Education*, vol. 28, no. 3, pp. 439–46.

Campbell, W.G., Ballou, S.V. & Slade, C. 1986, *Form and Style: Theses, Reports, Term Papers*, 7th edn, Houghton Mifflin, Boston.
    Chapter 3 discusses the use of quotations in academic writing.

Eichler, M. 1991, *Nonsexist Research Methods: A Practical Guide*, Routledge, London.
    This book provides a comprehensive review of the ways in which research practices can be sexist. It also includes a discussion of sexism in language (chapter 7).

Harrison, N. 1985, *Writing English: A User's Manual*, Croom Helm, Sydney.
    Chapter 6, 'Making the text live', is an extensive review considering the uses of punctuation.

International Committee of Medical Journal Editors 2004, *Uniform Requirements for Manuscripts Submitted to Biomedical Journals: Writing and Editing for Biomedical Publication* (online), Available: <http://www.icmje.org/> (18 August 2005).

Li, X. & Crane, N.B. 1993, *Electronic Style. A Guide to Citing Electronic Information*, Meckler, Westport, Connecticut.

Electronic media such as CD-ROMs, electronic journals, email messages, and conversations via bulletin boards present special difficulties in referencing. Although no standard has yet been established, comprehensive and helpful guidelines are outlined in this book. Drawing from the referencing principles of the American Psychological Association (APA), the book outlines forms of citation for electronic media material. Unfortunately, APA referencing style differs a little in format from that of the Australian Government Publishing Service upon which material in this chapter is based. Nevertheless, it is a simple task to make stylistic modifications to provide consistency of format.

Library of Congress 2005, *How to Cite Electronic Sources* (online), Available: <http://lcweb2.loc.gov/ammem/ndlpedu/start/cite/index.html> (18 August 2005).

Miller, C. & Swift, K. 1981, *The Handbook of Non-Sexist Writing for Writers, Editors and Speakers*, rev. edn, Women's Press, London.

An extensive, fascinating, and useful review of sexist language, its influence, and ways to avoid it. Well worth reading.

Mills, C. 1994, 'Acknowledging sources in written assignments', *Journal of Geography in Higher Education*, vol. 18, no. 2, pp. 263–8.

Mohan, T., McGregor, H. & Strano, Z. 1992, *Communicating! Theory and Practice*, 3rd edn, Harcourt Brace, Sydney.

Peters, P. 1985, *Strategies for Student Writers: A Guide to Writing Essays, Tutorial Papers, Exam Papers and Reports*, Wiley, Brisbane.

Chapter 9 includes a detailed review of punctuation.

Preston, N. 2001, *Understanding Ethics*, 2nd edn, Federation Press, Sydney.

Snooks & Co. 2002, *Style Manual for Authors, Editors and Printers*, 6th edn, John Wiley & Sons Australia, Canberra.

At the time of writing this was the most recent official Australian government style guide. It is the updated edition of the 1994 Australian Government Publishing Service's *Style Guide*.

Walker, J.R. & Taylor, T. 1998, *The Columbia Guide to Online Style*, Columbia University Press, New York.

glossary

abstract

a library resource, which lists articles from periodicals under subjects and includes a summary of the article; a short statement outlining the objectives, methods, results, and central conclusions of a research report or paper. This latter form of abstract is limited in its length (usually about 100–250 words) and is designed to be read by people who may not have the time to read the whole report, who wish to get a quick impression of the paper's content, or who are working out whether the content is sufficiently interesting for them to read the entire document.

account for

explain how something came about and why.

acknowledgment

statement recognising the people and institutions to which an author is indebted for guidance and assistance. May be incorporated into the preface/ foreword. (See also *citation*.)

acronym

a word made up of the first letters of a group of words (e.g. SCUBA—Self-

Contained Underwater Breathing Apparatus).

analyse

explore component parts of some phenomenon in order to understand how the whole thing works. It can also mean to examine closely. (Contrast with *synthesise*.)

annotated bibliography

list, in alphabetical order by each author's surname, of works (books, papers) on a specific topic. Each work is summarised and commented upon.

apostrophe

punctuation mark, used to indicate possession (e.g. the girl's book, the three boys' books) and the omission of a letter or letters from a word (e.g. can't, you'll, we'd).

appendix

supplementary material accompanying the main body of a paper, book, or report. Typically placed at the back of the document. Includes supporting evidence that would detract from the main line of argument in the text or would make the body of the text too large and poorly structured.

appraise

analyse and judge the worth or significance or something.

argue/argument

a debate which involves reasoning about all sides of an issue and offering support for one or more cases. Typically, you will be asked to present a case for/against a proposition, presenting reasons and evidence for your position. In an argument you should also indicate opposing points of view and your reasons for rejecting them. An argument may be written or spoken.

assess

conduct an evaluation, investigating the pros and cons or validity of some issue or situation. You are usually expected to reach some conclusion on the basis of your research and discussion (e.g. is some situation under consideration, right or wrong, fair or unfair).

author–date system

system of referring to texts cited. Comprises two parts: (i) in-text references, which provide a summary of the bibliographic details of the publication being cited. This comprises author's surname, year of publication, and page references; (ii) alphabetically ordered list of references, which provides complete bibliographic details of all sources referred to in the text. (Compare with *note system*.)

bar graph

general name given to those graphs in which plotted values are shown in the form of one or more horizontal or vertical bars (column graph) whose length is proportional to the value(s) portrayed. (Contrast with *histogram*.)

bibliography

complete list of works referred to or found useful in the preparation of a formal communication (e.g. essay, book review, poster, report). Less commonly, a bibliography refers to a book listing works available on a particular subject. (See also *references (cited)* and *annotated bibliography*.)

blog

see *weblog*.

cadastral map

specialised map showing surveyed land tenure (from *cadastre*, an official register or list of property owners and their holdings (Robinson et al. 1984, p. 11)).

capital letters

used at the beginning of sentences, proper names, and titles (e.g. On Monday, Jane Smith went home).

caption

explanatory material printed under an illustration. May also refer to the title or heading above a map, figure, or photograph.

cartogram

form of map in which the size of places depicted is adjusted to represent the statistics being mapped. For example, if one was to produce a map of the world showing sheep populations, New Zealand and Australia would appear to be very large compared with most other countries. Although the physical sizes of places will be altered in the production of a cartogram, efforts are made to preserve both their locations relative to other places and their shapes.

CD-ROM

(Compact Disc Read Only Memory) a compact disc which can store large amounts of information (text, music, graphics).

choropleth map
a cross-hatched or shaded map used to display statistical distributions (e.g. rates, frequencies, ratios) on the basis of areal units such as nations, states, and regions.

circle graph
see *pie graph.*

citation
formal, written acknowledgment that you have borrowed the work of another scholar. Whenever you quote verbatim (i.e. recite word for word) the work of another person and when you borrow the idea(s) of such people, you must acknowledge the source of that information using a recognised referencing system.

clincher
that part of a paragraph that concludes the paragraph's argument. (See also *topic sentence* and *supporting sentence.*)

colon
punctuation mark (:). The colon means 'as follows' and is used to indicate lists and examples (e.g. 'We read: books, articles, essays, and magazines').

comment
make critical observations about the subject matter.

compare
discuss the similarities/differences between selected phenomena (e.g. ideas, places). Be quite sure that you know what you are meant to be comparing. (Often used in conjunction with *contrast.*)

concept
thought or idea that underpins an area of knowledge. For example, the concept of evolution underpins much of biology. The idea that new communications technologies 'compress' distance is significant in geography.

conceptual framework
the logic that underpins an argument or the way in which material is presented. A way of viewing the world and of arranging observations into a comprehensible whole. May be imagined as an intellectual skeleton upon which flesh in the form of ideas and evidence are suspended.

conclusion
that part of a talk, essay, poster, or report in which findings are drawn together and implications are revealed.

consider
reflect on; think about carefully.

continuous data
observations which could have any conceivable value within an observed range. Thus, includes fractional numbers, such as halves and quarters. (Compare with *discrete data.*)

contrast
give a detailed account of differences between selected phenomena. (Often used in conjunction with *compare.*)

corroboration
support or confirmation of an explanation or account through the use of complementary evidence. (Compare with *replication.*)

criticise
provide some judgement on strengths and weaknesses. Back your case with a

discussion of the evidence. Criticising does not necessarily require you to condemn an idea.

critique
see *criticise*.

database
large amount of information stored in a computer and organised in categories to facilitate retrieval.

data region
that part of a graph within which data is portrayed (usually bounded by the graph's axes).

define
explain the basic points or principles of something to provide a precise meaning. Providing examples may enhance your definition.

demonstrate
illustrate and explain by use of examples.

describe
outline the characteristics of some phenomenon. Usually, a description might be imagined to be a picture painted with words. What does the phenomenon look like? What patterns are evident? How big is it? Shape? … There is no need to interpret.

discrete data
phenomena which may be quantified in whole numbers only, for example animal and human populations. (Compare with *continuous data*.)

discriminatory language
treats people differently, or excludes them, on the basis of gender, race, religion, culture, age, or disability where it is unnecessary or inappropriate to do so. (Contrast *non-discriminatory language*.)

discuss/discussion
examine critically, using argument. Present your point of view and that of others. May be written or spoken.

distinguish
make clear any differences between two or more phenomena.

domain name
unique name that locates an organisation or other entity on the Internet. Always broken into two or more parts, separated by dots. For example, <iag.org.au> is the domain name for the Institute of Australian Geographers.

dot map
map in which spatial distributions are depicted by dots representing each unit of occurrence (e.g. one dot represents one person) or some multiple of those units (e.g. one dot represents 1000 sheep).

edit
revise and rewrite. Sometimes implies that some material needs to be deleted.

electronic mail
exchange of computer-stored messages by telecommunications.

ellipsis
punctuation, written as three full stops (…), placed in a quotation, for example, to indicate that words from the original source have been omitted.

email
see *electronic mail*.

endnote
short note placed at the end of a document and identified by a symbol or numeral in the body of the text. A textual 'aside', endnotes provide a brief elaboration of some point made in the

text but whose inclusion there might be inappropriate or disruptive to the flow of text. In the *note system* of referencing, endnotes may also include details of reference material cited in the text.

enumerate
list or specify and describe clearly.

essay
brief literary composition which states clearly what you think and have learned about a specific topic.

essay plan
preparatory framework outlining the basic structure and argument of an essay.

et al.
abbreviation of the Latin phrase, *et alii*, meaning 'and others', used to reduce a list of people's names.

evaluate
appraise the worth of something. What are the strengths and weaknesses and which are dominant? Make a judgment.

evidence
information used to support or refute an argument or statement. In forming an opinion or making an argument at university you may need to abandon some practices that may have been considered satisfactory in the past. For example, it is not acceptable for you to state such things as 'it is widely known that … ' or 'most people would say that … ' since in these statements you have not provided any evidence about who the people are, why they say what they do, how they came to their conclusions, and so on. In other words, you need to present material that supports or refutes your claim.

examine
investigate critically. Present in detail and critically discuss the implications.

explain
answer 'how' and 'why' questions. Clarify, using concrete examples.

extrapolate
to estimate the value of some phenomenon beyond the extent of known values. Typically, this is done by extending historically known trends into the future. For example, if house prices in Dunedin had been increasing at an average rate of 5% per year for the last twenty years and the median value of a house at the end of last year was $200,000, you might extrapolate from the trend to suggest that the median Dunedin house value will have risen to $210,000 by the end of this year. (Compare with *interpolate*.)

footnote
short note placed at the bottom of a page and identified by a symbol or numeral in the body of the text. A textual 'aside', footnotes provide a brief elaboration of some point made in the text but whose inclusion there might be inappropriate or disruptive to the flow of text. In the *note system* of referencing, footnotes may also include details of reference material cited in the text.

foreword
message about the main text of a book. Usually disconnected from that text because it is written by a different author or because it does not contribute directly to the textual content. (Distinct from *preface*.) An example of a foreword might be a statement by a prominent politician about the timeliness and value of the published volume in which the foreword appears.

freewriting
sometimes used as a step in the production of an essay. Involves (i) 'stream of consciousness' writing without concern for overall structure and direction, followed by (ii) careful revision.

full stop
punctuation mark, used to indicate the end of sentences and some abbreviations.

generalisation
a comprehensive statement about all or most examples of some phenomenon made on the basis of a (limited) number of observations of examples of that phenomenon.

Harvard system
see *author–date system.*

histogram
graph in which plotted values are shown in the form of horizontal or, more commonly, vertical bars whose area is proportional to the value(s) portrayed. Thus, if class intervals depicted in the histogram are of different sizes, the column areas will reflect this. (Contrast with *bar graph.*)

home page
the main or 'front page' of a web site. Usually sets out the content and other characteristics of the site. (See also *web site* and *web page.*)

HTML (Hypertext Markup Language)
set of instructions in computer files that tells WWW-browsing software how to display a web page's words and images.

HTTP (Hypertext Transfer Protocol)
set of rules for exchanging text, graphic, sound, and other multimedia files on the *WWW.*

hypothesis
supposition or trial proposition used as a starting point for investigation. Usually begins with the word 'that' e.g. My hypothesis is that Mount Ruapehu's 1995 eruption promoted tomato growth in horticultural regions of New Zealand's North Island.

ibid
abbreviation of the Latin word *ibidem,* meaning 'in the same place', sometimes used in footnotes and endnotes.

illustrate
make clear through the use of examples or by use of figures, diagrams, maps, and photographs.

index
alphabetical list of names and subjects, with page references, at the back of a book. Also a library resource, which lists citations to periodicals, articles, and other information alphabetically, according to subject.

indicate
focus attention on or point out.

Internet
a worldwide network of computer networks which enables communication between computers connected to the network.

interpolate
estimate a value of some phenomenon between, and on the basis of, values which are already known. For example, if you knew that the median price of a house in Darwin was $210,000 in January and $220,000 in December, you might interpolate the June value to have been about $215,000. (Compare with *extrapolate.*)

interpret
make clear, giving your own judgment. Offer an opinion or reason for the character of some phenomenon.

introduction
first section in a piece of formal communication (e.g. poster, talk, essay) in which author/speaker tells the audience what is going to be discussed and why.

inverted comma
see *quotation marks*.

isoline map
map showing sets of lines (isolines) connecting points of known, or estimated, equal values. Common examples include topographic maps, which show lines of equal elevation (contours), and weather maps, which commonly show isobars (lines of equal atmospheric pressure).

jargon
most commonly, technical terms used inappropriately or when clearer terms would suffice. Less commonly, words or a mode of language intelligible only to a group of experts in the field.

journal
publication issued at regular or irregular intervals, on an ongoing basis (e.g. *Australian Journal of Environmental Management, New Zealand Geographer*). Also called periodicals, magazines, or serials.

justify
provide support and evidence for outcomes or conclusions.

key
see *legend*.

legend
also known as a key. A brief interpretive statement making sense of the symbols, patterns, and colours used in a map or diagram.

line graph
a graph in which the values of observed (x,y) phenomena are connected by lines. Used to illustrate change over time or relationships between variables.

listserv
a software program that automatically redistributes *email* to names on a mailing list. It also allows users or an administrator to add and remove subscribers to the *mailing list*.

literature review
comprehensive summary and interpretation of resources (e.g. publications, reports) and their relationship to a specific area of research.

loc. cit.
abbreviation of the Latin phrase, *loco citato*, meaning 'in the place cited', sometimes used in footnotes and endnotes.

logarithmic graph
graph with one (semi-log) or two (log–log) logarithmic axes. Key intervals on logarithmic axes are based on exponents of ten.

log–log graph
see *logarithmic graph*.

mailing list
a list of email addresses identified by a single electronic address, such as <iag-list@flinders.edu.au>. When an email message is sent to the mailing list address it gets distributed automatically to all addresses on the list.

map
graphic device which shows where something is. Graphic representation of a place.

narrate
say what happened in the form of a story.

newsgroup
an online discussion group. Notices and messages often follow a particular theme or topic (known as a thread) within the broader interests of newsgroup members.

non-discriminatory language
uses forms of expression which do not exclude or denigrate anybody on the basis of gender, race, disability, religion, culture, or age.

northpoint
graphic indicator of direction north on map.

note identifier
symbol or numeral used in text to refer a reader to a reference or to supplementary information in endnotes or footnotes.

note system
system of referring to texts cited. Comprises a numeral in superscript within the text which refers the reader to full bibliographic details of the reference provided as a footnote (at the bottom of the page) or an endnote (at the end of the document). Compare with *author–date system*.

online
connected to, under the control of, or accessible by, a computer.

op. cit.
abbreviations of the Latin phrase, *opere citato*, meaning 'in the work cited', used rarely in footnotes and endnotes.

orthophoto map
maps created from a mosaic of aerial photographs and overlain with information such as contours, transport routes, and place names.

outline
describe the main features, leaving out minor details. Alternatively, an outline can be a brief sketch or written plan.

paragraph
a cohesive, self-contained expression of an idea usually constituting part of a longer written document. Typically comprises three parts: *topic sentence*, *supporting sentence(s)*, and *clincher*.

paraphrase
summarise someone else's words in your own.

parentheses
punctuation, written as round brackets, placed around a group of words (such as these) which is interpolated into a sentence, but of which the sentence is independent.

periodical
see *journal*.

pie graph
also known as circle graph. Circular-shaped graph in which proportions of some total sum (the whole 'pie') are depicted as 'slices'. The area of each slice is directly proportional to the size of the variable portrayed.

plagiarism
presenting, without proper attribution, someone else's words or ideas as your own.

population pyramid
form of histogram showing the number or percentage of people in different age groups of a population.

poster
piece of stiff card to which textual and graphic materials such as maps, tables, and photos outlining the results of some piece of research are affixed.

PowerPoint
proprietary software to aid public text/graphics presentations. Includes word processing, outlining, drawing, graphing, and presentation management tools.

précis
brief summary of a piece of writing or a talk.

preface
section at the start of a book or report in which the author states briefly how the book came to be written and its purpose. The preface will also usually include acknowledgments unless they are presented separately elsewhere.

prove
demonstrate truth or falsity by use of evidence.

quotation
verbatim (i.e. word for word) copy of someone else's words.

quotation marks
'inverted commas' which are placed around words reproduced exactly from someone else's speech or writing. They may be 'single' or "double" but their use must be consistent. Quotation marks may also be used to draw the reader's attention to a word that is somehow out of the ordinary. This device should not be overused.

references (cited)
complete list of works referred to or found useful in the preparation of a

formal communication (e.g. essay, book review, poster, report). Usually, a list of references includes only those sources actually cited (i.e. formally acknowledged). See also *author–date system* and *note system*.

relate
establish and show the connections between one phenomenon and another.

replication
with respect to the conduct of research, an account or explanation of some phenomenon may be given weight by experiments or studies that repeat the initial study and yield similar results. (Compare with *corroboration*.)

representative fraction
a form of scale which expresses the relationship between distances on a map or diagram and distances in reality in the form of a fraction. For example, the representative fraction 1:10 000 (or 1/10 000) means that any one unit of distance on the map (e.g. 1 mm, 1 inch, 1 metre) represents 10,000 of those same units in reality (e.g. 10,000 mm, 10,000 inches, 10,000 metres).

review
make a summary and examine the subject critically.

RF
see *representative fraction*.

scale
an indication provided on a map or diagram of the relationship between the size of some depicted phenomenon and its size in reality. A scale is used most commonly to provide a statement of the relationship between distances on the ground and distances shown on the map. Three forms of scale can be

distinguished: (i) a simple statement such as, 1 cm represents 1 km (ii) a graphic device which illustrates the relationship (iii) a representative fraction (e.g. 1:15 000).

scattergram
graph of point data plotted by their (x,y) co-ordinates.

search engine
software comprising a 'spider' ('crawler' or 'bot') that 'reads' WWW pages; an indexing program; and a search request program. Together, these receive a user request for WWW information, compare that with an index of pages consulted by the spider, and return to the user a list of WWW sites relevant to the information request. Examples of some major search engines include: AltaVista (<http://www.altavista.com>), Excite (<http://www.excite.com>), Google (<http://www.google.com>), and Lycos (<http://www.lycos.com>).

semicolon
punctuation mark (;), which indicates a longer break in a sentence than a comma, but is not as final as a full stop. It is now used mainly to mark the separations between long items in a list. It is not used to indicate the beginning of a list. (Contrast with *colon*.)

semi-log graph
see *logarithmic graph*.

sentence
a group of words which expresses a complete thought; begins with a capital letter; ends with a full stop, exclamation mark, or question mark; and contains a subject and a finite verb.

serial
see *journal*.

show
demonstrate in a logical sequence why or how some phenomenon occurred or came to be.

sic
Latin word which means, literally, *'thus'*. It is used after a direct quotation if the quotation contains an error or a questionable statement. The word usually appears in italics and is placed in square brackets: [*sic*]. It is used to indicate 'this is the way it appeared'. If only one word is wrong in the quotation, [*sic*] appears directly after that word: 'He done [*sic*] great work on the field today'.

state
express fully and clearly.

summarise
present critical points in brief, clear form.

supporting sentence(s)
that part of a paragraph in which discussion substantiating the paragraph's claim(s) is presented. (See also *topic sentence* and *clincher*.)

synthesise
build up separate elements into some comprehensible whole. (Compare with *analyse*.)

table
systematically arranged list of facts or numbers, usually set out in rows and columns.

topic sentence
that part of a paragraph in which the main idea is expressed. (See also *supporting sentence(s)* and *clincher*.)

topographic map
common, general purpose map that typically depicts contours, physical (e.g.

rivers, peaks) and cultural features (e.g. roads, churches, cemeteries).

trace
describe the development of a phenomenon from some origin(s).

URL (Uniform Resource Locator)
string of letters and numbers that make up the address of documentary, image, and other resources on the WWW. For example, <http://www.ssn.flinders.edu.au/geog/geos/RICHARDS.htm> is the URL for a paper (written by N. Richards) published electronically by GEOS, the geography and environmental studies student society at Flinders University.

viva voce
oral examination.

Web
see *World Wide Web*.

weblog
a web application that allows single or multiple authors to post news, information, musings, personal diaries, political commentary, photographs … on a common web page. Typically accessible

to any Internet user. Known also as a 'blog'. One of the oldest blogs on the WWW is Daniel Drezner's at <http://www.danieldrezner.com/blog/>.

web page
HTML document that may be grouped with other related web pages to form a web site. (Compare with *web site*.)

web site
collection of related and linked WWW files. See, for example, <http://www.iag.org.au>, which is the web site for the Institute of Australian Geographers. Usually a web site includes a beginning file, known as a *home page*, which sets out contents of the rest of the site.

why
reasons for.

word processing
use of a computer to create, edit, and print documents.

World Wide Web (WWW)
all resources and users on the Internet adhering to *HTTP* conventions.

WWW
see *World Wide Web*.

index